# Woggins for Supper

## (And other tasty tales)

## Travel and Adventure Outside the Comfort Zone

ORLA
KELLY
PUBLISHING

### DERMOT J DOUGLAS

Orla Kelly Publishing.

27 Kilbrody, Mount Oval,

Rochestown,

Cork

# Dedication

This one is dedicated to my children, Helen and Niamh, to my grandchildren, Holly and Liam, and my son-in law, Michael, who are my inspiration and who have accompanied Mary and me on a number of our adventures. We love you all!

# *Acknowledgements*

There are so many people we have met and who have helped us, guided us and shared our adventures in all the places to which we have travelled that it would require a separate volume to name them all. You know who you are -my heartfelt thanks to you all.

Once again to Mary, my wife, the axis upon which my world spins, all my love and thank you for your patience; and for giving me the space and encouragement to write these books. Without you, these books would never have been written.

Thanks are due to all those who have read the drafts and made so many helpful and constructive suggestions

- To Mary. You are always willing to be the first to read the drafts and diligently undertake the tedious task of proofreading, as well as having to put up with me on a daily basis, my deepest thanks.

- To my sister, Irene Geraghty, for reading and correcting the drafts and for her very helpful comments;

- To my friend Vincent Lennon, who thought he had given up this type of tedious task when he retired – thanks for your unstinting help and (mostly) useful comments;

- To my friend Maurice Doran for his companionship at the end of the world, you made that trip even more memorable;

- To my friend Karena Maguire for her steadfast support and encouragement.

- To Helen, Niamh, Michael, Holly and Liam – this book is not only dedicated to you but it is also, partly, about you. I hope you are happy with it?

- To Orla Kelly, my publisher (www.orlakellypublishing.com) – your professionalism, enthusiasm, encouragement and support has made the process of translating my musings into a book both enjoyable and relatively painless. Many thanks also for putting up with my warped sense of humour.

All of the people mentioned above have contributed to the attempt to make this book the best it can be. If, despite their best efforts, errors remain, some grammar is poor and some of the punctuation is risible, the fault is entirely mine. If you notice any of these things, please keep it to yourself; leave me with the delusion that I have done, at least, a passable job.

# Contents

# Photographs

Tree climbing goats, Morocco

Harpy Eagle high in a Kapoc tree, Peru.

Kaka, an endemic bird from New Zealand

Kea, another endemic bird from New Zealand

Jumping salt water crocodile, Adelaide River, Australia

Across: Singsing, Wamut Village, Papua New Guinea

Nuku Hiva dancers at the giant banyan; French Polynesia

Mudman, Papua New Guinea

Children in village beside the Karawari River, Papua New Guinea

Fashionable headgear beside the Karawari River, Papua New Guinea

Huli Wigmen, Papua New Guinea

Melpa women preparing for a Singsing Papua, New Guinea

Megapode egg collector and betel nut chewer, New Britain, Papua New Guinea

Secretary bird, South Africa

Elephants warning us off

Lions feasting on a wildebeest

# CHAPTER 1

# Kinetosis, Truth Drugs and the Devil's Breath

Mary, my wife, would get motion sick in a bath! She suffered so badly, when we travelled by sea, that at times she became almost catatonic. Whether it was a big ship or a small boat, calm water or turbulent water, the outcome was always the same. Every summer, when we were bringing up our children, we would vacation in France. This meant we had to take the ferry from the south of Ireland directly to France, a trip that could take up to 20 hours, or take two ferries – one from Dublin to Holyhead in Wales, taking four hours, followed by a 600km drive, and another ferry from Dover to Calais, taking another two hours. The shorter ferry trips were preferable, but were bookended by two bouts of seasickness. Nothing we tried seemed to alleviate this condition. Each year was a 'grin and bear' it trial until we arrived in France. Then we had to face the return journey and the anticipation of the kinetosis to come magnified the reality when it arrived. All the time the children were growing up we failed to find a cure for this condition. So bad was the anticipation of what it might be like that Mary wouldn't travel with me to the Galapagos Islands, as it involved living aboard a small motor boat, or accompany me on the trip she gave me for my 60th birthday to Antarctica, as it involved living aboard ship for three weeks in some of the roughest seas on the globe. Although I was accompanied by my eldest daughter Helen and her husband Michael to the Galapagos and my good friend Maurice Doran, when I went to the

1

Antarctic, these were the only adventures I had without Mary for company, and in a small but significant way, it diminished them.

When Maurice and I set sail from Ushuaia in Tierra del Fuego (Argentina) we noticed a number of people wandering the decks with small circular patches that looked like 'Band-Aids' behind one of their ears. Seeing so many of them, I began to speculate as to what they might have been covering, as it was unlikely that all of them would have injured themselves in the same place at the same time. Had they suffered the same mysterious fate that the nine members of the crew of the schooner *Demeter* did when Dracula was being transported from Varna, on the Black Sea, to Whitby in England?

Patches covering up vampire bites suddenly seemed plausible. Fortunately, this turned out to be a paranoid delusion on my part. What they were sporting so jauntily behind their ears were patches given them by the ship's doctor to ward off sea-sickness. I had never seen this before and felt that the voyage we were about to take, in some of the roughest waters in the world, would be an excellent test of their effectiveness. By the end of the trip, I had not heard of a single case of *mal de mer* aboard and was in awe of the effectiveness of this simple remedy.

When I got home I told Mary of my discovery. She was more than interested as she had come across a trip from Bergen to Kirkness in Norway, aboard the Hurtigruten Ferry, that promised excellent sightings of the *Aurora Borealis* – something we had both wanted to see for some time.

I did some research into the patches and discovered that they were infused with scopolamine and, when placed on a hairless bit of bare skin behind the ear, the chemical slowly diffuses through the skin and has its magical effect. Each patch is good for 3 days.

I knew it worked but we both wanted to know HOW it worked – given that so many other remedies had failed. Now for the scientific bit: Scopolamine also known as hyoscine is an alkaloid that can be extracted from plants of the nightshade family. When used as a dermal patch the active ingredient is absorbed through the skin. With motion sickness, it appears that locating the patch behind the ear is key, as the vestibular part of the ear[1] is important for balance. A person who suffers from sea-sickness on experiencing motion sends a nerve signal from the vestibule to the vomiting centre in the brain. *Voila!* The victim spews.

Transmission of signals between nerves involves a chemical called acetylcholine being released from one nerve and drifting across the small gap between it and the next nerve. This then stimulates the adjoining nerve to transmit the signal further. It appears that scopolamine blocks this communication between the nerves so signals fail to reach the vomiting centre of the brain. Given its role in blocking neurotransmission, dosage is very important and some people experience side effects that range from mild to severe. So, as a cure for motion sickness scopolamine doesn't work for everyone. Unfortunately, it is not a panacea. However, when it does work, it works exceedingly well. Fortunately, Mary is one of those people for whom it is a godsend. We did make the trip on the Hurtigruten ferry and as we sailed through a force 8 gale and many of our dining companions rushed to the rail or their cabins to evacuate the contents of their stomachs, Mary and I continued to tuck into a tasty dinner and toast her new found freedom from *mal de mer* with a very nice red wine. In previous years she would have honked before we even left the harbour.

This was not a once off happening. We subsequently enjoyed long sea voyages to the Arctic and from Tahiti to the Marquesas in the Pacific. Putting a patch on did the job each time. The Food and Drug Administration in the USA had approved the transdermal patch for motion sickness and the prevention of nausea as far back as 1979. Had we known about it earlier it would have saved us a lot of misery, not to mention the cleaning.

I now have the perfect excuse, if I ever needed one, to go back to the Galapagos, this time accompanied by my wife. I can't wait to share the

---

1 Where the semicircular canals converge, close to the cochlea

wonders of that special place with her. Bookings have already been made for Mary, our younger daughter, Niamh, and me to make this trip in autumn 2018.

Scopolamine's history also has its dark side. In 1916 an obstetrician named Robert House noticed that the drug induced a 'twilight sleep' in a woman who was experiencing labour during a home delivery. House had asked her husband to get a weighing scale to weigh the newborn infant. He couldn't find it anywhere. However, his wife still drugged and under the influence of scopolamine, told him exactly where it was. This convinced House that scopolamine could make anyone answer a question truthfully and began extolling its value as a 'truth drug'. A number of physicians noted that women in 'twilight sleep' answered questions accurately and often volunteered exceedingly candid remarks. Surprisingly, when I attempted to interrogate Mary when she was under the influence of the drug, I had little success. Her candour only extended to telling me to 'Aw Stop it!' and 'let me sleep!' The next time I will make her wear a patch behind each ear.

Scopolamine has also been implicated in murder. Filson Young[2] published a book about the trial of the American homeopath, Dr Crippen, who was hanged in London for murdering his second wife Cora in 1910. This case was the first where the suspect was captured with the aid of wireless telegraphy. Young outlines the forensic evidence thus

*'Dr Willcox (the senior scientific analyst to the Home Office) found a quantity of hyoscin, sufficient to show him that there must have been in the body of the person whose remains these were more than half a gram of hyoscin hydrobromide, which was the form in which hyoscin was used for medical purposes.'*

Dr Crippin was known to have bought some hyoscin hydrobromide (scopolamine) at the beginning of the year.

2 Young, Filson, ed. (1920). The Trial of Hawley Harvey Crippen; Notable Trials Series; Edinburgh: William Hodge & Company

In an interesting development in 2007,[3] DNA analysis cast doubt on whether the body found in the coal cellar was that of Cora Crippen. The scientists who undertook the work are positive that it could not have been Cora Crippen, as they were convinced that the body was, in fact, that of a man. They maintain that Dr Crippen was innocent of the crime for which he was hanged. The results continue to be disputed by other scientists and criminologists.

The Nazis were said to have used the drug in interrogations during the Second World War, and the infamous Dr Joseph Mengele, the so-called *Angel of Death*, in Auschwitz, is believed to have used it during experiments he carried out on Jewish prisoners.

After the war, scopolamine was one of a number of drugs evaluated in a CIA run operation to test whether mind-control drugs could be useful for the interrogation of Cold War prisoners. This programme was discontinued in 1973, or so we are told, but information on the efficacy of these drugs for such perverted purposes remains 'classified'.

The ŠtB (State Security) was the plainclothes secret police force in former Czechoslovakia from 1945 until its dissolution in 1990. It is known that they used scopolamine to assist them obtain confessions from those considered anti-state conspirators.

A classic case is reported in the book *Encyclopedia of Cold War Espionage, Spies, and Secret Operations* by Richard Trahair and Robert Miller.[4]

Not long after the six days war between Israel and the Arab states of Egypt, Jordan and Syria in 1967, Charles Jordan[5] allegedly committed suicide in Prague, in what was then Czechoslovakia. Apparently, Jordan was abducted by four Egyptian guerrillas, accompanied by Czechoslovak State Security

---

3 https://www.theguardian.com/uk/2007/oct/17/ukcrime.science

4 Trahair, R. C. S & Miller ,R. L (2012); Encyclopedia of Cold War Espionage, Spies, and Secret Operations; Enigma Books

5 The Director General for the Zionist Joint Distribution Committee for Jewish Relief

officers, and was taken to the Egyptian Embassy. State Security officers surrounded the embassy. While in the embassy, it appeared that Jordan had been injected with scopolamine before being murdered. His body was dumped into the Vltava river at about 3am. On the instructions of the Czechoslovakian government, the Egyptian murderers left for home and the authorities carried out a post-mortem and claimed Jordan had committed suicide.

This outraged many in the west, and the Americans in particular, and a second post-mortem was carried out by the independent Swiss pathologist Ernst Harmeier. This post-mortem discovered scopolamine in Jordan's pancreas. Not long after, Harmeier was found frozen to death near his car in Switzerland. It now appears that this was a double murder carried out by the Egyptian Mukhabarat.[6] The Russian dominated Czechoslovakian government continued to peddle the line that it was a double suicide in order to protect their relationship with Egypt.

That scopolamine is still in use as a truth drug and whether it is effective is documented in the text of a lecture leaked by *Wikileaks* in 2009. It provides chilling reading. This document was written in 2005 by a Dr Larry Forness, of the American Military University, and is titled *TORTURE, INTERROGATION AND INTELLIGENCE*. In it, among other things, he highlights one of the fallacies he addresses in the paper thus '**Fallacy #4.** *These things called 'truths serums' don't really work.*'

He then goes on to state that '*They do work to varying degrees of success.*' Regarding scopolamine he has this to say:

*To use scopolamine most effectively to get a prisoner to tell you what he or she knows, the key is where you inject it, and in what amounts. Normally it is introduced into the body by a transdermal patch or intravenously in the arm. However,* **if you inject it into the spine (amount classified), it causes absolutely incredible**

---

6 The Egyptian Intelligence Agency

**pain, accompanied by violent convulsions and seizures.**[7] *If injected into the spine in the appropriate amount, more than 95% of all prisoners will tell the truth -- not something fabricated to stop the pain -- within 24 hours (Source: classified)'......*

---

and

---

*'There is no known training that will allow anyone to resist scopolamine, when injected into the spine in the correct amount.' Later in the document he states 'When time is not a consideration, and when used in conjunction with skilled interrogators on a prisoner who has not been trained to resist the effects, sodium pentathol (sic) and sodium amythal (sic) will get you the truth in approximately 10% to one third of the cases. When the truth absolutely positively has to be there within five days, forget them – use scopolamine injected into the spine.'*

---

Until I read this chilling piece of detached arrogance and inhumanity, I thought that scopolamine as a truth serum was just an interesting piece of history that had utility only in spy novels and movies. My opinion has certainly changed. The arrogance, the xenophobia and the abnegation of the rights of others and the arrogation of the right to torture on the basis of 'suspicion' has all the hallmarks of the things Americans profess to despise in other less 'free' cultures. To ordinary people, among whom I class myself, it is really becoming a case of Walt Kelly's famous Pogo the possum's quote 'We have met the enemy and he is us' extending to those we really hoped were keeping us safe.

Scopolamine is one of the oldest plant-derived alkaloids in the world. It is listed by the World Health Organization as an 'essential medicine', and has proven beneficial to thousands of people. Yet, ignoring its dubious use as a 'truth drug', it has now gained a reputation as being one of the world's most dangerous drugs. In this context it is known as Devil's Breath or the Zombie Drug.

---

7 His emphasis

The drug, also referred to as Burundanga in its native Colombia, can be extracted from the flowers and seeds of the Borrachero, or 'get-you-drunk', trees. These plants belong to the genus *Brugmansia*, which consists of seven species of semi-woody small trees and shrubs in the *Solanaceae* family. All seven species are listed as Extinct in the Wild on the IUCN[8] Red List. They are, however, still popular as ornamental plants and continue to exist in many places as an introduced species. They have large pendulous and fragrant flowers that are commonly known as angel's trumpets – an interesting paradox, given that the misuse of the scopolamine extracted from them is commonly described as the Devil's Breath - a botanical example of a fallen angel, no doubt.

Devil's Breath is being used to further the commission of crimes such as robbery, kidnapping and sexual assault. It is estimated that in Colombia there are up to 50,000 scopolamine-related criminal assaults every year and in the city of Bogotá 20% of Emergency Room visits are because of scopolamine poisoning. The danger has encouraged the US Department of State, and the Government of Canada, to issue a warning to travellers. Criminals using Devil's Breath often use attractive young women to target men that they believe are wealthy. Most commonly, the victim is given a scopolamine-laced beverage to render him unconscious and unable to resist the robbery. The drug is reputed to leave people in a zombie like state and, conveniently for the criminal, blocks memories from forming. After the drug wears off,[9] victims have no recollection as to what happened and thus little chance of obtaining justice. According to the British Journal of Clinical Pharmacology, scopolamine causes the same level of memory loss as *diazepam*.

This problem is not just confined to Columbia. In 2015, three Chinese people were arrested in Paris for the illegal use of the drug. It appears that they blew scopolamine powder in the faces of elderly people and then took advantage of their weakened mental condition to rob them.

---

8 The International Union for Conservation of Nature

9 The drug is undetectable in the blood of victims within 2 to 6 hours and undetectable in the urine after about 12 hours

In the past two years cases of the criminal use of scopolamine have been reported in both Spain and France. In December 2017, the Daily Mail[10] published an article on the use of scopolamine in the UK and provided testimony from the English actor Robert Lindsay, who described how a friend of his daughter was attacked by three men outside a London night club. Unprepared she inhaled the drug that was blown into her face and that within seconds she lost all her senses and couldn't remember anything. Fortunately, friends nearby came to her aid and prevented further harm.

Easily and cheaply purchased online (one European vendor offers 1g for £11), scopolamine is not a controlled substance under the UK Misuse of Drugs Act.

For Mary and me, scopolamine is something of a blessing. It means we can travel together on the ocean without fear and the anxiety and discomfort of the past. For others it is a curse. It has been used to viciously assault them and to rob them. For a small number of others, it is torture – literally. Depending upon the use to which it is put, scopolamine, in reality, is both the cloud and the silver lining.

---

10 http://www.dailymail.co.uk/news/article-5158857/Colombian-Devils-Breath-drug-UK-online-11.html#ixzz53mZyZ7z1

# CHAPTER 2

ⵒⵕ

## Woggins for Supper

---

*... 'at 1 PM Sent our Boat on Shore After Some refreshments She returned with A Plenty of Woggins we Cooked Some for Supper' ...*

---

This observation, dated the 20th December 1792, was recorded in the logbook of Silvanus Crosby of the ship *Asia* out of Nantucket, Massachusetts, at that time sailing near the Desolation Islands (Kerguelen Islands – currently part of French Southern and Antarctic Lands), in the Southern Indian Ocean. These Islands were frequented by British, American and Norwegian whalers and sealers who hunted the relatively slow southern right whale and fur seals, and in the 18th century elephant seals, to the point of extinction.

And what is a woggins, you may well ask? That the word, from its first recorded mention in 1762 until the 1860s, was equally and fairly commonly used among American whalers, who hunted the Northern oceans, as well as those like Silvanus Crosby, who hunted in the Southern oceans, was demonstrated in research carried out by Storrs L Olsen and Judith N Lund.[11] Olsen and Lund discovered an entry in the Journal of Micajah Coffin of the sloop *Sandwich*, also out of Nantucket, dated the 19th April 1762 which stated

---

11 Olson, S.L. and J.N. Lund (2007) Whalers and woggins: a new vocabulary for interpreting some early accounts of the great auk and penguins. Archives of Natural History 34: 69-78.

*.... 'wind Started to Northward got on the Banks On the Latter Part Calm. Caught 10 wogens.'*

The 'Banks' referred to here are most likely the Outer Banks of North Carolina, a rich hunting ground for sperm whale at that time of the year.

A clue to the meaning of the word was found by Olsen and Lund in an entry, dated the 17th of November 1798, in the Journal of Christopher Almy of the *Barclay*, a ship of New Bedford, Massachusetts, and relating to the Island of Santa Maria, off the coast of Coronel, Chile

*... 'There is sea fowl in abundance of all kinds. There is one sort the whalemen call woggins, commonly called Penguins that cannot fly, neither have they any feathers, but have stubs like wings which they have to defend themselves with and when they walk hold them up and for that reason look like small boys a walking. Their nest is in every hole in the side of the hills.'*

The penguins alluded to here were, most likely, either Humboldt or Magellanic penguins (or possibly both).

The term woggins seems to have been exclusively used by American whalers and does not appear to have been in common use by English or European whalers who hunted these same waters. The fact that it was used in both the North and the South Atlantic is problematical as penguins, by and large, are confined to the southern oceans, with only one species, the Galapagos penguin, straying above the equator and doing so only because the cold Humboldt current swings around the islands bringing cold, nutrient rich water with it. Penguins that breed in tropical or temperate regions lay their eggs in burrows, caves or crevices to avoid the heat of the sun and maintain a constant moderate temperature to support egg development.

The name 'penguin' originated in the 16th Century to describe a large, flightless, black and white bird, called the great auk, that roamed the cold waters of the North Atlantic along the coasts of the United States, Canada, Greenland, Iceland, the Faroe Islands, Norway, Ireland, The United Kingdom , France, and Spain. Its derivation is still a matter of conjecture and dispute.

The great auk (*Pinguinus impennis*) is the only modern (non fossil) species of the genus *Pinguinus*. Easy to catch, these birds and their eggs were harvested for 100,000 years, since Neanderthal times, for food, for their down feathers, and, wastefully, as fishing bait. Great auks were powerful swimmers and efficient catchers of fish, which they consumed whilst floating on the surface of the sea. On land they were slow and clumsy and only came ashore, on a small number of suitable islets, to breed. The scarcity of available breeding sites meant that they bred in huge colonies. They were vulnerable to human exploitation, both on land and at sea, and they were slaughtered in huge numbers – particularly in the 18th and 19th centuries. Consequently they became extinct in 1844, with the last pair being killed on Eldey Island, Iceland on the 3rd of July.[12]

When European sailors saw similar flightless birds in the Southern Oceans, it is not surprising that they called them by the same name and attempted to exploit them in the same way. Thus all flightless black and white ocean going birds became known as penguins – although they are not related to the great auk.

Penguins were harvested for their eggs, meat, oil and skin. Their oil was a particularly valuable resource, being useful as fuel, lighting material and for tanning leather. The skin was used to make handbags, slippers, and hats; the feathers were used to fill pillows and mattresses or decorate some clothing.

Early mariners thought that the great auk and penguins were fish - not birds - and for this reason the Catholic Church, for a while, granted

---

12  https://www.nationalgeographic.org/thisday/jul3/great-auks-become-extinct/

believers an exemption that allowed them eat great auks during Lent without breaking the rule of abstinence from meat. Breast meat, in particular, was favoured for its delicate flavour and high nutritional value – largely because of the amount of fat present. Accounts of Antarctic explorers suggest that, in taste and texture, penguin breast resembled chicken or other poultry; meat from the back was said to be similar to beef and other parts of the body were said, after proper preparation, to be indistinguishable from fish. The meat could be prepared by boiling (the preferred method due to its toughness) and the flavour boosted with spices and herbs. Some cooks preferred to slice the meat thinly and fry it in oil or fat with slices of bread and a beaten egg. Indeed the eggs of penguins were often more valued than the meat and could be harvested without killing the bird – a much more sustainable method of harvesting. However, given the enormous size of breeding colonies I feel that this would not have been a consideration for the ancient mariners who slaughtered them. Most of the meat taken by mariners was not intended for immediate consumption. A large amount of it was salted and dried by the sailors and consumed weeks or even months later.

Although they are birds, penguin's wings have become modified as flippers and are useless for flying. The bones are flattened and the joints at the elbows and wrists have fused. Thus, unlike a normal bird, the wing cannot be folded. The flippers provide the main source of propulsion through the water with the legs, set well back on the body, acting as rudders. On land the rear set legs forces them upright and, when walking, to adopt a rocking waddle. When conditions are right they will toboggan on their bellies over snow and ice, or race downhill – always in imminent danger of crashing - or when conditions demand they can progress uphill and over rocks in a series of standing jumps. In the water they are expert swimmers and divers reaching speeds of up to 25 kilometres per hour. They may frequently be seen in open water porpoising. The purpose of this behaviour is uncertain as it is less energy efficient than staying completely submerged. However, it is believed that it has the benefit of allowing the penguin breathe more regularly and therefore swim much longer distances at greater speeds. It is also believed that it may be used to confuse and disorient both predators and prey. The fact that it may be seen in a number of species when approaching land lends credence to this view, as the edge of the shore is a region often patrolled by orca and leopard seals that would regard a plump penguin as a tasty snack. The penguin's distinctive 'tuxedo' colouring—black body with white belly—helps camouflage the bird in the water as it searches for food. When seen from below the white of its belly matches the lightness of the sky, and when viewed from above the darkness of its back blends in with the dark substrate of shallow seas.

Tony Soper,[13] provides an eloquent description of the anatomy of the penguins' body….

*Their compact streamlined bodies have a deep keel for a breastbone and massive paddle muscles. Their feathers are reduced in size and stiffened, with a fluffy aftershaft at the base. The down creates an insulating layer of air over a thick layer of blubber and skin. Their heads retract to create a perfect hydrodynamic shape. Effectively their bodies are packed in blubber, with a string vest and a windproof outer parka.'*

Penguins have been around for millions of years. Indeed, the ancestral penguin is thought to have evolved a mere five million years after the demise of the dinosaurs. It appears that there are at least 24 genera of extinct penguins,[14] containing a somewhat larger number of extinct species. Gaps in the geological record and a considerable number of unclassified fossil specimens will, undoubtedly, see these numbers grow in coming years.

One species, known as the colossus penguin (*Palaeeudyptes klekowskii* Myrcha, Tatur and del Valle 1990), was huge, standing up to 2m tall and

---

13 Soper, T. (2009) Antarctica – A Guide to the Wildlife, Bradt Travel Guides UK.

14 Jadwiszczak, P (2009), Penguin past: The current state of knowledge; https://www.researchgate.net/publication/230873362

weighing a hefty 116kg (18 stone). This huge bird was twice as tall and almost three times as heavy as the largest living penguin, the Emperor penguin, and it roamed the southern oceans 37 to 40 million years ago during the Eocene Epoch.

Penguins are predominantly aquatic creatures spending up to three quarters of their lives at sea. They feed by catching krill (small shrimp), small fish, squid and crabs within 20 metres of the surface, grabbing prey with their beaks and swallowing it whole whilst swimming. This doesn't mean that penguins cannot dive to great depth – the king penguin, the second largest species can dive to depths of up to 300 metres (1,000ft).

While a number of species may be seen loafing on ice floes or on shore, others only leave the water to moult (i.e. shed old feathers and grow new ones) and to breed.

Finding a single penguin is rare, although it happened to me, as the only Adélie penguin I saw on my trip to Antarctica was a loner standing on a lump of ice near the shore in Neko Harbour – ice conditions had prevented us from visiting the breeding colony in the Antarctic Sound. Seeing a single Adélie was unusual and probably represented an animal that had become isolated or lost from its group.

In New Zealand I was lucky to spot a single yellow-eyed penguin perched on the breakwater at the 'Whale Watch' marina, near Kaikoura. This was an uncommon, but, seemingly, not an unusual sighting, as others have reported seeing this species at this location. Couple the fact that it is an endangered rare bird, with it being the least social of the 17 recognised living penguin species, this was a real thrill.

Penguins are social animals and normally spend their life in colonies, or at least in groups that swim and feed together. During the breeding season several species form large 'rookeries'. The king penguin colonies I visited in South Georgia were vast. Saint Andrew's Bay has the largest colony – up to 300,000 birds; while Sailsbury Plain has up to 200,000 birds and is the second largest colony in the world. The sight is 'gobsmacking'. Hundreds of thousands of very large birds crushed together producing a cacophony of noise, a miasma of noisome fishy poo and a blur of black and white, fluffy brown (of downy chicks) and the flashing of orange/yellow necks and beaks as they head shake and bow in greeting to their mates.

Finding your mate or your chick would be impossible in such colonies save for the fact that each penguin has a distinct call which mates and chicks can hear and distinguish, even in the mewling din of the colony.

King penguins, like emperor penguins (their slightly larger cousins), lay only one egg at a time, which they insulate from the ground by balancing it on top of their feet and protect from the elements by tucking it into a flap of abdominal skin called a brood pouch. All other species of penguin lay two eggs.

I have been privileged to have seen penguins on four continents - the Galapagos, Humboldt and Magellanic in South America; the African along the south and western coast of South Africa; the little (or fairy) penguin in both Australia and New Zealand; the yellow-eyed penguin in New Zealand; and in the Antarctic - Adélies, chinstraps, and gentoos. The rest of my sightings were on the Falkland, South Georgia, South Orkney and South Shetland Islands, as well as individuals and groups porpoising through the freezing southern ocean or resting on ice floes. These include, among those already mentioned, king, macaroni, and rockhopper.

Edward Adrian Wilson who travelled with Scott on both the Discovery (as junior surgeon and zoologist) and Terra Nova (as Chief of Scientific Staff) expeditions noted that the main distinguishing feature of penguins was their head. This is the only place colour, if you disregard the feet of some, other than black and white, is to be found. Knowing that, and allowing for size then it is easy to distinguish species. The table below, and the illustration in the insert (page 161) provide a guide to identification.

| Species | Distinguishing features | Size |
|---|---|---|
| Emperor Penguin | The largest penguin species; short bill, large pale lemon yellow neck patch ; iris dark brown<br><br>Long 'trousers' i.e. white feathers go right down to the black feet. Back bluish-grey | 100 – 130cm |
| King Penguin | The second largest penguin; long slender bill<br><br>Bright orange ear patches; iris brown<br><br>White 'trousers' cropped above ankles. Black feet; back silver-grey | 85 – 95cm |
| Gentoo Penguin | Red bill; white 'bonnet' on top of the head; iris dark brown; orange-red bill; red-orange feet | 75 – 90cm |
| Adélie Penguin | Angular head and tiny black, red tipped bill; conspicuous white eye-ring; pink feet | 70 – 71cm |
| Chinstrap Penguin | White face black bill and conspicuous black line running from underneath the chin to connect with the black cap behind the ear; iris dark orange-brown, pink feet | 68 – 76cm |
| Rockhopper Penguin | Black face and reddish bill; bright yellow eyebrow begins well behind the bill and ends as long yellow plumes that fall sideways just behind the eye; iris bright red; pink feet | 45 – 58cm |

| Species | Distinguishing features | Size |
|---|---|---|
| Snares Penguin | Bright yellow stripe starting at the bill and running above the eye and forming a slight bushy crest behind the eye; massive red bill has bare pink skin at the base; iris bright red-brown; pink feet; | 51 – 61cm |
| Fiordland Penguin | This is the only crested penguin with white cheek-stripes; large orange-red bill; iris reddish-brown; feet pinkish-flesh coloured | 55 – 60cm |
| Erect-crested Penguin | Broad, bright yellow eyebrow starts at the base of the massive red bill - which has bare pink skin at the base - and forms a erect brush like crest above and behind the eye; iris dark reddish-brown; feet pinkish-flesh coloured | 60 – 67cm |
| Macaroni Penguin | Golden-orange eyebrow plumes start above the eye where they join and, on either side of the head, reach behind the eye where they droop; massive red-orange bill with bare pink skin at the base; iris dark reddish-brown; feet pinkish-flesh coloured | 71cm |
| Royal Penguin | Plumage similar to the Macaroni but the face is white tinged with grey; it is the only pale faced crested penguin; massive reddish orange-brown bill with pink skin at the base; iris is blackish brown and the feet are pinkish-flesh coloured | 65-75cm |

| Species | Distinguishing features | Size |
|---------|------------------------|------|
| Yellow-eyed Penguin | Pale yellow eye with a narrow red orbital ring; with a yellow bonnet that runs from the eye to the back of the head; upperparts pale dusky slate blue; long flesh coloured bill tipped red-brown; feet are pinkish-flesh coloured | 56 – 78cm |
| Little Penguin | Blue grey above, and on the head to just below the eye, white underneath; stout slightly hooked greyish-black bill; iris is whitish-grey; feet greyish. | 40 – 45cm |
| African Penguin | Black face bordered with white; a black band runs from the forehead to the nape; a broad black band on the chest and sides of the belly; black eye has a distinct pink orbital ring that extends as a patch forward towards the base of the bill; stout black bill has a sub-terminal band close to the tip; feet a mixture of pink and black flesh. | 60 – 70cm |
| Magellanic Penguin | Very similar to the African penguin but with TWO distinct black breast bands, the first across the base of the neck and the second, narrower band on the lower breast and flanks; black eye has a distinct pink orbital ring that extends as a patch forward to meet bare pink skin at the base of the bill; bill has a sub-terminal band close to the tip; blackish-grey feet | 70cm |

| Species | Distinguishing features | Size |
|---|---|---|
| Humboldt Penguin | Black head with a narrow white border that runs above and behind the eye, around the black ear-coverts and chin, and joins at the throat; a black breast-band that extends down the flanks to the thigh; fleshy-pink base to the broad black bill; bill has a sub-terminal band close to the tip; blackish-grey feet | 56 – 70cm |
| Galapagos Penguin | The second smallest penguin; black head with a narrow white border running from behind the eye, around the black ear-coverts and chin, to join on the throat; the throat is dark; a second narrower, and irregular dark band runs across the upper breast and down the flanks; the bill is dark; the feet are black – sometimes with flecks of flesh colour. | 50cm |

Edward Wilson (known as 'Uncle Bill' by the men on the expedition) died along with Scott, in March 1912, trapped by a blizzard, while returning to the Terra Nova from the South Pole. Wilson, Scott and three others, reached to South Pole on 18th January 1912, only to discover that the Norwegian explorer, Roald Amundsen, had beaten them there by a month. None of Scott's party survived the return trip.

To date, I have seen twelve of the seventeen known species of penguin in the wild. Those I have yet to see include the Fiordland penguin (the rarest of all), which occurs in south New Zealand, Stewart Island and adjacent islets; Snares penguin, which is found on Main and Broughton Islands some 200 kilometres south of New Zealand's South Island; the erect-crested penguin, which is found on Antipodes (860km south east of Stewart Island and New Zealand's most distant subantarctic island) and Bounty islands (9670km east-south-east of South Island New Zealand) - the latter named after his ship by Captain William Bligh some months before the famous mutiny); and the royal penguin which is confined to Macquarie Island and adjacent islets (politically part of Tasmania, Australia, it lies about half way between New Zealand and Antarctica). In order to make good this deficit, it looks like I will have to organise a trip from New Zealand to the Ross Ice Shelf. I better start planning!

# CHAPTER 3

# Cachalots, Humpbacks, Razorbacks, Pikeheads, and Sea Canaries

S ticking out like a finger pointing east across the relatively narrow and shallow Bering Strait is the Chukotka Peninsula in Siberian Russia. It is separated by approximately 85 kilometres of sea from the equally finger-like Seward Peninsula, which points west from Alaska in the United States of America. These two bits of bleak and barren land are not only separated in space but also in time, as the International Date Line, as well as the border, runs between the Diomede Islands plonked in the middle of the Strait. The smaller of these, Little Diomede, is USA territory and the bigger one, some 4 kilometres away and a day later in time, belongs to Russia.

During the Pleistocene Ice Age, which ended less than 12,000 years ago, the Bering Land Bridge occupied this space and formed a connection between Asia and the Americas. This land bridge permitted the passage of plant, animal and human migrants from further east. Archaeological studies in the area show that people have been living in the region for thousands of years – the Siberian (Chukotkan) Yupik in the west and Inupiat people in the east, both of whom depended on subsistence hunting and fishing for survival.

In 2007 a joint Russian-American team undertook an archaeological excavation at a site known as Un'en'en, located near the Chukchi whaling village of Nunligran, on the southern shores of the Chukotka Peninsula. Researchers searched for evidence of the Old Whaling culture; the only previously known Old Whaling culture site is on Cape Krusenstern, north-western Alaska. While excavating a wooden building, much to their delight, they found, buried beneath the collapsed roof, a 50 centimetre long ivory carving depicting a variety of animals and humans, and included scenes of people in umiaks[15] harpooning whales. Radiocarbon dating of roof timber in direct contact with the ivory carving showed it to be 3,000 years old. They also found the remains of whales and walruses, and tools that could have been used for hunting and butchering them. All of this, they suggest, is proof of whaling in the region up to 1,000 years earlier than previously believed. The location of the ivory carving beneath 3000 year old wood doesn't prove that the ivory is the same age but is strong circumstantial evidence. What is not in doubt, however, is that people in this area have hunted whales for millennia.

The topography of the Bering Strait is such that it acts as a choke-point between the Bering Sea to the south and the Chukchi Sea to the north – rather like the waist in an hourglass.

The Bering Sea supports a variety of whale species. Among these are the bowhead whale, gray whale, humpback whale, beluga whale, killer whale and the minke whale, as well as the vulnerable sperm whale, the endangered blue whale, fin whale, sei whale and very rare North Pacific right whale. The Chukchi Sea also supports bowhead, beluga, gray, humpback, fin, minke, and killer whales.

---

15 A Yupik and Inuit open boat made of a framework of driftwood or whalebone pegged (with ivory or antler) and wrapped with walrus or bearded seal skin. Up to seven seal skins, scraped free of hair, are required for a 9metre boat. These are sewn together using a waterproof stitch, stretched over the framework, tied in place with caribou sinew and allowed to shrink dry. Seal oil was used to waterproof the seams. These boats were traditionally rowed by women, although often paddled by men.

Records show that Arctic beluga and bowhead whales migrate south to spend winter in the Bering Sea, while humpback, fin and killer whales all travel north through the Bering Strait to feed in the biologically rich Chukchi Sea.

Given the former abundance of these species, it is not surprising that indigenous coastal communities hunted them. To catch a single whale would provide food, oil, bone and baleen that would last for months. It is most likely that they either shot the whale with an arrow or speared it with a harpoon to which was attached a drogue made from an inflated sealskin or a wooden drum. The whale would be shot or speared repeatedly as it surfaced to breathe. The drag of a series of buoyant floats would, over a period of time, weaken and exhaust the whale allowing it to be approached on the surface and killed. Blood spouting from its blowholes was a sign that it was finished. While brutal and gory, this type of hunting was entirely sustainable. The real problem arose when the activity reached industrial levels in the 17th to the 19th centuries.

Archaeological evidence suggests that people have been whaling for thousands of years. Norwegians were among the first to hunt whales in the Atlantic Ocean, as early as 4,000 years ago. The Japanese may have been doing so in the Pacific Ocean even earlier. *Kojiki*, (An Account of Ancient Matters), written in the 7th century AD appears to be the earliest mention of whaling in Japan. The Japanese hunted four species predominantly-the North Pacific right whale, the humpback whale, the fin whale and the gray whale.

The earliest records of Europeans being involved in whaling come from the Basque country and date from about 1000 AD. Basque whaling was initially an inshore operation targeting the North Atlantic right whale (*Eubalaena glacialis*). It was hunted and caught during its migration from November to February. This whale is one of the baleen whales (Mysticetes), which lack teeth, as opposed to the toothed whales (Odontocetes). Baleen whales have hundreds of comb-like baleen plates[16] hanging down from their upper jaw. The plates overlap in the mouth and each terminates in a fringe of bristles that act as a sieve to extract food from the water. These whales feed by scooping massive volumes of water, containing their preferred prey, into their huge gaping mouths. When it partly shuts its mouth and presses its tongue against its palate, the water is forced to escape sideways through the sieve of baleen and the gap between the upper and lower jaw of the partly closed mouth, while the prey, trapped on the other side of the baleen, is swallowed. Among the baleen whales, the streamlined and extremely fast rorquals are distinguished by having a series of longitudinal folds of skin running from below the mouth back towards the navel. This allows the mouth to be hugely expanded during feeding, thus enabling them engulf even greater volumes of water and food in a single scoop. Among this group are the two largest animals that have ever lived, the blue whale (*Balaenoptera musculus*), a giant 33 metres in length and 190 tonnes in weight and the fin whale (*Balaenoptera physalus*) at a slightly smaller 26 metres and lighter 74 tonnes.[17]

The North Atlantic right whale, to its detriment, was not a rorqual. It was a docile baleen whale that tended to stay close to the coast and often fed using a slow surface-skimming technique. Its high blubber content (which also makes it float when killed[18]) made it ideal prey for whalers.

During the calving season, these whales entered the shallow water of preferred bays. This provided the young with some protection from their only known natural predator - sharks - but left them vulnerable to human

---

16  Commonly called 'whalebones' by whalers – although they are not bony but are composed of keratin, a structural protein that is present in two forms α keratin in skin, hair, wool, finger and toe nails, animal claws, horns and hooves and the harder β keratin found in the nails, scales and claws of reptiles, the shells of tortoises, turtles and terrapins; the feathers beaks and claws of birds; and the quills of porcupines. Keratin in baleen is of the hard α keratin type.

17  The largest dinosaur to have lived was the sauropod Argentinosaurus at 23 meters in length and 36 tonnes in weight.

18  and which produces high yields of whale oil when rendered

hunters. If whalers spotted a mother and a calf, they would deliberately go after the calf, in the full knowledge that the mother wouldn't abandon it, thus making her easier prey for the hunters. This type of hunting took place near the shore using relatively small boats to harpoon the whale. It is estimated that up to a third of the North Atlantic right whales captured were calves. Obviously, this had drastic effects on stock replenishment and this, together with the enormous hunting pressure these whales suffered over several hundred years, has resulted in the North Atlantic right whale currently being on the cusp of extinction, with many regarding them as being functionally extinct in the eastern North Atlantic. It is not for nothing they were called 'right whales'. This appellation was deliberately chosen as they were the right whales to catch.

The Basques dominated whaling for five centuries. Their vessels, or the English, Dutch and Danish vessels they served on as whaling experts, ranged from the South Atlantic to the North Atlantic (as far north as Spitsbergen[19]) and as far west as Terranova (Newfoundland and Labrador).

When the English and Dutch took up whaling in earnest in the early 17th century, they hired Basque whalers to teach them what to do. Once the transfer of knowledge had been completed, they squeezed their former tutors from the richer hunting grounds. As a result, Basque involvement in large scale whaling declined throughout the 18th century and virtually disappeared by the 19th century.

Whaling by the Dutch concentrated in Spitsbergen and competition between them and the British saw armed gun-boats guarding the inshore whaling grounds. Other less protected fleets, such as the French, Spanish and Danish were forced to hunt and catch whales in the open sea – a more difficult and hazardous operation, with the whales having to be processed and rendered on board ship.

---

19 This was the former name for all the islands of the Svalbard Archipelago in northern Norway. Now it is only used to describe the largest and most populated island of the group.

The Dutch enjoyed the comfort of a land based processing station at Smeerenburg, on Amsterdam Island. This is now part of the North-West Spitsbergen National Park. The station operated between 1614 and 1655 but fell into decline as the whales diminished in number and was abandoned when the processing of blubber to oil transferred back to the home port of the whalers.

The name Smeerenburg translates from the Dutch as 'blubber town' reflecting its primary purpose in its heyday. When we visited in 2013, there was little sign of the settlement. This is not surprising as most of the sixteen or so buildings and the fort had been constructed from timber. Blubber Town never got very large. At its height there were probably no more than 200 men employed in flensing whales, boiling blubber into oil, and coopering barrels for onward transportation of the whale oil.

The location of the settlement is an austere and bleak place, planted on a barren windswept headland, otherwise occupied by the occasional beached walrus, but with sublime views over water to glaciers and snow-capped mountains. Whale vertebrae and bones, bits of timber and flotsam decorate the shore. Some of these, undoubtedly, are the remnants of its glory as a bustling whaling village. As this is a national monument, visitors are required to watch where they step and not to touch anything for fear of disturbing artefacts that represent cultural heritage. The most obvious remaining signs of the old settlement are the large circular concretised remains of whale oil that built up around the kettles in which the blubber was boiled. The rest of Smeerenburg has largely disappeared under the sand.

As we sailed the waters around Svalbard we were lucky to spot a variety of whale species. What was surprising was how close to the ship these leviathans came. We had only just left Longyearbyen, the capital of Svalbard, when we spotted a small pod of five or six beluga whales (*Delphinapterus leucas*). These small whales (5.5 metres long) are unlikely to be confused with any other because of their creamy-white colour and lack of a dorsal fin. This makes them relatively easy to spot in a calm blue sea but difficult to pick out among the whitecaps of rougher water or floating ice. They are among the most vocal of the whales; their clicks, and whistles and twitters being easily heard both above and below the water; this explains why they were known by another name – the Sea Canary. Belugas are toothed whales that feed mainly on fish but will also eat clams, crab, shrimp, squid and octopus. Their natural predators are killer whales and polar bears. Their white colouration provides some protection for them as they are invisible from above to polar bears stalking across the sea ice and from below against the sea ice by killer whales. While they were commercially hunted during the 19th and early 20th centuries, they have been hunted by the native peoples of North America, Greenland and Russia for many centuries. This continues today.

Seven days later, and early in the bright Arctic morning, we saw a super-pod of at least 100 Beluga Whales. Their white backs stood out against the dark blue of the ocean. As we were sailing parallel to the coast, the vista of snow covered mountains on land and the ice floes all around at sea presented a stunning backdrop to their activities. We were able to draw reasonably close (we didn't want to approach too close and disturb them) and watched as they ignored us and hunted cooperatively for their breakfast. After an hour of observation, we headed to the galley for ours.

Not long after our first sighting of belugas, we spotted a common (or Northern) minke whale (*Balaenoptera acutorostrata*), a species that I have seen a number of times at home off the south and the west coasts of Ireland. This is the smallest (10 metres), but the most abundant, of the rorquals. We were to see this species again in Woodfjorden. This whale is also known by the less flattering name of 'pikehead'.

The minke is now the only whale being hunted commercially and is also taken by the Japanese whaling fleet in the Southern Ocean under the guise of so called 'Scientific Whaling'. The Japanese claim that their efforts are strictly for research purposes, yet the great bulk of what they catch and kill is offered for sale as whale meat through supermarkets. What this catch lacks in terms of providing meaningful and useful new knowledge, it replaces by pandering to a minority and dying appetite for what is increasingly viewed as an inappropriate food source.

The eight nations that continued whaling 'legally' – i.e. within International Whaling Commission (IWC) rules - killed and introduced into the human food chain, in the 30 years leading up to 2015, some 47,677 whales.[20] This killing continues today. The futility of this abhorrent practice is underscored by the fact that, even in Japan, the desire to eat whale meat is diminishing. A poll commissioned by Greenpeace in 2006 found that 95 percent of Japanese people very rarely or never eat whale meat. It also revealed that the amount of uneaten frozen whale meat stockpiled in Japan between 2002 and 2012 doubled to 4,600 tons.[21]

Norway is another country that still hunts whales. Proclaimed to be both culturally and historically important, whale meat, however, only makes up a small fraction of the Norwegian diet. In 2014, one of the 'best' years for catching minke whales, the country experienced significant difficulty in moving the 700 tons harvested.[22]

The other main whaling country is Iceland. Whale meat is common on menus throughout the country. Surprisingly, according to Whale and Dolphin Conservation (WDC), only 1.7% of Icelanders eat whale meat (given the small population this equates to about 5,600 people). Even more surprising is that 35-40% of visitors to Iceland eat whale meat, most likely out of unthinking curiosity.[23] This now also appears to be falling, according to the International Fund for Animal Welfare (IFAW). A lot of whale meat harvested by the Icelanders goes uneaten and much of it remains frozen for years and some is exported to Japan.

---

20  This total does not include so called 'illegal' killing, i.e. killing that is not sanctioned by the IWC.

21  https://www.wired.com/2015/12/japanese-barely-eat-whale-whaling-big-deal/#comments

22  https://munchies.vice.com/en_us/article/kbxv7m/whale-meat-is-a-tough-sell-in-norway

23  http://www.bbc.com/earth/story/20151203-why-do-some-countries-still-hunt-whales

The IWC allows Denmark (including Greenland), Russia, the United States and the Caribbean nation St Vincent and the Grenadines to conduct aboriginal subsistence whaling.

Our first sighting of the beluga was to prove a red letter day. Not only did we see minke whales but were interrupted at dinner by the appearance close to our ship of a humpback whale (*Megaptera novaeangliae*). The captain slowed the ship down and we were able to observe this large (16 metre, 30 tonne) rorqual at close quarters. With a distinctive body shape, exceptionally long white flippers that have knobs on the leading edge, and a knobbly head this whale is easily identified. It habit of breaching[24], fluking[25], lobtailing[26] and flipper slapping is distinctive. Males produce a complex song lasting 10 to 20 minutes, which they repeat for hours at a time. Its purpose is unclear. Bio-acoustician Dr Roger Payne released the best-selling album *Songs of the Humpback Whale* in 1970,[27] selling over 100,000 copies.

The particular whale we were watching was swimming in fairly shallow water (40-60 metres deep). We saw it surface, blow[28] several times and then fluke, a prelude to diving. The whale was probably feeding because it fluked a number of times.

Humpbacks have some of the most diverse and spectacular feeding techniques of all baleen whales. Commonly, they lunge at shoals of the krill (in the southern hemisphere) or fish that form the bulk of their prey, hoovering up huge mouthfuls. They may even stun prey with flipper slapping or lobtailing. However, their most ingenious method is 'bubble fishing'. This involves the whale diving beneath a shoal of fish and then swimming upwards in a spiral while blowing out air from its two distinctive

---

24  leaping clear of the water

25  Flipping up their flukes (tail) and showing their black and white pattern on the underside

26  Forceful slapping of the flukes on the water

27  CRM Records, Capitol Records

28  Blowing or spouting refers to the act of breathing. This is an explosive exhalation producing a cloud of water droplets above the animals head. The whale inhales immediately after blowing.

blowholes. This creates a circular net of bubbles that surrounds their prey. The whale continues to swims upward through the centre of this circular bubble net, mouth agape. The pleated grooves, typical of rorquals, in the whale's mouth increase capacity and allow it capture thousands of fish in one gulp. The bubble net appears as a circle on the surface of the water and, if seen, acts as a prelude to this huge mammal lunging towards the surface like a dart heading straight for the bull's-eye.

Bubble fishing is sometimes undertaken cooperatively by several Humpbacks, enabling them exploit huge shoals of fish.

Humpback whales are known to migrate up to 25,000km each year. They feed in rich polar waters, and migrate to tropical or subtropical waters to breed and give birth. Indeed they are frequently seen along the coast of Ireland as they pass up and down on their migration and now support, particularly in the south west of the country, active whale watching enterprises. It is a matter of pride that in 1991 the Irish Government declared all its territorial waters to be a whale and dolphin sanctuary. This is an example that has yet to spread to the rest of the European Union.

Populations of humpback whales exist in both the northern and southern hemispheres but these whales do not normally cross the equator, although it is known that some mixing may occur between sub-populations in a particular hemisphere.

Like other large whales, the humpback was a target for the whaling industry. Once hunted to the brink of extinction, stocks have partially recovered. However, the species is not totally free from hunting. One hundred and eight Humpback Whales have been killed under the rubric of 'Aboriginal Subsistence Catches' since the moratorium on whaling came into force in 1985. It is debatable, whether there is still a need for this type of exploitation. One of the reasons given is the preservation of cultural traditions, but I can think of many cultural traditions that have been abandoned as people progressed from subsistence to a more sustainable form of existence, and to a more enlightened view of the role our progressively diminishing biodiversity plays in the balance of global ecosystems. Activities that were the norm in the past are now looked upon with horror. Examples that readily spring to mind include killing elephants for ivory, tigers for body parts, rhinos for their horn, and American bison for their skins. Recent research has shown that humans are directly responsible for some 322 species of reptiles, birds, and mammals becoming extinct in the past 500 years. Included among these are the dodo, which was killed for food; the Caribbean monk seal, the Japanese sea lion and Stellar's sea cow, which were killed for oil, meat and fur; the passenger pigeon whose teeming millions were slaughtered for 'sport'; and the thylacine which had a price on its head to prevent it attacking introduced sheep - to name a few. Human behaviours that were once seen as normal in some societies, such as, slavery, infanticide, geronticide, human sacrifice, head hunting and ritual suicide are now completely beyond the pale. I may be accused of not comparing like with like and exaggeration, but this depends on your view of the value we should place on all life. I cannot see a clear case for continuing the practice in these indigenous communities as it is clearly evident that they could survive without them – as they have to do in some years when the animals do not turn up or the weather is too bad to permit hunting. Just liking the taste of a particular rare animal's meat is a poor justification for killing it. Continuation of the practice seems to me, to have more to do with political expediency than necessity.

Whales do not appear to be frightened of ships – many are quite indifferent to them. This was brought home to us when four fin whales surfaced beside our ship. These massive animals cruised back and forth near the vessel for more than an hour. It is not surprising, therefore, that the fin whale is the species of great whale that is most frequently struck by ships.[29] It is difficult to appreciate the sheer bulk of these animals when

---

29 https://www.greateratlantic.fisheries.noaa.gov/shipstrike/whatsnew/Laist%20et%20al_2001.pdf accessed 16/03/2017

you see them in the water. A couple of years ago, I photographed a dead, beached, fin whale on Keel Beach on Achill Island in Ireland, and was in awe of its huge size. Interestingly, northern hemisphere fin whales tend to be bigger than southern hemisphere ones. It was easy to appreciate that it was the second largest animal that ever existed. It is one of the rorquals and is sometimes known as a 'Razorback' because of the distinctive ridge that extends from behind the dorsal fin to the flukes. The baleen of this whale is interesting. The plates reach a maximum length just shy of a metre and on the right side the baleen plates in the first third of the mouth are white and the ones in the remaining two thirds are dark grey. All the baleen plates on the left side of the mouth are dark grey. It is a fast swimmer capable of reaching sprinting speeds up to 40km/h, although their cruising speed is considerably lower. The former director of the American Museum of Natural History, Roy Chapman Andrews,[30] in 1916 called the fin whale *'the greyhound of the sea..... for its beautiful, slender body is built like a racing yacht and the animal can surpass the speed of the fastest ocean steamship.'* This very speed protected them from the early whalers who couldn't keep up with them. Even when caught, their tendency to sink rather than float made them a poor option.

Like a number of the other great whales, fin whales are highly migratory. In spring and early summer they can be found in colder waters, where productivity is high and food plentiful (such as the North American coast and Arctic waters around Greenland, Iceland, northern Norway and the Barents Sea). In autumn and winter they move to warmer waters to mate and give birth (the Caribbean and the Gulf of Mexico and from southern Norway to Spain). Research has shown that interbreeding can and has taken place between fin whales and blue whales, despite the fact that the two species separated several millions years ago. Fin whales feed mainly on crustaceans (such as krill and other euphausiids), squid and small schooling

---

30 January 26, 1884 – March 11, 1960; allegedly one of the real life models upon which the movie character of Indiana Jones was based.

fish. Feeding on up to two tonnes of food a day, they need to make every mouthful count. To improve efficiency of catch, they sometimes circle schools of fish at speed, herding the fish into tight balls which they can then engulf in their expanded mouth and throat. In order to do this they often roll onto their right side to feed.

While secure from early whalers as a result of their speed, the invention of the steamship and exploding harpoons shot from cannons was a disaster for the bigger and faster species such as the blue whale, fin whale and the sei whale. Populations were heavily depleted by humans who hunted them to near extinction in the first half of the 20th century. Various estimates indicate that between 10,000 to 30,000 fin whales were slaughtered each year between 1935 and 1965. Another figure shows that around 704,000 fin whales were caught in Antarctic whaling operations alone between 1904 and 1975.

Even since the IWC zero catch limits came into force in 1985, fin whales continue to be hunted. Iceland has killed a total of 843 over the intervening period and West Greenland, under the derogation of Aboriginal Subsistence Catches, has taken 356.

During the 16th to the 20th century whaling was not just the prerogative of European Nations. The Americans were also deeply involved. American whaling appears to have begun in the area around New York and New England, with hunters in small boats pursuing whales from the shore. By the 18th century, this had developed into a significant industry, centred on Nantucket in Massachusetts.

The origin of whaling in Nantucket is described by Obed Macy[31] in 1835 thus:

*The sight of whales playing near the shore led the inhabitants to contemplate the advantages which would arise, could they become possessed of the proper means of taking them.'*

31 Macy, O., The History of Nantucket (1835); Boston, Hilliard, Gray and Co.

The first whaling expedition was undertaken by some of the original purchasers of the Island sometime between 1660 and 1670 when, according to Macy

---

*'A whale of the kind called 'scragg,' came into the harbour and continued there for three days.....'* To prevent its escape and to capture it *They accordingly invented and caused to be wrought for them, a harpoon with which they attacked and killed the whale. This first success encouraged them to undertake whaling as a permanent business; whales being at that time numerous in the vicinity of the shores.'*

---

Paul Dudley in 1725[32] gave a description of the 'scrag' whale that permits identification as to what species it might have been:

---

*The Scrag Whale is near akin to the Fin-back, but instead of a Fin upon his Back, the Ridge of the Afterpart of his Back is scragged with half a Dozen Knobs or Nuckles'*

---

The aforementioned 'scrag' was most likely a gray whale (also known as a Devilfish). These whales are now confined to the Pacific; the North Atlantic population was rendered extinct by the late 17th to early 18th century.

Macy writes of an agreement between the owners of Nantucket Island with one James Lopar that marked the beginning of organised commercial whaling. This agreement dated the 5th of April 1672 stated:

---

*James Lopar doth Ingage to carry on a design of Whale Citching on the Island of Nantucket.....'*

---

Inshore whaling had been taking place in neighbouring Cape Cod for some time and, finding that these whalers were more successful than the

---

32 Dudley, P (1725). 'An essay upon the natural history of whales' : Philosophical Transactions of the Royal Society. 33 (381–391): 256–259. doi:10.1098/rstl.1724.0053. JSTOR 103782

Nantucket Islanders, they, in 1690, employed a man with the splendid name of Ichabod Padduck to teach them how best to kill whales and to extract their oil. The Nantucket islanders made use of the local Indians in this enterprise as there weren't sufficient whites to support this growing enterprise and the Indians, themselves, took to it like ducks to water as they had a long history of fishing in the area. The main species they hunted near the shore was the North Atlantic right whale. As with whaling in the eastern North Atlantic, right whales in the western North Atlantic were brought to the cusp of extinction. Currently, they are among the most endangered of the whale species. It is thought that only some 400 individuals survive in these waters, migrating annually up to 2500km each way, between their traditional feeding grounds in the Gulf of Maine and their winter calving waters off the coast of Georgia and Florida.

The first sperm whale (*Physeter macrocephalus*), or 'Cachalot' (meaning 'big head') encountered by the Nantucket Islanders was found dead, washed up on one of the island's beaches in the southwest. Macy does not, in his history of the Island, indicate when this occurred but it is apparent that the islanders prized it for the amount of oil they were able to get and there was considerable dispute over who owned the rights. The sperm whale is a toothed whale and its teeth were considered to be very valuable. Macy states that these '*had been extracted by a white man and an Indian, before any others had any knowledge of the whale.*'

The first sperm whale actually harpooned by the Nantucket whalers is reputed to have been killed by one Christopher Hussey sometime around 1712, after his boat had been blown some distance from the coast. Hussey's capture of this prized beast encouraged others to set sail in larger vessels. By 1715 six sloops[33] were engaged in the business. As the industry expanded bigger sloops and schooners[34] were added to the fleet. Hunting

---

33 a sailing boat with a single mast and a fore-and-aft rig. A sloop has one head-sail and one main sail.

34 a sailing ship with two or more masts, typically with the foremast smaller than the mainmast

whales expanded southwards and eastwards of the Grand Banks. As whaling continued to increase, boats sailed further and further, reaching Davis' Straits (Labrador Sea, 1746), Disco Island in Baffin Bay (Greenland, 1751), the coast of Guinea (West Africa, 1763) and the coast of Brazil (1774). By 1775 a number of large brigs[35] were added to the fleet allowing whales to be hunted much further afield. In the late 17th century whalers from Nantucket were hunting whales from the Arctic to the coast of Africa, Brazil, the Pacific and as far south as the Falkland Islands. The first Yankee whalers rounded Cape Horn in 1791, entering the Pacific Ocean in pursuit of the cachalot. By 1792 the sperm whalers had reached the coast of Peru, and in 1820 extended west to hunt sperm whales midway between Japan and Hawaii, the latter island being used as a rest and repair stop, to engage more crew and stock up on fresh fruits and vegetables. Many of the whalers who hunted these waters came from Nantucket.

Such was the fame of Nantucket as a centre of whaling that there is some evidence that Herman Melville drew on Obed Macy's history to inform the section on Nantucket in his novel *Moby-Dick*. Melville didn't actually visit Nantucket for the first time until six months after his book had been published. Melville had personal experience of whaling in the Pacific as in 1840 he signed aboard the whaler *Acushnet*. However, in 1842, eighteen months into the four year voyage, he and shipmate Richard 'Toby' Greene jumped ship on Nuku Hiva in the Marquesas, French Polynesia. Melville wrote of his time there in his first novel, *Typee,* an embellished account of his 'life among the cannibals'. Now generally forgotten, during his life it was by far his most famous publication; *Moby-Dick* when it was published barely made a ripple.

Mary and I visited Nuku Hiva aboard the *Aranui 5*, which services the Marquesas from Tahiti, in 2016. We landed in Taiohae the administrative capital of the Islands which Melville described thus in *Typee*

---

35 a sailing vessel with two square-rigged masts. The main mast of a brig is the aft one. To improve manoeuvrability, the mainmast carries a small (gaff rigged) fore-and-aft sail.

> 'No description can do justice to its beauty. …From the verge of the water the land rises uniformly on all sides, with green and sloping acclivities, until from gently rolling hill-sides and moderate elevations it insensibly swells into lofty and majestic heights.'

Despite French annexation and Melville's fears that it would ruin the island, time has treated it well. Showing just a little bit of modernisation to the town and the dock, the bay of Taiohae looks much the same today as it must have in Melville's time and the people are still happy and friendly but in a major change from the people depicted in *Typee*, disinclined to eat you. Ironically, almost in a direct line from the town jail across the bay is a monument, erected in 1992, commemorating the 150th anniversary of Melville's arrival on the Island. In effect, the jail points to a monument to a deserter. If he had been unlucky to have been caught he would have been subject to federal laws providing for his forced return to his ship and would also have been subject to any other punishment deemed fit by the ship's master for desertion.[36] The vessel's master could discipline a seaman through loss of earnings and goods, confinement or beating.

Melville's experience as a sailor and working on a number of whalers gave him plenty of material for *Moby-Dick*.

The eponymous whale of *Moby-Dick*, albeit a rare white whale, was a sperm whale, and the story relates the obsession of Captain Ahab, master of the *Pequod*, in hunting the animal[37] that on the previous voyage bit off his leg at the knee. The story has a basis in fact. There was a well known hard to catch white whale in the Pacific known as Mocha Dick,[38] which was reputed to have destroyed many whaleboats with his 'immense flukes' or 'crushed in his powerful jaws' before he was finally killed in 1838.

---

36  https://www.law.upenn.edu/journals/jbl/…/Gutoff9U.Pa.J.Lab.&Emp.L.87(2006).pdf

37  Deemed a 'spouting fish' by Ishmael, in the book

38  J. N. Reynolds. 'Mocha Dick: or the White Whale of the Pacific: A Leaf from a Manuscript Journal,' *The Knickerbocker, or New-York Monthly Magazine*. Vol. 13, No. 5, May 1839, pp. 377–392.

Attacks by sperm whales on ships, though infrequent, were known at the time. In 1820 George Pollard Jr, a Nantucket captain lost his ship, the *Essex*, when it sank after it was rammed by a sperm whale. At this time, most of the crew were in small whaleboats, away from the mother ship.

We didn't see live sperm whales while we were in Polynesia or the North Atlantic, though one dead specimen washed ashore a couple of years ago, in Blacksod Bay, in Ireland, not too far from where we have a house. Their habit of hunting in very deep water beyond the continental shelf means that, except in very specific locations, they are rarely casually observed.

Whaling in Australia and New Zealand started in the late 18th century. There is no record that the native people of Australia or New Zealand hunted whales before the arrival of white men although it is known that the Māori did eat stranded whales. Whaling never became a significant industry in New Zealand, but in Australia from the time of colonisation, and for about 70 years, the whaling industry enjoyed some commercial success. Thereafter, petroleum superseded whale oil and workers abandoned the oceans to pursue gold, following the 1850s gold rush. Although whaling continued into the 20th century it was never a major industry in either country. Since 1978, the Marine Mammals Protection Act saw whales protected within New Zealand's 370km Exclusive Economic Zone. In April 1979 Australia followed suit and banned whaling.

The town of Kaikōura on the South Island of New Zealand has become a major centre for watching sperm whales. Mary and I visited Kaikōura in February of 2016 and took a trip offshore to see the sperm whales that frequent these waters.

The Kaikōura whale sanctuary, which extends 45 kilometres both north and south of the Kaikōura peninsula and 56km out to sea, is intended to protect the animals that frequent the area. What makes the Kaikōura sanctuary unique is its underwater topography and the water currents that collide in it.

Just offshore, the continental shelf drops rapidly into a series of canyons and troughs – the Kowhai Canyons to the east of the peninsula, the Conway Trough to the south, and sandwiched in between the 60km, u-shaped trench of the Kaikoura Canyon. Starting close to shore, this canyon quickly plunges to a depth of up to 2000 metres and extends to 800sq km. A complex mixture of currents supports a huge biomass of creatures not expected at these depths. Bristle worms, heart urchins, spoon worms and sea cucumbers are abundant, and support bottom feeding fish. Cold Antarctic currents flowing up the east coast of the South Island clashing with warm sub-tropical currents flowing down from the north produce an abundance of nutrients close to the surface. Eddies in the deep water of the canyon continually stir the sediment and allow the upwelling of even more nutrients. These nutrients fuel phytoplankton (minute floating plants), which in turn supports zooplankton (minute invertebrate animals) and these in turn support larger animals and birds. When all these surface water animals die, their remains sink to the bottom and provide nutrients for the life living there. The closeness of the canyon to the shore allows for additional nutrients, in the form of run-off from land, to enter the canyon. This results in the Kaikōura Canyon being able to support a deep water biomass that is 100 times greater than that observed at these depths anywhere else in the world.

This is ideal habitat for the deep-water loving sperm whale. This is the largest toothed whale and the largest living toothed predator. Reaching up to 20m in length, it has a huge boxy head that comprises one third of the body length. This unique shape, together with its angled, bushy blow from the single blowhole on the left of its head, makes it easy to distinguish at sea. Sperm whales can be found anywhere in the oceans of the world, but their distribution is patchy. In summer, there is a general move towards the poles and in winter they move back to warmer waters. They prefer deep water in the submarine canyons at the edge of the continental shelf. Here they can hunt for their preferred prey of giant squid (*Architeuthis dux*) and colossal squid (*Mesonychoteuthis hamiltoni*), both of which provide a substantial meal worthy of the effort put into catching them. Both the whale and the squid are capable of diving to enormous depths – down to 2250m.

Characteristic features distinguishing between these two huge cephalopods are that the giant squid's eight arms and two tentacles have suckers lined with small teeth, while the colossal squid , as well as having a larger beak than its cousin, has arms with tentacles that have the additional armoury of swivelling, as well as three-pointed sharp hooks. The sharp beak of a squid may sometimes lodge in the whale's intestine. Irritation of the intestines may lead to the production of ambergris - a solid, waxy, grey brown substance. Its name *amber gris* comes from the French for amber (a plant resin) and grey. Ambergris is eventually expelled along with the faeces or, more rarely, vomited through the mouth. This used to be highly valued as a fixative by perfumers that allowed the scent to last much longer. Herman Melville in Moby-Dick mused on the irony that '*fine ladies and gentlemen should regale themselves with an essence found in the inglorious bowels of a sick whale.*'

Although ambergris has largely been replaced in perfume manufacture, it is still a valuable substance. Sometimes found washed up on beaches, a lump weighing 1.1kg was found on a beach in Wales and was subsequently sold at auction in September 2015 for £11,000.

Circular shaped scars on the skin of sperm whales are believed to have been caused by the suction cups of both species of squid and the hooks on the arms and tentacles of the colossal squid are reputed to be the cause of scars on the back of sperm whales. Tasty though these huge molluscs are, the bulk of the whale's diet consists of medium sized squid, as well as octopuses and rays.

The large square head of this species, its main distinguishing feature, contains a huge cavity, called the spermaceti organ.[39] This is believed to be

---

39 Whalers originally knew this whale as the spermaceti whale

a buoyancy aid and also may be used to focus the sonar clicks made by the whale. It is packed with web-like tubes filled with a yellowish wax. It is believed by some, but hotly disputed by others, that shrinking the density of the wax by sucking cooling water into the blowhole helps the whale sink; increasing the density as the wax heats up helps it rise. Others hold that the main function of the spermaceti is in focusing the whale's echolocation when it is deep in the dark ocean during a dive.

Spermaceti was prized by whalers as it was used in the manufacture of the highest quality candles, ones that burnt with a very bright flame. Oil from spermaceti was deemed to be the best lubricating oil on earth and was used in watches and sewing machines and in the automobile industry. There is some suggestion that, because of its very low freezing point, sperm oil saw widespread use in the aerospace industry until the use of whale oil was banned in the USA in 1972.

We were very lucky to see one of these magnificent animals several kilometres offshore over the Kaikōura canyon. While there were no signs of the animal on the surface, the captain of our vessel had detected its presence using a hydrophone – a sort of underwater microphone that picked up the clicks the whale uses to echolocate. Dives rarely last more than 45 minutes (although the whale can stay underwater more than twice as long as this) and the whale frequently surfaces near where it began the dive. Some studies indicate that the whale may hunt by swimming upside-down when it reaches the bottom of its dive, allowing squid to be seen above them highlighted against the dimly lit surface.

After we waited about 15 minutes I saw, and heard, the whale blow as it surfaced. This 15 – 16m leviathan stayed relatively motionless on top of the water for some time as it breathed. It remained in this position for fully 15 minutes (not unusual for these whales who breathe at about 20 second intervals and need to spend enough time at the surface to take in sufficient oxygen for a dive). After raising its head slightly for a final breath it straightened out its body, arched its back and flipped up its flukes high into the air to dive vertically back into the abyss. What a glorious sight.

In November of 2016, Kaikōura was struck by a 7.8 magnitude earthquake, making it second in strength to the 8.3 magnitude Wairarapa earthquake which, in 1855, struck just to the north in the Cook Strait area. The earthquake resulted in damage to buildings, major land slips, road blockages, and the closure of key rail and road links for many months. Although dozens of people were injured, there were only two recorded fatalities. Viewing the extent of the damage from the air the Prime Minister, John Key, described a scene of 'utter devastation' that he believed would cost billions of dollars to repair. Leaving out public works, some $1Bn of insurance claims have already been made.

One useful outcome to emerge from this earthquake was the amount of scientific data obtained. It was one of the best recorded earthquakes anywhere in the world. While it brought the communities of affected areas together in adversity it also brought them together in a more physical sense; a findings of the scientific research that has taken place has shown that, as a direct result of the earthquake, parts of the South Island are now more than 5m closer to the North Island.

Despite the damage, Kaikoura has reopened for business and whale watching in this unique place has resumed.

As they became scarcer in the late 18th and early 19th centuries, hunting for whales and in particular, the sperm whale, forced whalers to sail farther and further from home. Eventually, whalers were found everywhere, covering all the oceans of the globe.

This effort hit its peak in the mid to late 19th century with the invention of gun-loaded harpoons, explosive harpoons, fast steam-powered catcher boats, and steam winches. The efficiency this brought to the industry led scientists to estimate that more whales were killed in the early 1900s than in the previous four centuries combined. As seen everywhere when efficiency and greed is introduced into hunting or fishing enterprises, stock levels rapidly become diminished and the enterprise becomes economically unsustainable. This is what happened with whaling. It became too efficient, too successful and went far beyond the ability of the stock to replace itself by breeding. It reduced entire whale populations to near extinction.

Antarctic whaling really began on a large scale in 1904 when a whale processing station was built by the Norwegian sea captain Carl Anton Larsen at Grytviken, South Georgia. When my friend, Maurice Doran, and I visited in 2010, this had become a massive heap of rusting whale oil boilers, corrugated metal and splintered wood. Half-sunk vessels, including the whale-catcher 'Petrel', whose rusted harpoon gun points uselessly inland towards the nearby mountains, flake out their end on the edge of the beach, as their metal plates turn to rust.

Littering the shore and some of the inflowing streams are the bones of the slaughtered. These remains of long dead ocean-going behemoths provide enduring testament of a brutal endeavour. Deserted by humans, this formerly thriving centre of commerce is now reclaimed by its original occupiers - Antarctic fur seals (*Arctocephalus gazella*).

While we were in Grytviken, we drank a toast to a fellow Irishman – Ernest Shackleton – buried in the small whaler's cemetery. His plot is marked by a simple granite column. As we drank, we poured a libation for the 'Boss' to share. We would have preferred to have shared a drop of good Irish whiskey with him, but the Russian crew of our ship had only provided vodka. Ah Well! Any port in a storm, I'm sure he would agree.

A number of Antarctic shore-based stations were in operation, with some kind of regulation regarding catches, in the early years of the 20th century. We visited one of these on Deception Island. Here the whales were stripped of their blubber, baleen or anything else that was useful and anything that remained was left to drift away. The smell of rotting flesh in the shallow water, or on-shore if the carcass was washed ashore would have been disguised by the even stronger smell of rendering whale blubber. Such was the extent and intensity of this enterprise, over a relatively short period that, in some places, the beaches consisted almost entirely of whale bones. A plaque on Signy Island in the South Orkneys group gives details of catches in South Orkneys and South Shetlands for the years 1911 – 1930. This period saw the slaughter of 78 right whales, 61,336 blue whales, 48,023 fin whales, 1,796 sei whales, 6,742 humpback whales and 184 sperm whales for a grand total of 118,159 whales in just under 20 years. This averages 6,219 whales each year in this fishery alone.

The first 'factory ships' were built in 1925, permitting the entire whaling process to take place at sea and rendering the shore based stations all but obsolete. As the whalers were operating entirely in the open ocean and not within the territory of any particular country, regulation did not exist. No restrictions existed as to species that could be taken, catch size, sex of the animal or even its age. This free-for-all resulted in a swift and progressive decline of species as the 'low hanging fruit' was harvested and depleted and the whalers then moved on to the next species. Initially, the slow moving humpback was the catch of choice. As its numbers dwindled, whalers went after the much faster blue whale; as they became scarce attention was turned to the second largest whale, the fin whale, and then the sei whale.

It wasn't until the late 1970's, when International agreement banned the taking of fin and sei whale, that whaling ships turned to the much smaller minke whale. These creatures continue to be slaughtered to this day, both in the name of so-called scientific research and commercially by the current whaling nations (Japan, Norway and Iceland).

A moratorium on commercial whaling was established by the International Whaling Commission (IWC) in 1982, and came into effect for the 1985/1986 season. From then up to 2014 (the last year for which data is available) commercial catches (under objection or reservation by the IWC) amount to a total of 24,381 whales killed. Most of this results from catches made by Norway and Iceland. Given the nature of its establishment, the IWC is a fairly toothless organisation and the most it can do is indicate its displeasure by stating that these catches are either under objection to the moratorium decision, or under reservation to it.

What is encouraging is the number of countries who are vehemently opposed to any form of whale catching. As a result of their efforts and agreement in the IWC, the stability of whale populations - though still parlous in a number of cases - shows distinct signs of improvement. The eighteen day trip Maurice and I took from Ushuaia to the Falklands, South Georgia, the South Shetlands and the Antarctic Peninsula resulted in us observing a total of 71 individual whales, comprising five different species. We saw 3 fin whales – one of which had three hourglass dolphins bow-riding on its nose; a pod of 6 orca in Neko Harbour in the Antarctic Peninsula stalking a mother humpback whale and her calf;[40] 14 Antarctic minke whales at various places on the peninsula and in the Southern Ocean; 5 southern right whales near Shag Rocks – 240km west of the main island of South Georgia; and a grand total of 43 humpback whales - the first of which we saw on our second day out of Ushuaia, but the bulk of which we saw in the Southern Ocean (60% of the total was recorded on one day viz. 17th February 2010) .

The sighting in Neko Harbour was my first, and so far only, encounter with orca (*Orcinus orca*), known in the past as the Grampus, and more commonly now as the killer whale. The sight of its huge triangular dorsal fin cutting through the water surface is, for many creatures, a harbinger of imminent death. Orcas are apex predators, meaning that they themselves have no natural predators. They often hunt in groups, known as pods, earning them the soubriquet of 'the wolves of the sea'. Orcas occur globally but have a patchy distribution, preferring deep water, but in some cases coming right onshore in the surf while hunting seals. They will eat squid, many species of fish, including rays and sharks, birds, sea turtles, seals, and

---

40 She initially swam alongside our zodiac to confuse them and then used our ship as a screen – it was wonderful to be within touching distance of this magnificent creature

dolphins. They are known to attack the calves of great whales and even adult minke whales and gray whales. Less commonly they will attack sperm whales and even the huge blue whale. They have a unique trick of holding captured sharks upside-down inducing 'tonic immobility'. In this position the shark is helpless, unable to defend itself or injure the Orca and suffocates in about 15 minutes. Even the most feared predator in the ocean does not appear to be a threat. The Australian Broadcast Company (ABC) on the 5th February 2015 reported a *'Great white shark 'slammed' and killed by a pod of killer whales in South Australia.'*

To refer to this animal as a whale is somewhat misleading. Although labelled a 'whale', the orca is really the largest member of the dolphin family. It is believed by some[41] that this error arose when the term *'asesina-ballenas'* used by Spanish whalers in the 18th century was mistranslated as 'killer whale' instead of 'whale killers'.

While the international moratorium on whaling has been successful in averting the extinction of whale species due to over-hunting, contemporary whaling is subject to intense debate. Pro-whaling countries wish to lift the moratorium on stocks that they believe have recovered sufficiently to sustain limited hunting. Anti-whaling countries and environmental groups contend that the species in question are still vulnerable; as well as insisting that whaling is immoral and should be banned regardless of whether hunting is sustainable.

To bolster their position, pro-whaling countries, and in particular Japan, are incentivising countries to join the IWC and vote with them. Research by Christian Dippel in 2015 provides evidence suggesting *'that Japan rewards joining the pro-whaling bloc, and that countries who recently experienced aid reductions from the three big anti-whaling donors – the U.S., the U.K., and France – are more likely to join the pro-whaling bloc.'*[42]

---

41  http://animals.about.com/od/cetaceans/p/orca.htm – accessed 28th February 2017

42  Christian Dippel (2015) Foreign Aid and Voting in International Organizations: Evidence from the IWC; Journal of Public Economics, December 2015

You do not need to have been involved in whaling to become a member of the IWC, any country can join, from the smallest independent island nation to the largest, and each has an equal vote. Indeed eight current members of the IWC are completely landlocked.[43]

Membership in the IWC has doubled since 2001 with an average of almost 6 states per year joining from 2002 to 2008. As of July 2013 there were 88 members. Opinions among them vary greatly, arguments are divisive and currently there is disagreement on all major issues between the pro-whaling nations and the anti-whaling nations. Fortunately, the pro-whaling lobby is not yet getting its way.

The anti-whaling nations and all those of us who support their position should be more vocal and more active in demanding that this obscenity be stopped completely. It is clear that the meaning of a moratorium in IWC language is elastic. Whaling continues under three headings today:[44]

**1. Aboriginal subsistence whaling** – not subject to the moratorium as it does not seek to maximise catches or profit.

Its purpose is to enable aboriginal people to harvest whales **in perpetuity** at levels appropriate to their cultural and nutritional requirements.

**2. Special permit whaling** - the IWC does not regulate special permit whaling. Any Contracting Government (i.e. IWC member) may grant to any of its nationals a special permit authorizing that national to kill, take and treat whales for purposes of scientific research subject to such restrictions as to number and subject to such other conditions as the Contracting Government thinks fit, and the killing, taking, and treating of whales in accordance with the provisions of this Article **shall be exempt from the operation of this Convention.**

**3. Commercial whaling** - The IWC is responsible for setting catch limits for commercial whaling. However, in 1982 the IWC decided that

---

43 Austria, Czech Republic, Hungary, Laos, Luxembourg, Slovak Republic, Mali and Mongolia

44 Source: IWC website for text and data: https://iwc.int/home

there should be a pause in commercial whaling on all whale species from the 1985/1986 season onwards. This is often referred to as the commercial whaling moratorium, and it remains in place today.

Norway and Iceland take whales commercially at present, **either under objection to the moratorium decision or under reservation to it.** These countries establish their own catch limits but must provide information on their catches and associated scientific data to the Commission. The Russian Federation has also registered an objection to the moratorium decision but does not exercise it. The moratorium is binding on all other members of the IWC.

Norway takes North Atlantic common minke whales within its Exclusive Economic Zone, and Iceland takes North Atlantic common minke whales and also North Atlantic fin whales, again within its Exclusive Economic Zone.

To put this into perspective, since the moratorium began, IWC figures for the period 1985/86 to 2014 show aboriginal subsistence whaling accounted for a total of 10,139 whales, Special Permit whaling accounted for 16,235 whales and Commercial Whaling accounted for 24,381 whales. This means excuses have been found to permit a total of 50,755 whales to be killed without sanction. In lay man's terms, the moratorium *sort of* means what it says, but not really because it tries not to upset long standing (redefined as *traditional*) practice.

There is no rational argument to continue whaling. Eating whale meat is pandering to an unnecessary and selfish food fashion. The gratification of the few should not be allowed to dictate the continuation of an intolerable behaviour. Synthetic products have made whale oil redundant and the development of plastics and other polymers has left whalebone[45] obsolete. This being so, let us add our voices to the protest. There is no justification for whaling. Aboriginal subsistence whaling is not conserving a tradition it

---

45 Baleen

is preserving a practice that can and should be stopped. Any detriment to the population is easily addressed in other modern and more humane ways. The case for commercial whaling died last century and the fallacy being peddled by the Japanese that they can only do science by killing the objects of their study is self-serving, disingenuous and untrue. Since the moratorium, they have killed a total of 15,315 whales of five different species.[46] In 2017, in the North Pacific alone, they planned to kill at least 174 minke and 140 sei whales and to continue at this level each year for the next twelve years. This is a lot of dead animals for very little scientific information of substance, but I suppose the whale steaks were good, when the bits needed for science were removed and the remainder of the corpse went into the human food chain. In spring 2017 the Japanese whaling fleet returned from Antarctica having completed another so-called 'Scientific Expedition' with a bag of 333 minke whales. The sham/scam continues.

It is incumbent on us, if we value the rapidly diminishing biodiversity of our planet, to bring these countries into the light and persuade them to make their money through whale watching rather than whale killing. Proper protection of whale populations will see their numbers rise and provide for successful and profitable enterprises, successful sightings and amazed and grateful whale watchers.

Notwithstanding this, the diminishing appetite for whale meat, especially in the most ardent whaling countries, may be the best hope for the survival of these gentle cetaceans and may yet achieve where regulation has failed.

---

46 Bryde's whale, minke whale, sperm whale, sei whale and fin whale

# CHAPTER 4

———— ✽ ————

# Wingless Midges and Swimming Elephants

O
ur fifth largest continent, and twice the size of Australia, Antarctica is the coldest, driest and windiest place on earth. It is such a remote and hostile environment that it has no permanent residents; the only humans that spend time there are scientists carrying out research. It is virtually a desert as far as land animals are concerned. The native land fauna is entirely composed of invertebrate animals. These are dependent on plant colonisation of areas that have become relatively ice free, so are not widely distributed. Among the tiny little animals that few people have heard of are the minute heliozoans (sun-animalcules), rotifers (wheel animals), tardigrades (water bears or moss piglets), nematodes (roundworms), and ciliate protozoans. The single celled protozoans dominate the soil and freshwater communities. These simple single celled organisms and microscopic multicellular animals are known as extremophiles because they thrive in the extreme conditions found at these latitudes.

The terrestrial macrofauna, or large animals, scarcely deserves this appellation. It consists entirely of arthropods. Among these are mites and springtails, which live under stones and feed on plant material; the parasitic biting lice, sucking lice and fleas that live on the birds and seals that occupy the littoral fringe of the continent; and the true flies - represented by a single species of non-biting midge.

Indeed, the largest entirely terrestrial animal is the flightless midge *Belgica antarctica*, which grows up to an 'enormous' 6mm in size. The midge belongs to a family known as chironomids, constituting an important group of insects that can be found in terrestrial habitats but more frequently in freshwater. I studied freshwater chironomids in some depth when researching for my PhD thesis in Ireland.

Unfortunately, when my good friend Maurice Doran and I travelled to the Antarctic in the winter of 2010, I never got to see *Belgica*. Arriving at the end of the Austral summer, as we did, it was probably too late to observe adults. Spreading ice prevented us from landing at a number of sites where they probably occurred, and the places we visited on shore were generally rocky and ice covered and lacked the type of habitat the larvae of *Belgica* normally occupy - such as the smelly black soils associated with seal colonies; the guano of penguins; the rhizomes of the grass *Deschampsia antarctica*, and the feathery debris that frequently accompanies gull and petrel nests. Although we toured these types of habitats on the sub-Antarctic islands we visited, I neglected to grub around in the substrate to search for these midges, as both Maurice and I found it difficult to tear our eyes away from the spectacular colonies of penguins, skuas and seals that crowded the foreshore. Ah well! There is always the next time.

While the structure and venation of insect wings are important features in identification, *Belgica* is brachypterous, meaning that its wings are reduced to two useless tiny short strips. The flight balancing organs, or halteres,[47] that are a vestige of the hind wings of true flies are also absent – largely because they are not needed as *Belgica* cannot fly. However, as it is the only species within its family, and is the only true fly present on the 'Frozen Continent,' identification is not much of an issue.

Chironomids have been used as indicator organisms of good or poor oxygen levels in the water column of lakes and rivers, with different species thriving at different levels of oxygen saturation. However, if tolerance of

47 The modified hind wings of true flies

52

lack of oxygen was a competition then *Belgica* would knock the socks off all comers as it can withstand total lack of oxygen for two to four weeks.

It spends most of its life, of up to two years, as a larva feeding on microorganisms, terrestrial algae, mosses, and organic detritus, and only lives for 10 days as an adult – during which time it must locate a mate and reproduce. When the temperature falls too low it can burrow into the vegetation and substrate on which it lives and overwinter below the surface to avoid the cold. These larvae can tolerate freezing[48] down to –10°C in these sheltered microsites, where the temperature is considerably warmer, even a mere 1cm down; a survival strategy that they share with the other members of the Antarctic terrestrial fauna. However, it does not approach the super-cooling capacity of some freeze-susceptible organisms - Antarctic mites and springtails can survive temperatures as low as minus 30°C by using alcohols and sugars as antifreeze.

In summer, male larvae moult to become adult a day or so before females. Mating occurs when the larger females join large groups of males, a ground-hugging version of the swarming behaviour of flying chironomids in more temperate climes.

Despite the fact that there are no large terrestrial animals living permanently on Antarctica, the coastal fringes and offshore islands teem with bird and large mammal activity in spring and summer. Here they find relatively mild conditions and a greater availability of liquid water. While the numbers of individuals in breeding colonies may be very large, there is relatively little diversity in Antarctica compared to the rest of the world. Antarctica, and its subantarctic islands[49], lacks indigenous fully terrestrial amphibians, reptiles or mammals. Eight species of penguins inhabit Antarctica and its

---

48 A range of cryoprotectants such as glycerol, erythritol, trehalose, glucose, fructose and mannitol have been extracted from *Belgica* larvae.

49 The ring of subAntarctic Islands that includes the Falklands, South Georgia, South Sandwich Islands, Tristan Da Cuhna, Crozet Islands, Kerguelen Islands, Amsterdam Isd, Macquarie Isd and Auckland Isd., among others , have populations of introduced cattle, horses, donkeys, reindeer, sheep, goats, pigs, dogs, cats, rabbits, hares rats and mice.

offshore islands. Four of the 17 known penguin species live and breed on the mainland and its close offshore islands. When we were on the Antarctic Peninsula, we saw three species of penguin, gentoo, Adélie and chinstrap, all of which breed there. The one species we did not see was the emperor penguin, the largest of all, which, in the area Maurice and I visited, breeds on the fast ice from March to December.

Flying birds nest on the milder shores of the Peninsula and the sub-antarctic islands.

Omnipresent at penguin breeding colonies are large predatory skuas. We spotted two species – the brown skua (*Catharacta antarctica*)[50] was common everywhere but it wasn't until we landed on Barrientos Island that we saw South Polar skuas (*Catharacta maccormicki*),[51] their slightly smaller but more aggressive cousin. Looking like large brown belligerent seagulls, skuas are renowned predators of penguin eggs and chicks and, in the case of the brown skua, weakened or injured adults. They feed on other birds, carrion and the afterbirth of seals, as well as chasing other birds in flight to cause them to release the food they have caught. The South Polar skua, although it does prey on penguins, is more of a fish eater; often robbing gulls, terns and other birds of their catch. The family name *Stercorariidae* is derived from this activity – *stercus* is Latin for 'dung' and early observers mistook the food disgorged by other birds, when chased by skuas, for excrement. In Neko Harbour, deep inside Andvord Bay on the Antarctic Peninsula, breeding South Polar skuas dive bombed us to keep us away from their chicks.

One of the birds that accompanied us on our journey in the South Atlantic, and which we saw near the peninsula and its off-shore islands was the elegant black-browed albatross *Thalassarche* [*melanophrys*] *melanophrys*.

---

50 The taxonomy of this group of birds can be confusing. The genus is often merged within Stercorarius. Its synonyms include Catharacta lonnbergi (Mathews, 1912) and Stercorarius lonnbergi (Matthews, 1912). Catharacta antarctica (del Hoyo and Collar 2014) was previously placed in the genus Stercorarius, following Chu et al. (2009), and split as S. antarcticus and S. lonnbergi, following Sibley and Monroe (1990, 1993).

51 *Catharacta maccormicki* (del Hoyo and Collar 2014) was previously placed in the genus *Stercorarius*.

Unfortunately this magnificent bird is now endangered, due largely to being an unfortunate by-catch of longline fishing as well as through increased over-fishing of its food resources. It is regarded as one of the smaller albatrosses, yet it has a wingspan of 2.5 metres (the large albatrosses, such as the royal and the wandering, have wingspans of up to 3.5 metres). Maurice and I marvelled at these graceful birds as they hung in the wind and glided effortlessly behind and abeam of our ship while we traversed the Southern ocean.

Another huge bird that we saw throughout our whole trip was the southern giant petrel (*Macronectes giganteus*), which has a wingspan of up to 2 metres.[52] The word petrel is derived from St. Peter and the biblical story of his walking on water. The name appears to have originated with the sparrow sized northern storm petrel, whose dangling webbed feet appear to walk on the water, as it hovers over the surface in search of food.

The bills of petrels are split into between 7 and 9 horny plates. This makes it difficult to have nostrils located on the side. As a result, these birds normally have horny, tube-like sheaths attached to the upper bill. These are called naricorns and protect the nostrils. During feeding, all petrels imbibe salt water as they eat. To prevent accumulation of toxic levels of salt in their bodies, a salt gland, situated above the nasal passage, helps them desalinate by excreting a concentrated saline solution through their noses.

The southern giant petrel has a very large bill atop of which is a single long tube-like nostril. The bird was well known to seafarers and whalers and went by a variety of less prosaic names such as 'Mother Carey's goose',[53] the stinker, or stinkpot, glutton and vulture of the seas. These referred to its penchant for eating anything and everything as well as the defence mechanism it shares with other petrels of regurgitating smelly food and stinky oil

---

52  As big as a Golden Eagle (1.9 - 2.3 metres)

53  Mother Carey is the personification of a cruel sea in folklore; her 'children' was the name given by English sailors to birds which they suppose are fore-runners of a storm

at an opponent, or at anyone who gets too close to its nest. These birds are both scavengers and predators, often eating from penguin and seal carcases on land but also killing live birds on land or at sea by grabbing them by the head. Its habit of trying to pilfer bait from longlines often results in it being caught and drowned.

Allied to the southern giant petrel is the Cape petrel (*Daption capense*), which is extremely common in the Southern Ocean. We saw these birds nearly every day we were at sea and also observed them nesting in Paradise Harbour on the Antarctic Peninsula. It has previously, but inaccurately, been called the Cape pigeon.[54] My preferred name, of all those it is known by, is the pintado or painted petrel. Its upper-wings are black with white patches and speckles and it has a black and white speckled back. In contrast, its under-parts and under-wings are white and its head is entirely black. Its tail is white with a terminal band of black. This plumage is unique and makes it an unmistakeable and readily identifiable bird. It is also a large bird with an impressive 90cm wingspan.

In common with other petrels, pintado produce oil in their stomachs. This smelly concoction is used as a weapon against competitors and against predators. It also provides an energy rich food (being rich in triglycerides[55] and wax esters[56]) that can be regurgitated to feed chicks or act as a fuel reserve for adult birds during long flights.

Offshore, we frequently saw its much smaller cousin Wilson's storm petrel (*Oceanites oceanicus*), one of Mother Carey's chickens and another of the ocean 'walkers'. Mariners believed that these birds were the souls of dead seamen. This is one of the most abundant bird species in the world and may be found in both the southern hemisphere (during our winter) and

---

54  From its habit of pecking at the water for food

55  Triglycerides are the main constituents of body fat in humans and other animals, as well as vegetable fat. In humans they have been linked to atherosclerosis and high levels are thought to increase the risk of heart disease and stroke.

56  Wax esters are a normal part of the human diet and are found in unrefined whole grain cereals, seeds, nuts, fish roe and some fishes.

northern hemisphere (in our summer). It travels huge distances from the Antarctic to the edge of the Arctic but, as it spends most of its time at sea, it is rarely seen by anyone other than sailors. Despite its small size and fragile appearance it is at home on the roughest of seas, flying in the troughs of the waves during storms. Weighing in at about 40g, it is the smallest warm-blooded animal that breeds in the Antarctic region. Interestingly, we also saw black-bellied storm petrels (*Fregetta tropica*) nearly every day as we sailed down the Antarctica peninsula and back. This was a surprise to me as my guidebook to the birds of the Antarctic[57] indicated that this was outside its normal range. It showed that the closest it came to the peninsula was the South Shetland Islands. After breeding on subantarctic islands they migrate to tropical seas. Their scientific name was based on birds taken just south of the equator in the Atlantic. I have also seen these birds when sailing to the Marquesas Islands in French Polynesia.

Another unmistakable bird we saw along the coast of the Antarctic Peninsula was the Antarctic shag[58] (*Phalacrocorax [atriceps] bransfieldensis*). It is one of the blue-eyed shags and the only one to occur this far south. It is a large black backed and white bellied bird with a black cap which sports a longish, wispy and erectile crest. It has a white face and piercing blue eyes; yellow nasal caruncles (knobs) adorn the forehead above the beak; and it sports dark pink to red legs and feet. It is an elegant bird. It is unique among Antarctic and subantarctic birds in that it maintains a nest year-round, particularly in areas where the sea remains relatively ice-free. Additionally, as it never ventures far from its nest site out to sea, seeing it in any number means that land is nearby. It feeds on fish in inshore waters. Frequently, cooperative hunting sees them forming a 'raft' that may consist of dozens or hundreds of birds. This behaviour is thought to confuse the

---

57 Shirihai, Hadoram (2007) A Complete Guide to Antarctic Wildlife; 2nd Ed. ; A&C Black Publishers Ltd. ISBN 978-0-7136-6406-5

58 Shags and cormorants are similar and belong to the same family the *Phalacrocoracidae*. There is no consistent distinction between "cormorants" and "shags" as these names appear to have been assigned to different species randomly.

fish and make them easier to catch. Unlike penguins, which 'fly' underwater, shags tuck in their wings and propel themselves with their powerful webbed feet, as they chase after fish. Antarctic shags nest in colonies and make tall nests of seaweed cemented together with mud. These increase incrementally each spring as they are added to by the adults. A hollow at the top provides shelter for chicks from the weather. This is especially important as, uniquely amongst Antarctic birds, the chicks are born naked. We spent some time observing a nesting colony of these birds on cliffs in Paradise Harbour. This place was so named because of the beauty of the chiselled icebergs and surrounding snow splashed mountains that reflect in the glassy grey still water. It is an astonishingly beautiful place, and we took a slow zodiac trip around it just to drink in its unspoiled beauty.

Earlier in our voyage, as we sailed from the Falkland Islands and were some 1500km east of Tierra del Fuego heading for South Georgia, we came across a set of six steep, jagged rocks sticking out of the South Atlantic, which were completely covered by some 4000 of the very closely related South Georgia shags (*Phalacrocorax [atriceps] georgianus*). This has resulted in these isolated outcrops being named Shag Rocks. What seems to distinguish the 8 to possibly 14 species within the 'blue-eyed shag' complex is geographical isolation. As the guide books put it, individual species are unmistakable in their range; no other blue-eyed shag overlaps it. The easy rule of thumb for identification is, therefore, where you see it determines what it is – it couldn't be easier.

When we landed at the then unoccupied Argentine station 'Almirante Brown', located on Sanavirón Peninsula in Paradise Harbour, and named after the Irish-born Argentine admiral William Brown,[59] we saw our first snowy sheathbills of the trip. This is the only land bird native to Antarctica. It lacks webbed feet and seeks all of its food on land. This very tame,

---

59  He was born in Foxford, County Mayo, Ireland, on 22 June 1777. He emigrated to the USA in 1786 with his family and didn't return to Ireland again until 1847, when he visited his native Foxford accompanied by his daughter. Brown is renowned as the creator and first admiral of Argentina's maritime forces and is known as the 'Father of the Navy.'

medium sized, plump, hen-like bird has pure white plumage, a strong yellow beak and a patch of pink warty facial caruncles,[60] extending from the front of the eye to the base of the forehead and down to the top of the beak. Its Latin name *Chionis albus* translates as 'snow white'. However, being a messy eater, it frequently tarnishes its pristine smock and, consequently, must spend much of its time cleaning and preening its feathers.

Usually found on the ground, where it struts around, bobbing its head as it goes, it is completely unafraid of humans. Indeed, while we were there a couple even had the effrontery to peck at my boots, maybe because I had trodden in some penguin poo and this to them was nectar. Sheathbills are omnivores eating anything they can find, living or dead. A renowned scavenger, it feeds on carrion, animal and bird faeces, feathers, and in places occupied by people, human waste. It is an accomplished kleptoparasite, stealing krill[61] and fish from penguins as they return to shore and, when the opportunity arises, will eat their eggs and their fluffy down-covered chicks. In the harsh environment where it lives, nutrition is all important and it doesn't pay to be finicky. Snowy sheathbills carry this to an extreme not noticed with other birds, as they have been recorded eating tapeworms that lived in a chinstrap penguin's gut and have been seen sipping milk that had spattered around an elephant seal pup's mouth.

A colony of Antarctic terns (*Sterna vittata*) nested not far from the station. They protected their territory with vigour and screamed and chased every errant south polar skua that dared to intrude into their air space. Very similar in appearance to the Arctic tern, it is stockier, and the wing tips are grey instead of black. Unlike the Arctic tern, Antarctic terns do not undertake spectacular migrations after breeding, but tend to remain close to the breeding sites throughout the year.

---

60 small, bulbous, fleshy protuberances

61 These are small crustaceans of the order *Euphausiacea* that are found in all the world's oceans. They are near the bottom of the food chain feeding on phytoplankton (microscopic plants). Antarctic krill, *Euphausia superba*, is among the species with the largest total biomass- some 389,000,000 tonnes. Half of this is eaten by whales, seals, penguins, squid and fish each year, and is replaced by growth and reproduction.

On our way to the Antarctic Peninsula we had skirted the top of Weddel Sea at 62° south. We travelled in strong gales for several days and were prevented from entering the Bransfield Strait by advancing pack ice. This meant that we couldn't reach the Antarctic Sound, where we had hoped to visit a large colony of breeding Adélie penguins. The advancing ice pack forced us to detour west and southwest around the South Shetland Islands. One bonus of the detour was that we saw a couple of Arctic terns (*Sterna paradisaea*). This is a strongly migratory bird that travels each year from its northern breeding grounds to the Antarctic coast for the southern summer and back again about six months later for the northern summer. This bird lives in perpetual summer but does so at an exhausting cost. Recent studies, using geolocators attached to seven captured birds, show an average annual roundtrip of about 90,000km for birds that nest in the Netherlands.[62]This is by far the longest migration known from the animal kingdom. Having seen them many times in the Arctic and Europe, I felt privileged to see them again at the southern end of their peregrination.

As well as birds, we had the good fortune to see quite a number of mammals on the peninsula and its nearby offshore islands. Of these, the only ones to appear on land were pinnipeds, or seals.

Seven seal species inhabit Antarctica. We saw a small number of the largest of these, indeed the largest of all seals, the southern elephant seal (*Mirounga leonina*) on Barientos Island and Livingstone Island in the South Shetlands. These large, earless, oceangoing seals were hunted to the brink of extinction by the end of the 19th century. Fortunately their numbers and those of the northern elephant seal[63] have recovered. Earlier in our trip we had observed large numbers of these huge animals grumpily moulting on

---

62  Fijn, R.C.; Hiemstra, D.; Phillips, R.A.; van der Winden, J. (2013). "Arctic Terns Sterna paradisaea from the Netherlands migrate record distances across three oceans to Wilkes Land, East Antarctica". Ardea. 101: 3–12. doi:10.5253/078.101.0102

63  Mary and I saw the slightly smaller Northern Elephant Seal (*Mirounga angustirostris*) from the boardwalk at Piedras Blancas about 7 kilometres north from Hearst Castle on California's Highway 1. Some 17,000 animals call this place home.

beaches in the Falkland Islands and in South Georgia. The scars of previous battles for mates were still obvious on some of them.

Named for their great size (males grow up to 6 metres in length (20ft) and weigh up to 4,000 kilograms) and for the bull's large and prominent proboscis, these are truly impressive creatures. Even more so if you are standing close to two bulls in the throes of a bad-tempered scrap.

The male elephant seal's huge nose is used to make extremely loud roaring noises, especially during the mating season, when males compete to gather harems and become beach masters. Adversaries charge at each other in a tidal wave of rippling blubber, rear up and slash with their pointed canines and bite with their sharp teeth. Fights are loud, brutal and frequently bloody, but rarely end in death. It quickly becomes clear who is the winner, when the battered, bruised and frequently lacerated looser wobbles away hastily in defeat.

Although the largest member of the Order *Carnivora*[64] in the world, southern elephant seal pups, juveniles and even adults may fall prey to orcas, the so-called killer whale (*Orcinus orca*), the apex predator of the oceans.

The shoreline of Barientos Island was also home to a number of Antarctic fur seals (*Arctocephalus gazella*). When we were on South Georgia, where about 95% of the world's population breeds, these pugnacious seals, particularly females with pups, chased after us and tried to nip us, and we only managed to keep them at bay by holding our backpacks between us and them.

These are the smallest of the seals found in Antarctica reaching only 150 kilograms in weight and 1.9 meters in length (males). Like the southern elephant seals, they generally live north of the sea ice, and breed in harems on beaches. In late summer and early autumn along the Antarctic Peninsula, males form groups while moulting. The discomfort this seems to occasion makes them narky, snappy and ill-tempered.

---

64 Includes all dogs, wolves, foxes, badgers, skunks, weasels, otters, bears, red pandas, seals, cats (including lions, tigers, leopards etc), linsangs, hyaena, civits, fossa, mongoose, falanouc, walrus, and sea lions

The other four species of seal found in the Antarctic can live on the sea ice. We were fortunate to see three of these, the crabeater seal (*Lobodon carcinophagus*), the Weddell seals (*Leptonychotes weddellii*) and the leopard seal (*Hydrurga leptonyx*).

We didn't get to see the Ross seal (*Ommatophoca rossii*), which was unsurprising as it has a range confined entirely to the pack ice of Antarctica. In summer its main breeding range seems to be confined to the heavy pack ice in the Weddell Sea and the Ross Sea where it appears to live a fairly solitary life. It is also the least abundant and least well known of the Antarctic seals. Interestingly, females appear to be larger than males, reaching a size of 2.5 metres. In contrast to the harem forming southern elephant seals and Antarctic fur seals, where the males are considerably larger than the females, all the species that live on sea ice have females that are generally larger than males.

Paradise Harbour was a good 'sealing' spot for us as we observed five leopard seals, ten crabeater seals, and two Weddell seals as they rested on ice floes. One large female leopard seal, less than five metres from where we were standing, rolled, shuffled and slithered all over her personal ice floe as she tried to get comfortable. Several times she gave a wide gaping yawn displaying her formidable armoury of sharp teeth. We had also seen a leopard Seal on a floe in Neko Harbour but the sighting wasn't nearly as good as this.

We spent the next morning at Deception Island in the South Shetlands. The Island is what remains of the caldera of an active volcano. It is currently classified as a restless caldera with a significant volcanic risk. As it is possible to sail right into the flooded crater through a narrow gap in the walls of the caldera, called Neptune's Bellows, it provides a natural harbour that is mostly free from ice and wind. This was used by whalers up until the 1920s. Once ashore and rapidly becoming accustomed to the sulphurous atmosphere that pervades the caldera, some of us made the fairly easy but steep scramble up the volcanic slope to the notch that is known as Neptune's Window. This provides unimpeded views across the Bransfield Strait and as far as the Antarctic Peninsula, as well as providing an elevated vantage from which to view the caldera itself. Our anchorage was in the only geothermal lagoon in Antarctica. The beach here is strewn with whale bones and boiled krill that fails to survive in the geothermal waters bubbling up from the abyss. Rusted buildings, skeletons of wooden boats, the remains of an old wingless, tailless and engineless aeroplane, resting alongside its derelict hangar, and piles of barrel staves, litter the shore.

A short distance away is Livingstone Island, where we spent the afternoon. We landed at Hannah Point and strolled along the beach of Walker Bay. The site was noisy from bellowing southern elephant seal males displaying their strength and inviting all-comers to battle. This rarely consisted of more than butting each other with their heads and roaring and slobbering in each other's faces.

The large penguin colonies had attracted a huge leopard seal, probably female from the size, which patrolled the edge of the tide. It watched penguins rushing into the surf to go fishing and others body-surfing the waves as they came back from a fishing expedition. We watched as it caught and ate an unlucky gentoo. In typical leopard seal fashion, it grabbed the penguin by its feet and slapped it back and forth on the surface of the water to skin it before devouring it. It was an awesome display of ferocity and power.

The four seal species that inhabit sea ice are thought to make up half of the total biomass of the world's seals. Crabeater seals are believed to be one of the most numerous large animals on earth. Despite their name, crabeater seals do not feed on crabs, but their specialised finely lobed teeth (from which they get their Latin name of *Lobodon*) are adapted to filtering krill, their small crustacean prey.

The crabeater seal also serves as an important component of the leopard seal diet. The leopard seal is the only seal that feeds on other seals. It is believed that they are responsible for consuming up to 80% of crabeater seal pups.

Another abundant seal is the Weddell seal which is renowned for having the most southerly distribution of any mammal, being found as far south as 77°. Unlike other seals, it prefers fast ice[65] to free-floating pack ice. Uniquely, among Antarctic seals, Weddell seals can survive under fast ice by using their strong teeth to excavate and maintain breathing holes. This is very useful in winter as it allows them shelter from the worst of the weather. As it is easy to approach when resting on the ice, it has become one of the most studied of the seals.

Like the crabeater seal, the Weddell seal female is slightly larger than the male, but only just. Also like its cousin it has specialised lobed teeth that help it filter small crustaceans and other prey. It feeds on squid, krill, bottom-feeding prawns and other crustaceans, as well as fish. In the winter, when days are dark and it must hunt under the ice, it uses its highly specialised vibrissae (often called whiskers) to detect movement in the water and seek out prey. Here, it has been known to catch large Antarctic toothfish (*Dissotichus mawsoni*) at up to 300m depth. When on the ice, it is predator free and this probably explains its docility and approachability. In the water, however, the story is different. Here it can fall prey to orcas and leopard seals.

Many other places on earth support a much greater variety of animals and plants than the Antarctic. However, what is lacking in variety is more than made up in abundance. Although one of the most hostile places to live on the planet, even in summer, the abundance of food in the Southern Ocean supports a staggering number of a select variety of species. How long this will remain so is uncertain. The overwhelmingly negative effect of human

---

65 Ice that is "fastened" to the coastline, to the sea floor along shoals or to grounded icebergs

activity on the state of the planet and a collective reluctance among nations to adequately and comprehensively address anthropogenic problems of water quality and climate change does not bode well for the future. Let us hope that the coming generation, when compared to this one, is less rapacious, less xenophobic and insular, more tolerant and more enlightened. Without this, our demise will be confirmed in planetary history as the 6th mass extinction.

# CHAPTER 5

## Crispy Critters, Lemon Ants and Mopane Worms – A Brief Descent into Entomophagy

Sitting near the narrow mouth of the huge limestone cave, his partner nursing their infant at her breast, the Neanderthal man gnawed on another piece of raw horse meat as he warmed himself near the red-orange flames of his fire. It was bitterly cold outside and he could see the first flurries of snow that marked the onset of winter. The meat was welcome as he and the other members of his small group had lived on meagre rations as they hunted for most of the week before being rewarded with this protein bounty. Fast moving horses were difficult to catch and not as productive as the huge slower moving woolly mammoths they preferred to ambush. The mammoths, however, were becoming increasingly rare, and each year the tribe had to go after smaller but swifter prey.

If they were going to survive they had to eat what they could find as well as what they could catch. Many times they had to go hungry when food was scarce. When they could, they ate seals, rabbits, tortoises, small reptiles and carrion.

Although thought to be exclusively carnivorous, recent studies show that their diet was much more varied than we give them credit for. Most scientists now believe that they also ate honey[66] when they could get it. As is the case with hunter-gather cultures nowadays, bee larvae in the honeycomb were probably eaten together with the honey. It is highly likely that they also ate other insects, but the fact that honey and insects leave little fossil trace renders this speculative. Examination of fossil faecal matter of Neanderthals has shown that plant material played an important role in supplementing their predominantly meaty diet. It is now believed that they filled up on roots, tubers, nuts, berries seeds and fruits whenever available.

The search for evidence on how Neanderthals lived depends mainly on finding traces of their food preserved for thousands of years in the sediments of the places where they lived, or accompanying their skeletal remains. Differential preservation means that, in many cases, we are reliant on the breakdown products of long decayed or even digested food and inferring from this how they might have lived. While we might piece together some of the pieces of this jigsaw there will still be gaps and we may never fully appreciate all the things that they may have consumed. Clearly some of the things they ate may have left no identifiable remains or have decayed to a point that it is impossible to make anything other than the most general deduction.

To get a better understanding of what their lifestyle might have been, many researchers have used the lifestyle and behaviour of modern hunter gatherer peoples as an analogue. Like Neanderthals, these peoples also value energy-dense meat, whenever they can get it, as part of their diet, not only for the protein rich hit it gives them, but also for its flavour – both cooked and raw. Indeed the men of the tribe spend inordinate amounts of time in its pursuit.

---

66 Orangutans, gorillas and chimpanzees also like honey and bee larvae, often using sticks to extract the food from hives. If these primates are able to procure honey, Alyssa Crittenden says 'it is highly likely that early hominids were at least as capable of honey collection.' www/smithsonianmag.con/science-nature/humans-the-honey-hunters-9760262

However, with these modern tribes it is axiomatic that if '*man the hunter*' is not supported by '*woman the gatherer,*' then starvation is likely. There is little reason to believe, even if game was more prevalent in their time, that Neanderthal man faced any less of a challenge. It is likely that he, like modern hunter-gatherers, took food in whatever shape it presented itself, whenever it presented itself – be it animal or vegetable. Examples of the commonality of the eclectic nature of the aboriginal diet can be seen on those continents where hunter-gatherer cultures still exist.

In Africa the nomadic Mbenga pygmy peoples, the Aka and the Baka, whose groups are scattered in different territories spread through the Central African Republic, the Republic of the Congo, Cameroon, and Gabon, feast on a varied diet derived from twenty-eight species of game, sixty-three species plants - in addition to assorted nuts, fruit, honey, mushrooms and roots – and twenty species of insect.

The !Kung[67] of the Kalahari, members of the San people, will eat anything available in the dry and barren lands they occupy. They hunt for a variety of antelope, zebra, porcupine, wild hare, lion, giraffe, fish, tortoise, snakes (venomous and non-venomous), eggs and wild honey, flying ants and insects. In lean times they rely on tubers and mongongo nuts[68] (from the mongongo tree - *Schinziophyton rautanenii*) which can be stored for the lean times.

The Yansi people of the Democratic Republic of the Congo have a saying which will have little resonance in the West that goes '*As food, caterpillars are regulars in the village but meat is a stranger.*'

---

67 The ! in front of the word Kung represents an alveolar click sound or click consonant found in the Khoikhoi language. Click consonants of a variety of types are common in a number of languages in Southern Africa

68 The walnut sized and egg-shaped fruit ripen between March and May. Outside there is a thin layer of edible flesh around a thick, hard, shell. Inside the shell is a highly nutritious nut. The fruits can be collected when they fall from the trees and boiled to release the edible maroon coloured fruit and the shell roasted to release the nut, or the nut can be collected from elephant droppings having already been cleaned of the outer pulp through digestion in the elephant's stomach.

In South America, the Yąnomamö Indians of the Amazon hunt for snakes, wild pigs, monkeys, tapirs, deer, fish, crabs, and shrimp. They also feast on wild honey, plantain, sweet potato, cassava, and palm fruits as well as caterpillars, giant ants, termites, tarantulas and grubs. Often they will chop down a palm and let it decay in order to facilitate the growth of the two inch long grubs of the South American palm weevil *Rhynchophorus palmarum*.

In Australia the Aboriginal people hunt kangaroo and wallaby, possum and wombat, birds (and their eggs) and various turtles, lizards, frogs, fish, molluscs and crustacea. Their plant menu is equally varied and includes, among others, native cherry, native currant, water chestnuts, kangaroo apple, and vegetables such as the native potato and native carrot. Honey and insects such as ants, termites, bees, cicadas and grubs, such as witchety grubs and moths,[69] which are rich in fat, are important additions to the diet.

In South-east Asia one of the last remaining hunter-gatherer groups are the Penan[70] of Sarawak. Most harvest the starchy pith of wild sago palms (such as *Eugeissona utilis* or *Arenga undulatifolia*, etc.), which constitutes their staple carbohydrate. Sago harvesting is a destructive process as the tree has to be cut down and the stem split to get at the starchy pith inside. As the sago supply in an area becomes exhausted the group moves to a new area of the forest. The Penan hunt 45 different animal species including their favoured quarry, the bearded pig (*Sus barbatus*), and utilize over 300 species of plants. However, the loss of native forest, and the widespread felling of fruiting forest trees, as a result of progressive land clearance by settlers and oil palm plantation owners, has resulted in a decline in the pig popula-

---

69  Eaten by tribes in the mountains of New South Wales

70  We never saw Penan people when we were in Sarawak, but we did come upon recently abandoned *sulaps* (huts) in the Mulu National Park. Groups of nomadic Penan move through distinct clan territories, some groups are just a family of five or six; others have up to 30 people. Every month or so the Penan leave their old *sulaps* and exhausted sago supplies and move to another patch of forest, where a fresh camp is established. Sulaps are made from thick poles tied together with rattan strips and roofs made from palm leaves (or, more commonly now, tarpaulins for which they trade handicrafts or forest products with the Kenyan people at their longhouses). Typically the floors are four feet off the ground. Above a hearth of mud are two wooden racks for storing cooking equipment and drying fire wood. Each family usually has one hut for living and a smaller one for sleeping.

tion, with consequent negative knock-on effects for the Penan diet. Other species that the Penan hunt include barking deer, mouse deer, long-tailed and pig-tailed macaques, snakes - such as the reticulated python, monitor lizards, frogs, small birds and squirrels or anything else they can shoot with their blowpipes and poison darts or antique guns. They are particularly keen on honey and will readily eat insects, such as locusts and sago grubs.

The Nochmani of the Nicobar Islands, 150km north of Sumatra, were an unknown tribe until after the 2004 Indian Ocean Tsunami drove them from their villages into the mountains to escape the rising tide. They were spotted by aid helicopters flying over what was previously believed to be an uninhabited area. What surprised the aid workers and subsequent anthropological researchers is that they had subsisted for thousands, perhaps tens of thousands, of years on insects. It appears that they eat mostly beetles and worms, but also favour some kinds of spiders, centipedes, and locusts.[71]

It is projected that by 2050 the world will host 9 billion people. Current levels of food production will not be able to sustain this number – it will require at least double what we now produce. There isn't enough arable land to do this if we intend to meet the challenge by growing the same crops and animals we currently do. Seafood will not fill the gap as the oceans are overfished, becoming progressively warmer and more polluted and current fishing practices are unsustainable.

Worldwide there are nearly 1 billion chronically hungry people, and with climate change and regional conflicts this can only grow. We need, urgently, to find new ways of producing food.

It is estimated that, currently, some 2 billion people eat insects as part of their normal diet, with more than 1900 species being used as food. This practice, known as entomophagy, is common around the globe – but almost entirely absent in Europe! Why is this? Well the Food and Agricultural Organisation (FAO) in an important report in 2013[72] stated

---

71 http://www.nationalgeographic.com/foodfeatures/evolution-of-diet/

72 http://www.fao.org/docrep/018/i3253e/i3253e.pdf

> *'In most Western countries, however, people view entomophagy with disgust and associate eating insects with primitive behaviour. This attitude has resulted in the neglect of insects in agricultural research'.*

What is this disgust to which the FAO refers? Well, the Merriam-Webster dictionary indicates that the word comes from medieval French - *desgouster*, from *des-* dis- + *goust* taste, from Latin *gustus*; akin to Latin *gustare* to taste. So disgust and taste are intimately related. It is often referred to as a feeling of revulsion or strong disapproval aroused by something unpleasant or offensive. Charles Darwin wrote that disgust is *'a sensation that refers to something revolting.'* Disgust is experienced as a reaction to the sense of taste in particular but also to the senses of smell, touch, and vision.

We often pick up cultural cues to decide which things are acceptable and which are not. Perception, rather than experience renders many things taboo to us. Children note what the adults around them find delicious to eat and reflect these tastes in establishing their own boundaries of the acceptable and the disgusting. By the time one is an adult the delight/disgust reactions are hard wired into our psyches. Once this happens it is difficult, if not impossible, to break these long established behavioural boundaries.

As a general statement, insects are a highly nutritious food source with high fat, protein, vitamin, fibre and mineral content. Indeed, the European Food Safety Authority (EFSA) has proposed that, in order to bridge the food gap facing us, the solution doesn't lie in increasing livestock numbers or growing more arable crops but that the things with the *'greatest potential for use as food and/or feed in the EU include houseflies, mealworms, crickets and silkworms.'*[73]

It is ironic that we often call food 'grub' – as in 'grub's up' - but we would retch in disgust if we were actually offered grubs as food.

---

[73] https://www.efsa.europa.eu/en/press/news/151008a

In our travels, Mary and I have often tried to push our boundaries of food acceptability and from time to time we have indulged in a bit of entomophagy. We learnt, when we took a trip along La *Ruta Maya* in Mexico, Guatemala and Belize, that pre-Columbian civilisations, such as the Aztecs, weren't sustained by the best sirloin steak but rather wholesome dishes of protein-rich, fat-free stink bugs, mescal worms and fly eggs.

Our snack of choice consisted of *chapulines* (grasshoppers of the genus *Sphenarium*). *Sphenarium purpurascens* is a pest of alfalfa but also one of the most important edible insects in Mexico. These crispy critters are to be found all over Mexico and are the most popular of the many chitinous delicacies available in this wonderful country. They are easy to procure being sold in chic bars or roadside stalls, where they are piled up in trays alongside peanuts and other nourishing snacks. Harvesters catch them in conical nets during the season. *Chapulines* are brachypterous, which means they have reduced, non-functional wings but they can leap relatively long distances from plant to plant. The catching season lasts for three months, from hatching in early May until early autumn. The harvest of *chapulines* takes place very early in the morning when it is cool (04:00–05:00am) because they are active and difficult to catch during the hotter part of the day.

To prepare them, they must be thoroughly cleaned and washed. Then they are toasted on a smooth, flat cast-iron griddle or concave clay comal. The addition of condiments and spices such as garlic, lime juice, and salt containing an extract of agave worms, lends a sour-spicy-salty taste to the finished product. Sometimes the grasshoppers are also toasted with chilli, although this method can also be used as a cover up for stale *chapulines*. The ones we had were dusted with a mild chilli powder and squirted with lime juice.

We enjoyed these tasty and crunchy titbits in Oaxaca, which is renowned for the production and consumption of *chapulines*. While they are said to contain nearly as much protein as salmon, recent research has shown that they can also contain high and sometimes dangerous amounts of lead. Thus, in rock and roll parlance they may provide a veritable heavy metal snack.

Another entomophagous experience came when we were hiking through the thick, steamy jungle of the Peruvian rainforest. While sheltered from the beating sun by the dense canopy overhead, the humidity had us soaked in sweat within a short distance of starting. We followed a mud trail through thick forest draped in lianas, heliconias, orchids and bromeliads. In front of us there was a break in the dense green wall and we emerged into a clearing dominated by a lone tree. Indigenous people tend to avoid these places as they believe them to be the lairs of evil and malignant spirits and call them 'devil's gardens'.[74] In the Peruvian Amazon indigenous people believe that an evil spirit called the *Chuyachaqui* is responsible for cultivating the gardens. They believe him to be a dwarf distinguished by the possession of one human foot and one hoof. The *Chuyachaqui* is endowed with the power of shape-shifting, thus allowing him to transform into any likeness he chooses. If encountered in the forest, he may fool you by appearing in the guise of one of your friends or family members and lead you in circles until you are lost and, eventually, die.

Our guide sallied forth nonchalantly, broke off a small branch, split it apart with the tip of his machete and passed it to me. It was crawling with dozens of minute brown ants and soon they were swarming over my hand and arm. He told me they were very tasty and advised me to eat them. Like an anteater I licked and sucked them into my mouth. Once in my mouth, I couldn't claim to have chewed them as they were too small and despite the numbers I managed to ingest, I hadn't consumed a sufficient volume to make a biteable wad. However, as their fragile bodies burst inside my mouth, I got a distinct, but slight, bitter lemon taste. It is not for nothing that they are called 'lemon ants'. It seems that, when disturbed, the ants

---

74 A loose translation of the Quechua word *supay-chakra* (see David P. Edwards,Megan E. Frederickson, Glenn H. Shepard, and Douglas W. Yu; *A Plant Needs Ants like a Dog Needs Fleas.* Myrmelachista schumanni Ants Gall Many Tree Species to Create Housing; vol. 174, no. 5 the American Naturalist; November 2009)

produce a citronella pheromone as a warning to other members of the colony. It is this citronella that accounts for both the lemony odour and taste they produce when eaten.

It is the presence of formic acid that allows the ant and the tree to have a remarkable symbiotic relationship that results in the production of the 'devil's garden'.

The ants (*Myrmelachista schumanni*) and tree (*Duroia hirsuta*) cooperate to their mutual benefit. A single tree may support a colony of up to 3,000,000 worker ants servicing some 15,000 queens. The ants actively patrol the 'devil's garden' and when they come across plants other than their hosts, they attack them. Hundreds of worker ants bite into a leaf or a stem and then inject drops of formic acid from their stingers (gaster) into the holes they made. Within about 24 hours, bits of the plant begin to turn brown and, thereafter, necrosis progressively spreads along the vascular bundles and leaf veins, with the plant ultimately wilting and dying.

The ants are, in effect, mobile weed killing units that produce their own herbicide within their bodies. The ants' nesting plant benefits as the area around it is kept open to sunlight allowing it to grow and expand laterally as well as vertically and also retain exclusive rights to the nutrients in the surrounding soil. The ants benefit from the shelter given to them by the plant and, by preventing competition from other plants, the colony can expand as its 'condominium' grows. Being nest site limited, in order for the colony to expand, it must promote the growth and expansion of its nest site to create new housing.

Close to Africa's 'Four Corners' where Botswana, Namibia, Zambia and Zimbabwe meet, and lying on the south bank of the Chobe River is Kasane (Botswana). It is a small market town and the administrative centre of the Chobe District, and has a small claim to international fame in that it was the location of the remarriage of the movie stars Elizabeth Taylor and Richard Burton, in 1975.

I had stayed in our camp near the Chobe River updating my diary while, in the afternoon, Mary headed off with our guide, Hannes, into Kasane for some retail therapy. When she returned she had a small brown paper bag in her hand and nothing else. She explained that there was nothing she was interested in buying, but that, as I had been banging on about them, she bought us a treat. She held the bag out to me and on looking inside I saw that it was filled with dried mopane worms (*Gonimbrasia belina*). The mopane worm is not a worm in the true sense but is the brightly coloured caterpillar of the emperor moth, which is one of the world's largest moths. The caterpillar is about 10cm long and 1cm in diameter. The underlying colour of the caterpillar is black, but round scales in variations of white, red, green, blue and yellow patches or bands give it an overall colour that from a distance may range through yellow and green to blue. It is armed with short, black, red tipped, spines and is covered in fine white hairs. It lives primarily on the leaves of the mopane tree (*Colophospermum mopane*) – hence its name. Once dried it has a dusty yellow-grey appearance.

Mopane worms are a staple part of the diet in Southern Africa and, as they are a bivoltine species (i.e. producing two generations each year), there are two annual harvests. The major one takes place between November and January, and a second, smaller, harvest occurs between March and May. The worms are hand-picked or shaken off the trees, mainly by women and children. Sold in markets for local consumption they have, in recent times, become the basis of a multi-million Euro trade. However, overharvesting, tree cutting, and the frequent droughts experienced in the areas where mopane trees grow, has also led to local extinctions.

After harvesting, the caterpillars are squeezed like tubes of toothpaste to expel the slimy, green contents of their guts. They are then spread out on the ground and left for a few days to be sun dried. Once they've been dried out, they are ready to be eaten.

In Botswana people tend not to eat the head, a custom we were only too willing to emulate. We ate them dry and straight from the bag. They were as crunchy as potato chips but had little flavour. But as we continued to chew, the real flavour became evident and I detected a combination of dry soil, plaster and salt. It was rather unpleasant and, although we tried several each, we didn't finish the bag. Despite this blandness of taste, mopane worms are highly nutritious being comprised of 60% protein and high levels of iron and calcium.

For those who are really keen to order in a supply and can't travel to Africa, they are readily available, pre-packed and sealed, through the internet.[75]

If you are not partial to the thought of uncooked worms then they can be rehydrated by soaking overnight and then fried until crunchy; or alternatively they may be cooked with onion, tomatoes and spices and then served with pap or sadza.[76] They can also be cooked in a spicy or peanut butter sauce.

A recipe I found, but as I didn't try it, I can't vouch for it, is as follows:

Ingredients

1.  500 grams dried mopane worms;
2.  Three tomatoes, diced or 1 x 400g can of tomatoes
3.  Two onions, diced;
4.  1/2 teaspoon turmeric
5.  Three fresh green chillies, finely chopped
6.  Three cloves of garlic, finely chopped
7.  Tablespoon of fresh ginger, finely chopped.

---

75  www.crunchycritters.com/shop/edible-insects/mopane-worms-30-grams/

76  both are traditional names in for a porridge made from ground maize (mielie-meal)

Method:

1. Soak dried worms in water for 3-4 hours to reconstitute. Drain excess water.

2. Fry the onions in groundnut oil on medium heat until translucent.

3. Add turmeric, chillies, garlic and ginger and fry for a further five minutes.

4. Add the tomatoes and cook on a low heat for about 20 minutes until spices are well blended.

5. Add the drained worms and cook until they have softened a bit but still are a little crunchy.

6. Season with salt and pepper to taste

Serve with pap,

ENJOY!

# CHAPTER 6

## Bamboo Pipes, Big Horns and Fire Dragons

S eemingly endless grey, damp and miserable weather, steep and rugged mountainous terrain, and, until relatively recent times, one of the most backward and sparsely populated areas – these are the hallmark of the Guizhou region of southern China. So what was it that attracted us there in the middle of February of 2013? In a word - people. Although some 75% of the population consists of the majority Han people,[77] its isolation has ensured that the region contains a varied and rich complement of ethnic groups such as the Bai, Bouyei, Dong, Gelao, Hui, Miao, Shui, Tujiao, Yi, and Zuang. At this time, during the first lunar month, a number of festivals take place and we were hoping to attend some of them.

Straddling the banks of the Nanming River is the city of Guiyang, where we began our adventure. The city lies in a basin that is surrounded by the Miaoling Mountains. Despite the predominant drizzly and dull weather, its name translates as 'precious sun,' either in the optimistic hope that it will prevail; or else in honour of its all too fleeting appearance in this area.

Guiyang was developed as an administrative centre during the Ming Dynasty[78] and has grown to have a population in excess of 3 million.

---

77 92% of the overall Chinese population is Han, who in turn make up over 19% of the total global population.

78 1368–1644 AD

Needless to say, this growth, and China's burgeoning economy, has resulted in an urban sprawl of high rise blocks, creating towering walls of concrete with streets running far below like trails in canyons.

There are few attractions in this otherwise industrial city, but chief among the sights, is the Jiaxiu Tower. This Ming Dynasty edifice is a three-storey 20 metre tall wooden tower built on a large turtle-shaped rock outcrop in the middle of the Nanming River and linked to its banks by the Fuyu Bridge. Its white parapets, red columns, engraved windows and green tiles give it a striking, if somewhat incongruous, appearance against its backdrop of skyscrapers. The tranquillity of the setting is compromised by the incessant noise of traffic from the riverbank roads, but the islet containing the tower provides a sanctuary for the families of continuously cheeping russet sparrows that occupy it. The purpose of the tower was to provide a place of study for imperial examinations and its name is the title given to someone who gains first place in these examinations. As with most wooden buildings it has suffered from the ravages of time and has been renovated six times. At night the view of the tower, illuminated by lanterns and reflected in the river, is impressive. Inside, it is decorated with intricate woodwork, engraved stone tablets and examples of calligraphy. To the south of the tower a bridge leads to the Cuiwei Garden, which includes buildings from the Ming and Qing Dynasties. Not far from Jiaxiu Pavilion is the flower and bird market. Today, this market is a poor remnant of its former glory and very few stalls still sell flowers or birds. Closely packed stalls are protected by large red umbrellas and sell everything from handicrafts to antiques, cats, dogs, fish, food, and other bric-a-brac. Both in the market and the nearby side streets there are many snack stalls, offering an opportunity to taste local specialities.

A short walk west brings you to Renmin Square and its huge statue of Chairman Mao. Here we saw people practicing Kung Fu and Tai Chi. Some of those doing Tai Chi were armed with red fans and others had springy steel swords with long red tassels attached to the bottom of the hilt. A number of people flew kites, others practiced formation ballroom dancing and guards in black pants, red tunics and caps and white webbing strolled around seemingly confident that the orderly scene would remain undisturbed.

Not far away and tucked behind the Marriott Hotel is the Ming Dynasty Qianming Buddhist Temple. Rebuilt by the Emperor Qianlong (AD 1771), the monks were expelled and temple was destroyed during the Cultural Revolution. In 1981 it was declared an historical and cultural site by the city authorities, and later by Guizhou province, and money was allocated to its restoration. Currently, it is a functioning Buddhist temple and an important tourist destination. Located, as it is, in a bustling metropolis, it provides a rare, but welcome, oasis of tranquillity. The entrance gate is guarded by two carved stone lions and inside you are greeted by a large laughing Buddha and several large statues of warriors and bards. The main temple building is occupied by a statue of a golden Buddha, seemingly in tune with the zeitgeist as it sports a mop of blue hair.[79] It is seated in the 'Calling the Earth to Witness' pose, with the legs crossed, the left hand in the lap facing upwards, and the right hand pointing to the ground and with the palm facing inward toward the Buddha. This is probably the commonest pose found with Buddha statues, in that it depicts the moment of enlightenment for the Buddha. Engraved on its chest is a swastika. Known as a 'yungdrung' in ancient Tibet, it is a graphical representation of eternity and is a sacred and auspicious symbol in Buddhism.

Having exhausted the somewhat limited delights of Guiyang, we headed west, out of the city to Luizhi, which was to be our base for the next couple of days as we visited the 'Longhorn Miao' villages of Longga.

The Miao, with a population of over 7 million, is one the largest of the 56 minority ethnic groups in China. They are concentrated mainly in

---

[79] Gold is a common colour in Tibetan Buddhism; Blue is a sky colour that transforms anger into wisdom

the mountainous region of the South West. Geographical isolation, and a very poor transport infrastructure throughout historic times, has resulted in distinct tribes separating out from the main group and adopting an individual culture, dress and customs. Unique characteristics of their clothing, decoration and adornment formed the basis for naming these groups. Numbering some 4000 people, and living in 12 villages around Longga, are the so called Changjiao Miao. Literally translated, this means 'Long Horn' Miao. This comes about as a result of the custom whereby the young women adorn themselves by tying wooden horns into their hair and then wrapping them in a figure of eight pattern with yards and yards of ancestral hair, braided with wool, which has been gathered over generations, to fashion the huge 'horns' that they wear on special occasions. It was only with the building of the highway to Longga in 1994 that these people became more widely known in the West.

I first became aware of them through a 'Lonely Planet' programme in 2000, when the presenter, Justine Shapiro, visited the village of Lung Ga and saw the Long Horn Miao in traditional dress and recorded the young girls singing their ethereal song to lovers across the valley. This was a 'standing hair on the neck' moment for me. I later got a recording produced by Pilot Guides and listened to it frequently. While I loved it, Mary couldn't abide it. Ah well! Different strokes etc.

From that time I looked for an opportunity to visit the area and it came in 2013 when Explore Worldwide sent us early notification of a trip they were running to Southern China to meet some of the tribes and attend some of their festivals. Given that tourist infrastructure was basic, to say the least, and that few of the locals spoke anything but Chinese, the fact that we would have an English speaking local Chinese guide and a driver made it an unmissable offer.[80]

As we drove into the mountains around Longga we began to encounter people dressed in traditional costume and girls sporting the famous

---

80 This has now become a regular offer from Explore Worldwide and a number of other companies.

'long horns' all making their way to attend the *Tiaohuacha* (or Flower Danc-ing) festival. This takes place between the 4th and the 14th day of the first lunar month and the most important day is the 10th and final day, when locals from all the villages gather together dressed in their finery to sing and dance outdoors throughout the day. This time of year, when work in the fields is at a minimum, is intended to permit the single young men and women look for marriage partners. The final day festivities take place in a single designated festival site – colloquially known as a 'flower ground'. The girls from the surrounding villages descended in groups onto the 'flower ground' in the designated village, where they danced and sang to entertain the boys from other villages. This is known locally as 'fishing for partners'.

The dancing started once an extremely long string of firecrackers placed in the middle of the dancing ground, and attached to a trimmed and upright tree trunk topped with a small crown of remaining branches and red ribbons, was set off.

If a boy and a girl become attracted to each other, then an engage-ment is sealed with a presentation of gifts. This, however, is only the begin-ning of the process as the family of the potential groom has to convince the potential bride's family that it is a good match - often a drawn out pro-cess of negotiation. Sometimes, if the bargaining doesn't yield the desired result, a boy and girl may elope. If the marriage doesn't work out, divorce simply requires notice to be given to the elders and the couple are then free to pursue new partners.

The singing that takes place during the festival is quite repetitive and the dancing is simple – the girls hold hands in a large circle and walk, skip, bow to each other and turn as they progress. This continues for much of the day.

The traditional costumes that the girls and boys wear are distinct. These intricately decorated clothes provide an expression of the clan's individual identity. The cloth is carefully chosen and embroidered. An expert embroiderer or batik maker is highly valued in this society, and is seen as both hard working and a good catch.

Girls are dressed in skirts that are patterned with orange, black and white horizontal stripes. They wear a heavily embroidered and intricately patterned jacket of orange, pink and white and in front have a black felt apron or bag. The boys wear black trousers and black jackets embroidered with white flowers down the lapel edges and embellished with orange, pink and white pockets. Some of the boys wear white skirts over white tights and have belts and aprons decorated in the same fashion as the jackets of the girls.

Older members of the community, who aren't directly involved in the singing and dancing, wear simpler, but still colourful, traditional garb.

One of the more entertaining things to do during the festival is observe the activities of the huge crowd of spectators from each of the twelve villages as they enjoyed the day out with their families.

We noticed that many young men, who weren't participating in the festivities, were dressed like 1950's 'teddy boys' with tight jeans, jackets and, additionally, they had dyed their hair in bright colours and slicked it back to form huge quiffs. Whether these were Chinese visitors from other regions on a day out or locals stuck in a 1950's time warp we could not tell. Many of the girls who accompanied them were in western type dress and spent a good amount of time trying to get 'selfies' with us on their mobile phones.

The following day we headed out to visit the *Huangguoshu* (Yellow-Fruit Tree) waterfalls located on the Baishui River. These are among the largest falls in China and, at a total height of 77.8 meters and a total width of 101 metres, are reputed to have the longest drop of any falls in Asia.

Near the entrance and along the pathway Yao women sell souvenirs and fruit.

As you walk on the winding path, you can hear the falls long before you see them. The reveal is definitely worth the walk, as a broken, diaphanous curtain of water, some 80 metres wide drops 67 metres into a turquoise receiving pool. Smaller subsidiary falls and pools mark the decent of the river down the mountainside. There was less water falling, when we visited, than might be seen during the rainy season, but, in many ways, while less powerful, this seemed to make the falls even more beautiful.

Later in the afternoon we visited a Bouyi village. They are reputed to have lived in this region since the Stone Age. Here, unlike most of the Miao who use wood for their homes, the Bouyi build in stone. These were solid buildings that provided shelter against the cold and damp weather and they were roofed with intricate patterns of irregular slate tiles. We arrived in time to see a basketball match in the main square. Around the edges of the square locals dressed in round furry caps or berets and fairly ubiquitous blue aprons watched and cheered. In several places small wooden tables had been set up and older men played Chinese chess. One corner of the village was crowded with parked motorbikes, while their owners, looking like a group of 1950's rockers watched the game from a vantage point. A group of girls, bizarrely attired in miniskirts, and stiletto heeled boots looked on. Heavy dyed hair draped over one eye seemed to be the fashion of the day for both genders. I shudder to think of the age of the magazines from which they got their fashion tips. It is entirely possible that these were the same guys and gals I remarked upon above, who attended the Miao courtship festival on the previous day.

One thing is sure, however, things are beginning to change in this area and maybe not for the better. Whilst bringing many benefits to indigenous communities, the removal of isolation and access to modern communication technology is accelerating the homogenisation of society and is, unfortunately, removing much of value and interest from traditional cultures.

After the basketball match, which I believe was an inter-village event, there was a free dance show on a small stage set up at the far end of the village. Women, in bright red and yellow costumes danced against a painted backdrop showing a mountain scene with a flock of white doves flying in the foreground.

Following the show we drove to Anshun and there, again, encountered our 1950's biker group. Once again I photographed them.

From Anshun we travelled to a village near Kaili to attend a Lusheng courtship festival. This is one of the most important festivals in the area and runs from the 16th day of the first lunar month until the 20th. The festival features singing, bullfighting, horse racing, and dancing to the music of the Lusheng. The Lusheng is a Miao and Dong polyphonic musical instrument. It is made from bamboo pipes, fitted with a free reed, attached to a long hardwood blowing tube. The number[81] of bamboo pipes and reeds can vary, as can the length of the instrument – ranging from 0.3 metres to 3 metres - resulting in different pitches and tones. Lushengs with multiple reeds can produce tones that range from deep bass to a sweet treble. Musicians often dance or swing with their instruments during a performance. The Lusheng can be used to play rich and complex music, but at festivals the music tends to be simple, repetitive and somewhat monotonous.

Miao people from different villages attended the festival. The girls dressed in traditional costume, the colour and decoration varying from village to village. Miao groups are named for their unique clothing such as the Black Miao, Big Flowery Miao, Small Flowery Miao and White Miao, among others. Women's dress includes an embroidered blouse or long coat, trousers and at least one skirt, decorated with sewn on pieces of silver, broad waistbands, and embroidered shoes.

As the Miao do not have a written language, the complex embroidery on their clothes acts as a repository of their history, legends and culture. As well as traditional clothing, each of the girls participating in the dances was adorned with a complex beaten silver headdress. Some of these can weigh

---

81 Normally five or six pipes, each containing a single reed.

up to 10kg. Decoration also included waist length silver trains and chest pieces and many had two rows of beaten silver disks stitched to the front and back of their skirts. Most wore a couple of silver hoops around their neck. Only girls, who ranged in age from toddlers to older teenagers, took part in the dance. So complex were their costumes that most were accompanied by their mothers, or a female relative, to help them dress. The dance takes place in a circle with the girls on the outside and their accompanying musicians inside the ring. The musicians usually consisted of two older men or two boys – though in some cases there were several more – playing a repetitive two note tune - *Dah -Da, Dah-Da, Dah-Da, Da* and repeat – on their Lusheng flutes. The sound is similar to what you would get if you puffed seven times into the lower end of the scale on a western mouth organ. It is the rhythm rather than the tune that gives the cue to the dancers. The dance, like the music, is simple and repetitive. The girls shuffle forward several steps , step to the side and back, twist to the back and then to the front, step in place a couple of times, rotate, step in place and then shuffle forwards. This is repeated endlessly, with the Lusheng players mimicking the movements of the girls as they accompany them from inside the circle.

The dance is intended to promote both good health in the village and the prospect of a good harvest in the coming growing season. It also provides an opportunity for boys and girls from different villages to meet and possibly get to know each other, and perhaps make a match.

Nearby, in the Lusheng stadium, fights were taking place involving specially reared and groomed fighting animals known as 'king bulls' or 'holy bulls'. These bulls are pampered and fed to make them big and strong and their horns are allowed to grow to full size. Here, bullfighting is literal, as it involves two powerful male buffalo, generally from different villages, fighting head to head on the muddy stadium floor, to determine which is the stronger. A lot of pushing and horn twisting results in the stronger bull wrestling its opponent to the ground. The bull left alive – or the one that doesn't run away – is the winner.

Over the course of the festival, more than one hundred buffaloes participated. The bulls had large identifying numbers painted on their sides and some were decorated with ribbons and bells. A couple we saw bore the wounds of horns that had slipped from butting heads and gored them along their flank. A huge crowd packed the stadium and added to the cacophony with shouts and the banging of drums and gongs. Nearby food stalls catered to the masses. You could buy squares of barbecued pig skin, skewered sausages, chicken, kebabs, skewered chicken's feet (toenails and all) and whole roast dog. Some stalls sold prepared rice, noodle and vegetable dishes, but sited as they were amid the mud, litter and rubbish none whetted our appetites. Other stalls sold household items and souvenirs adding to the carnival atmosphere of this very authentic event.

Our next two nights were spent in Nande village, one of the oldest and most traditional of the Miao villages, in a home-stay, with a local family. Each house in the village is constructed on piles, or stilts, on the mountain slope above the river. Construction utilises locally sourced timber and other raw materials, and each house is planned in such a way as to allow it adapt to its local terrain. As the pyramid shaped village ascends the mountain side its structure of timber dwellings and cobblestone paths and piazzas underpins the harmony of the buildings with their surroundings. This type of construction is called *diaojiaolou* style and permits the houses avoid the negative impacts of steeply sloping terrain and floods in the river valley.

The family were very friendly but, mainly because of the language barrier, left us to our own devices. The three storey wooden stilt house in which we stayed was quite large. The ground floor housed the kitchen, fire pit, an animal fold and storage for agricultural equipment; the second floor, where our bedroom was located, provided the sleeping quarters; and the top floor was used for storage. Drying ears of corn and peppers hung from the balustrades. The buildings had fretwork windows, but no glass. As the weather was dull, misty and cold, this meant that our bedroom was freezing and that the supplied bedclothes were quite damp. We adapted by removing the soft mattress from another, unused, bed in the room and used it as a duvet.

Outside, a simple wooden hut was constructed over a long drop toilet. As there was no electricity in the house or any form of external lighting, after the sun went down, it made any nocturnal visits to the noisome sanitary services an adventure. This was heightened by a deep, uncovered pit dug adjacent to the door of the loo. Its purpose was something of which we are still ignorant. We got a couple of planks from the owner to cover this yawning chasm and provide safe passage on trips to use the facility.

In places like this, normal western concepts of hygiene do not apply, so it was no surprise that there was no running water in the toilet – or any-where else. Our obliging hosts, on request, provided us with a bucket of water that we were able to use for hand washing after using the toilet. The lack of knowledge of basic hygiene also extended to the food preparation. Fortunately, the extreme heat produced by the stove under the wok was sufficient to cremate any and all bacteria. Unfortunately, despite the best efforts of our hosts, and the abundance of fresh ingredients available from the village gardens, the food we were offered was barely palatable and we only picked at it. Our lack of appetite was more a reflection on us than on the hospitality of our hosts. This is the true meaning of home-stay – our hosts shared with us their shelter, their facilities and their food.

Indeed, when we arrived, the entire village turned out to greet us, the women and girls dressed in their traditional finery and the men in long black smocks and a type of black pillbox hat entertained us with music from their Lushengs and bamboo bassoons. Women offered us drinks of potent rice wine from a teapot as we ascended the stone path to the village gate. They were happy to offer refills as a token of their welcome and their pleasure in seeing us.

The next day, after strolling around the village and taking some pictures of the houses and the people, the whole village turned out to put on a display of traditional music, singing and dance for us. It was entrancing.

Following the home-stay, we moved on to visit Xijiang, the largest Miao village in China. This appeared somewhat contrived and less authentic. The reception was more choreographed and slicker than what we had received in Nande. The Miao here have become very aware of the benefit of tourism and have developed a 'cultural' product to exploit it. Tourism has helped them preserve their culture and traditions and brought back people who previously migrated to the cities for work, so it would be arrogant to dismiss their efforts as inauthentic.

The Miao of Xijiang are known as the 'drum people' due to their belief that their ancestors dwell inside percussion instruments. The welcome here, though staged for tourists, is genuine. As we arrived at the gate to the village we were greeted by male Lusheng players and women singing traditional songs of welcome. The women offered each of us in turn water buffalo horns full to the brim with potent rice liquor. The rule is that if you touch the horn you must drink its entire contents. The trick, if you want to remain sober, is to find the woman with the smallest vessel, as the big ones can contain huge volumes of booze. This welcoming ceremony is intended not only to welcome visitors, but offering a copious amount of strong spirits is believed to ward off bad luck.

In the square in front of the village, villagers provided us with another welcome dance, after which we strolled through the village, alongside the river and visited the main square and pagoda like drum tower. Nearby, we were able to see the impressive rice terraces laid out along the slope of the mountain. In the afternoon, we were treated to another cultural event in the main square. This was much more choreographed, stylised and varied than the ones we had seen before. It felt that we were seeing dances and traditions representing several Miao tribes. One group performed wearing the now common heavy silver headdresses, another group danced whilst twirling red parasols, and a final group, who sported conical straw hats, blue tunics and miniskirts over black leggings, gave us our only glimpse of representatives of the famous Datang 'short-skirt Miao' tribe. Normally, girls of this tribe wear short skirts, as small as 10cm in length and thigh high black leggings – both summer and winter. Why? Nobody knows; but they were dressing this way six hundred years before Twiggy sported a mini in 1960's London. It is likely that the leggings on show here were an attempt to preserve modesty in the eyes of an international group.

After the 'professionalism' of Xijiang, we explored the more basic activities of the villages of Shudian, Paika and Datang (the home of the famous short-skirt Miao). Here we got a better idea of the daily lives of these pastoralists as they went about their chores, tended their crops and livestock and practiced their crafts. We took a stroll through the fields and observed the simple waterwheels that are used to get water from the streams and into the fields.

As we drove from village to village we were able to observe some of the magnificent 'Wind and Rain Bridges' typical of the area (see p. 170). These wooden bridges get their name because of the pavilions built on them that provide shelter when crossing them from the wind and rain. On rainy days, the pavilions provide meeting places for the locals.

Our next stop was in Leishan for the infamous fire-dragon festival. During the afternoon teams garbed in red or yellow costumes danced with their huge paper and wood dragons in the crowded square. In the background the crack of exploding firecrackers was everywhere. We observed as children aged three and four lit the fuses with matches and lighters given them by their parents or older siblings, before they tossed them a couple of feet away to explode under any unwary passerby. We fortified ourselves for the evening's festivities by feasting on some excellent steamed dim sum in a local dumpling shop.

Once it got dark, we headed downtown to an intersection to watch the fireworks display. It was like World War III. The percussion of exploding rockets and 'bombs' was deafening and we were continuously showered in sparks. Health and Safety regulations had no place here. As the fireworks exploded over the nearby buildings, it was difficult to see how they continued to avoid causing a conflagration. Shops remained open and sold fireworks by the box-load to all comers. It was equally miraculous how the sparks from the explosions in the street didn't set off these retail 'arsenals'.

But the best was yet to come. When it got fully dark a dozen or more firework laden dragons danced through the town and through the doors of the hotels. These dragons, literally, spewed fire and were accompanied by followers who set off even more fireworks as they went. It was deafening. It was like a scene from Dante's inferno (see p.169). It was magnificent! The next morning we were able to photograph the burnt out skeletons of the 'dragons' as they rested on stands in the street.

We spent the next couple of days mooching through the Miao heart-lands and stopping at villages as we went. We visited Taijiang, Shidong and Zhenyuan and took time to stroll in the countryside and climb up the hill-sides. One of these walks took us to the Emerald Dragon Pool – providing a relaxing and peaceful interlude before heading back to another Lusheng festival. We drove via Shibing and Huangping to Kaili, stopping from time to time as sights and people captured our interest. From Kaili we headed to Zhouxi village where a major Lusheng festival was just beginning. After watching some more dancing, we headed down to the dry riverbed, where horse racing was taking place. The races followed a course along the stony bottom of the riverbed. Two or three horses raced at a time. The jockeys, generally young boys, some sporting helmets, some bareheaded, whipped their horses at breakneck speed from point to point along the designated course. Despite the inherent danger and the roughness of the terrain, there were no injuries while we were there. We sat on the wall some three metres above the course and had a magnificent view – both of the races and the stewards who were unarmed but were black garbed and curiously labelled on their backs with the gold letters -S.W.A.T. Was this a job-lot of seconds from the USA perhaps?

China, I love ya!

# CHAPTER 7

### ∽C∼2∾

# *Asleep with the Fishes*

*When Aquarius, or the Waterbearer, pours out his whole deluge and drowns us; and to wind up with Pisces, or the Fishes, we sleep. From Moby Dick (1851) by Herman Melville*

In Mario Puzo's 1969 novel[82] '*The Godfather*' there is a scene where Clemenza entered the room carrying a large dead fish wrapped in Luca Brasi's bulletproof vest. Michael Corleone asked what it meant and was told by Tom Hagen that '*The fish means that Luca Brasi is sleeping on the bottom of the ocean.*' He added that it was an old Sicilian message. In the film this is changed with Sal Tessio explaining that '*Luca Brasi sleeps with the fishes.*' This latter phrase has now become a metaphor to describe someone who is already dead or someone about to be 'whacked' – in underworld parlance.

Literally speaking, it is not surprising that the description lacks a basis in reality, as actually sleeping with the fishes would be rather difficult to do. Decomposing with the fishes would be infinitely more accurate, but may be less poetic. However, in West Africa they have come up with a practice that makes literal the figurative. Here, sleeping with a fish, or more literally, in a fish, is not an uncommon practice.

Having left Accra, the capital of Ghana, we headed for our camp site on the coast, near the mouth of the Volta River at Ada. En route, we

---

82 Published by G. P. Putnam's Sons

stopped off at Teshi, which was one of the original six independent towns of the Ga people.

Over one thousand years ago the area now occupied by the Ga was home to the Kpeshi people. Through displacement and intermarriage, the Ga replaced them. Originally farmers, the Ga brought the slash and burn system of cultivation with them, and they are also reputed to have replaced the tradition of growing millet[83] with cultivation of maize - probably as a result of their close contact with Europeans who brought it back from the Americas in the late 15th century. Maize is now the most widely consumed staple food in Ghana and accounts for more than 50 percent of the country's total cereal production. Over time, the Ga intermingled with a range of migrants and settlers from other areas of West Africa, with European settlers and even some immigrants from as far away as Brazil. This has given rise to the common saying that 'there is no such thing as a pure Ga.'

Many of the Ga who settled on the coast became involved in fishing. At first, they stayed relatively close to the shore fishing either off the beach or from small canoes. By the eighteenth century the Ga learnt from the Fante people of the south-western coastal region of Ghana how to use nets for fishing. Subsequently, this became a major occupation for many Ga, with the men catching the fish and the women selling them. Today, the fishing industry is dominated by powerful trawlers, many with multinational owners, and is big business. While small scale local fisheries still exist, they are under threat and continue to disappear. Despite its decline, the fishing tradition still remains important to the Ga people and their attachment to it and their respect for it can be seen in their funeral rites.

As well as farming and fishing the Ga were also known for trading. Ga merchants in Accra acted as middlemen between the Asante kingdom and the early European traders; first the Portuguese in 1471, who were then followed by the Dutch, Danes, Swedes and the Prussians. The British gained

---

83 Most likely Fonio

possession of all Dutch coastal forts by the last quarter of the 19th century, during which period (1860s)[84] they managed to stop the Atlantic slave trade (in which they themselves had participated actively until 1807, when they outlawed the practice). Up to that time, slaves, gold, ivory, and spices, such as pepper, were the most sought after items. Slaves were bought by both men and women - some of whom became very successful and rich. Despite their generally inferior status to men in Ga culture, their participation in trading activity appears to have paved the way for women to own and sell property without having to seek male permission. This position pertains to the present day where, even within marriage, women's property and wealth and men's property and wealth are separate. Marriage, unlike in western tradition, does not result in a cooperative husband-wife economic unit.

The arrival in the 1820s of European missionaries had a significant impact on the culture. By the mid-nineteenth century, many of the Ga had converted to Christianity. However, as in many other cases where Christianity and African traditional beliefs met,[85] syncretism took place, with elements of both traditions being combined. The Protestant sects that had the greatest impact, Methodism and Presbyterianism, together with Islam, provided, along with traditional animist beliefs and ancestor worship, a veritable cornucopia of beliefs that underpinned the development and proliferation of a variety of syncretic cults.

Marriage, as an institution, remains less important to the Ga than for many other cultures, as spouses don't share wealth, property or residences and espouse a facile and flexible divorce system. The main aim of getting married is to have children. The most common reason for divorce is non-support of the children by the husband. Gender separation is the norm, with men usually living with their patrilineal male relatives and women living with their matrilineal female relatives, along with their children. This

---

84 Despite this, as late as the early twentieth century, a few slaves were still being sold in or near Salaga Market in Central Accra.

85 See Vodou, Santeria, Candomble, New Orleans Voodoo - Chapter 11, p.127

separation is perpetuated when boys, sometime between the ages of six and twelve, leave their mother's house and go to live in their father's house - which could be several kilometres away. The physical and ideological separation between genders both enforces and reinforces the notion of the superiority of the male. Both Christianity and Islam have contributed to the rite of marriage but adherence to traditional beliefs has resulted in the development of new syncretic forms of ceremony. This is best exemplified in the marriages of wealthy or middle-class people, where customary rites often are accompanied by the trappings and ceremonies of Western middle-class marriages. Marriages among the poor classes generally follow local tradition and are often sealed by a simple gift of drink,

Among the most important of the Ga rituals are funerals. Propitiation of ancestral spirits, through libations or other offerings, is essential to ensure that they continue to take a benign interest in the living. Death has a cause. It may be entirely natural or attributable to the malevolent action of an angry spirit, or a combination of both. To the Ga, death is not the end but life continues in the next world in much the same way it did on earth. Spirits of the recently dead are believed to wander for a period before they can join the other ancestral spirits in the sky. Ancestors are thought to be more powerful than the living and able to influence their living relatives.

Families feel obliged do everything they can to ensure that a dead person is sympathetic towards them. The social status of the deceased depends largely on the size and the success of the burial service and, in the last 65 or so years, the usage of exclusive, individually designed coffins. They often symbolise the dead person's prior standing in the community, their occupation, their interests, their character traits or their vices. The purpose of the unique coffin appears to be to help them continue with their earthly profession in the afterlife. Design coffins first appeared around the 1950s, when Seth Kane Kwei (1925-1992) from Teshie built coffins in the shape of fish for local fishermen. This was the first time that a carved coffin had been crafted for someone other than a chief or community leader. They have now become an integral part of Ga burial culture.

Today, coffins can be crafted to resemble anything desired by the relatives of the deceased. They come in an infinite variety of corpse sized styles, limited only by the imagination of the relatives and the skill of the craftsmen asked to make them. I suppose that the choice of a design that would upset the spirit of the deceased is eliminated by the desire on the part of the relatives to ensure that he or she will be a beneficial influence for them in the spirit world.

These coffins or *Abebuu adekai*, meaning 'proverbial coffins' in the language of the Ga, are coffins that tell a story. We visited '*Hello Design Coffins*' breezy, second story showroom, just down the street from the more famous '*Kane Kwei Coffins*' established by Seth Kane Kwei. A short list of the finished coffins that we saw between the two workshops, all appropriately sized for their respective clients, included, among others, a pencil, an aeroplane (with wings, engines and tail), a car, a truck, an oil tanker, a cannon, a boat, a shoe, a sneaker, a saw, a vice, a chilli pepper, an ear of corn, fish (many varieties of this type of coffin were available), a lobster, a bible, a rooster, a lion, a soft drink bottle and a star beer bottle. Other designs that have become popular, but which we have yet to see are sewing machines, cell phones, tractors, elephants, and a hair dryer.

In exploring this funeral practice on the Internet, I came across an article where the author stated that his favourite *Abebuu adekai* was a shiny, polished uterus made for a deceased gynaecologist. I didn't see this one myself but I have no trouble believing it existed.

These coffins are not cheap. Ghana is still one of the poorest countries in the world, yet families can spend US$600 or more on a coffin, depending on the design. And this is only a fraction of the total cost that needs to account for food, musicians, drink, marquees, tables and chairs, microphones and amplifiers, and posters to advertise the funeral. As a result, families often have to delay the funeral as they save to pay for it. This postponement may last from two months to two years. During this period the family has to pay to have the body stored in a mortuary. The coffin may be ready long before the family has accumulated the resources to pay for the funeral and it remains in the workshop until the family is ready to claim it. Total funeral expenses, depending on how lavish the event is, can range from US$3,000 to US$20,000. As the funeral costs so much, all members of the family, relatives and friends are expected to contribute according to their means. In addition, guests are expected to offer some money to offset expenses.

Funerals in Ghana are huge celebrations and Ga funerals rank high among them for spectacle. Far from being sad, they are loud parties where knowing the deceased is not a requirement of attendance.

As with other elements of religious practice in Ghana, syncretism is easy to distinguish. Christian rites have largely taken over but elements of the old indigenous religion are generally incorporated into funerals. During a funeral, the coffin travels around the villages in an attempt to confuse the spirit to prevent it returning and haunting its friends and relatives – a practice seemingly at odds with the desire to have the spirit of the deceased exert beneficial influence in the after-world for his or her relatives.

It is interesting to speculate the use to which ex United States President Jimmy Carter intends to put the three coffins (an eagle, a fish and a bell pepper) he is reputed to have bought when he visited Teshie. If he intends to be buried in one, which will he choose – the eagle as a symbol of his presidency or the bell pepper as to signify his life as a farmer? Will he order a special peanut shaped coffin to signify the crop he grew? Or will conventional American funeral furniture triumph? Only time, hopefully far in the future, will tell.

# CHAPTER 8

## What is the difference between a dog and a fox?

The answer to this old, politically incorrect and extremely sexist, joke is '*about ten pints of beer.*'

Ever since early man had his first taste of meat he has had an interest in how animals behave – not least because an in depth knowledge of the characteristics and habits of prey animals enhanced his chances of success in the hunt. Being human, it would not have been unusual to interpret human characteristics and emotions in the animals he observed. This is called anthropomorphism.

Stephen Mithen (1999)[86] postulated that such empathy aided hunters in predicting animal movement and reactions and that it is exemplified in anthropomorphic works of art that have been manufactured since the Upper Palaeolithic times, about 40,000 years ago.

It is not a huge step from attributing human characteristics to animals to turning the argument on its head and attributing animal characteristics to humans. This is known as zoomorphism and often takes the form of viewing human behaviour in terms of the behaviour of animals.

Many examples can be found such as 'breeding like rabbits'; 'filthy as pigs'; 'sly like a fox'; 'timid like a mouse'; 'horny like a goat'; 'stubborn as

---

86 The Prehistory of the Mind: The Cognitive Origins of Art, Religion and Science; Steven Mithen (1999) Thames and Hudson

a mule' and so on. In this context, zoomorphism has become a common part of daily discourse. Indeed, we have become so familiar with this type of expression that the name of an animal has become synonymous with a particular behaviour – 'don't badger me'; 'stop wolfing down your food'; 'he outfoxed you'; 'she ferreted it out'. Often animal names are used linguistically as dysphemistic[87] epithets such as 'You Bitch!'; 'You Pig!'; 'You Rat!'; 'You Snake!' 'You Louse!'; 'You Worm!'; 'You Toad!'; 'You Chicken!' etc. Everyone understands what these insults mean. However, for a more academic explanation you need go no further than Allen and Burridge (2006)[88] who explain it thus 'dysphemistic uses of animal names takes some salient, unpleasant characteristic from the folk concepts about the appearance and/ or behaviour of the animal, which is then metaphorically attributed to the human named or addressed.'

Such musing was prompted by an earlier visit to a small museum in the city of Thanjavur, in the south Indian state of Tamil Nadu. This physical journey, lead me on a fascinating intellectual journey to derive meaning from an unusual and compelling exhibit.

Thanjavur is the location of the Brihadeshwara Temple- a 1000 year old Hindu temple dedicated to Shiva. Built by emperor Raja Raja Chola I[89] and situated in the centre of the city, it is one of the largest temples in India and an excellent example of Dravidian architecture. It is part of a complex of similar temples comprising the UNESCO World Heritage Site known as the 'Great Living Chola Temples'.

Not far from the temple is the Thanjavur Maratha palace. Unfortunately, this complex shows both its age and its neglect. Easily overlooked

---

87 A dysphemism is an expression with connotations that are offensive either about the subject matter or to the audience, or both. Dysphemisms contrast with neutral or euphemistic expressions.Dysphemism is sometimes motivated by feelings such as fear, distaste, hatred, and contempt (Wikipedia).

88 Keith Allen and Kate Burridge '*Forbidden Words: Taboo and the Censoring of Language*' (2006) Cambridge University Press.

89 Raja Raja translates to English as 'the King of Kings'.

WOGGINS FOR SUPPER

within the complex, but a shame to miss, is the Saraswati Mahal Library located just beside the lane leading to the palace. Visitors, however, are confined to the library museum. Within this small and dusty area is a sample exhibit from its collection of over 60,000 Indian and European manuscripts and books written on palm leaf and paper. The eclectic nature of the exhibits hints at the enormous variety available within the main library. This consists of a mix of artefacts, photographs, paper, canvass, wood, and glass paintings, portraits of the Thanjavur Maratha kings, drawings, maps, atlases, old manuscripts and books.

Reposing among these is a couple of bizarre and unexpected exhibits. One of these is an 1804 set of drawings and texts describing Chinese punishment techniques. Unfortunately, photography is forbidden in the museum so I was unable to record the techniques for personal use later.

On display also are the amazing physiognomic sketches of Charles Le Brun (1619 -1690).

What, you may well ask, made these drawings so interesting; and what is a bunch of medieval European drawings doing in a small dusty museum in south-east India? Indeed, for that matter, what is physiognomy?

Let us start with the last question first. The origin of the word, according to Collins Dictionary, comes from Old French *phisonomie,* via Medieval Latin, from Late Greek *phusiognōmia,* erroneous for Greek *phusiognōmonia,* from *phusis* nature + *gnōmōn* judge. Clear as mud, says you! Put more simply, physiognomy is the 'knowledge of nature,' or, more specifically, how you might assess human character through study of physical features. Are you any the wiser yet?

What is being hinted at is that the soul of a person is clearly reflected in his features and body and easily discernible to the trained observer. This concept has its roots in antiquity. As early as 500 BC, Pythagoras was accepting or rejecting students based on how gifted they looked.

101

*Physiognomonica,*[90] a Greek treatise of 300 BC (frequently attributed to Aristotle, but now believed to be by some other unknown author) was believed to be the earliest surviving work devoted to the subject, until texts preserved on clay tablets appeared to provide evidence of physiognomy manuals from the First Babylonian Dynasty (approximately 1500 to 1800 BC) during the Bronze Age.

While in all probability Aristotle did not write *Physiognomonica*, he did believe in the applicability of physiognomy. In his *Prior Analytics,*[91] written in 350 BC, he stated

*'It is possible to infer character from features, if it is granted that the body and the soul are changed together by the natural affections: I say 'natural', for though perhaps by learning music a man has made some change in his soul, this is not one of those affections natural to us; rather I refer to passions and desires when I speak of natural emotions. If then this were granted and also that for each change there is a corresponding sign, and we could state the affection and sign proper to each kind of animal, we shall be able to infer character from features.'*

He also wrote that large-headed people were mean; those with small faces were steadfast; broad faces reflected stupidity; and round faces signalled courage.

It was also believed that the character of man could be determined by comparing his features with those of animals. So we could state that his appearance is bull-headed or pig -headed, lion hearted, snake eyed, or has an aquiline (eagle like) nose, implying that these physical attributes give us a template against which we can measure character.

---

90 The Complete Works of Aristotle (2013) Delphi Classics - *Physiognomics (805a)*Translated by T. Loveday and E.S. Forster

91 Translated by A.J Jenkinson (1989), Hackett.

Whether Aristotle regarded it as a science in its own right is unsure but the unknown writer of *Physiognomica* certainly did. He attempted to present the process as both interpretive and predictive. His view of it as a practical scientific tool can be seen in this quote

---

*But still better instances of the fundamental connections of body and soul and their very extensive interaction may be found in the normal products of nature. There never was an animal with the form of one kind and the mental character of another; the soul and body appropriate to the same kind always go together, and this shows that a specific body involves a specific mental character. Moreover, experts on the lower animals are always able to judge character by bodily form: it is thus that a horseman chooses his horse or a sportsman his dogs. Now, supposing all this to be true (and it always is true), physiognomy must be practicable.'*

---

Even in ancient times, however, a real scientific basis for physiognomy was disputed. The general view in Aristotle's time was it was more an art than a science, and as such did not necessarily generate accurate information.

This is exemplified by the reaction of the intellectuals of the day, the students of the great philosopher Socrates, to a physiognomic assessment of their teacher. It deemed Socrates to be prone to intemperance, sensuality, and violent bursts of passion. Lacking the Socratic wisdom of their master, his students were appalled by this slur and they denounced the physiognomist, pronouncing the assessment as being based on unfounded lies.

Socrates, knowing better the truth of his character, restored harmony by admitting that though he was given to all these vices, his particularly strong self-discipline kept them buried deep.

Among the Latin classical authors Juvenal, Suetonius, and Pliny the Elder refer to the practice of physiognomy, and numerous allusions occur in the works of the Christian scholars, especially Clement of Alexandria and Origen.[92] As it developed, physiognomy evolved from the descriptive to the predictive and found itself allied with prophetic folklore and the magical arts, divination, astrology, chiromancy (palmistry), and alchemy.

During the middle ages, the writings of Albertus Magnus and his pupil St Thomas Aquinas were instrumental in bringing Aristotelian thought, and an acceptance of both physiognomy and chiromancy, into Christian belief and into wider general acceptance within Europe.

However, this view of the practicality and utility of physiognomy and chiromancy was not shared universally. By the middle to the end of the 15th century some leading intellectuals dismissed them as being without value. Leonardo Da Vinci was emphatic[93]

*'I do not concern myself with false physiognomy and chiromancy because there is no truth in them, and this can be proven because these chimera have no scientific foundations.'*

Despite widespread opposition, physiognomy continued to be widely accepted and taught in English universities right up to 1530. Thereafter it fell foul of the king - Henry VIII had no time for *'beggars and vagabonds playing subtile, crafty and unlawful games such as physnomye or palmestrye'* and outlawed the practice*s*.'[94]

Nonetheless, physiognomy continued to be popular and prevalent throughout Europe and had at least an equal standing with the new science of anatomy as it developed throughout the 16th and 17th centuries.

Contemporaneous with the great strides being made by anatomists to map the interior of the human body (most notably by Andreas Vesalius;

---

92 http://www.britannica.com/topic/physiognomy-divination (accessed 01/12/2015).

93 *Leonardo da Vinci (2002). André Chastel, ed. Leonardo on Art and the Artist. Translated from French by Ellen Callman. Courier Dover Publications. pp. 144–45. ISBN 0-486-42166-X. Unabridged republication of The Genius of Leonardo da Vinci, originally published by Orion Press, New York, 1961*

94 *Popular Law-making by Frederic Jesup Stimson - Full Text Free Book (Part 2/8). fullbooks.com*

1514–1564), Giambattista della Porta, in 1583, published a major work *De humana physiognomonia* illustrating how behaviour is associated to physical appearance and relating it to the shapes of animals. Porta's physiognomics purported to provide its practitioners with a key for decoding human characteristics encoded in the human face and by relating them to the shapes of animals[95] provide a predictive tool to character traits or failures. The more base the animal the more base the person; and the more noble the animal the more noble the person. For example, Porta held that a man with sheep-like features would have personality characteristics similar to that of a sheep - in his view a stupid and impious animal.

Porta's understanding of physiognomics went beyond the descriptive. He wrote

*Through this art, we have helped many friends avoid dangers and ascend to honours. Shortly before I wrote these things, I counselled a friend of mine to avoid the company of a certain ugly and unlucky man, an advice he did not want to hear, as his acquaintance had promised him riches; at the end of the day, they were caught by the governor producing counterfeit money in a hide-out and shortly afterwards both ended on the gallows.' (Coelestis physiognomonia, bk. 1, ch. 2)[96]*

On 28th March 1671, in an address he made to the Royal Academy of Painting and Sculpture, Charles le Brun - first painter to King Louis XIV - formally presented *'all of the various demonstrations that he has drawn, whether heads of animals or heads of men, making note of the signs that mark their natural inclination.'*[97] This set of drawings, minus the original text, is preserved in the Louvre.

---

95 Facsimiles of some of his drawings are available at https://www.nlm.nih.gov/exhibition/historicalanatomies/porta_home.html

96 http://plato.stanford.edu/entries/della-porta/#WorPhy

97 Procès-verbaux de l'Academie I : 358-359

An edition of engravings derived from the drawings was published in 1806.[98] A copy of these constitutes the exhibition in the Saraswati Mahal library.

It is almost certain that Le Brun was inspired in his efforts by the drawings and writings of della Porta. He, however, took this a step further and attempted to give it a firm mathematical basis when he elaborated a geometry that linked lines and angles of different features of the head (at its simplest an equilateral triangle running from the point of the nose to the tympanum of the ear and thence to the inside of the eye) which in turn pointed to emotions, faculties and character and amplified this by comparing geometries of drawn human heads with similar geometries of drawn animal heads. Human heads with similar geometry to an ass head indicated obstinacy; if related to an ox, it indicated both obstinacy and strength. Matching with a cat indicated that a person was obstinate, distrustful and fearful; matching with a ram indicated stupidity; while matching with a hog denoted lubricity (i.e. you were both licentious and slippery) and gluttony. To indicate intelligence you would need to match with the facial geometry of a camel or a monkey.

It is unclear whether the mathematical and geometric relationships shown in Le Brun's illustrations were derived from the drawings themselves or were a reflection of actual measurements derived from a large number of living animal and human specimens. Personally, I am inclined to the former and feel that the drawings were based on preconceived prejudice and adjusted to fit the measurements. This may explain why they resemble caricatures more than portraits.

It is interesting to note that Charles Darwin had occasion to consider Le Brun's drawings when writing his book *The Expression of the Emotions in Man and Animals* (1872; London, John Murray). He notes

---

98 The first 11 plates were engraved by Mr. [Louis-Pierre] Baltard and the others by Mr. André Le Grand' according to the title page of the 1806 edition; for the catalogue of a recent exhibition of the engravings, see Madeleine Pinault Sørensen, *De la physionomie humaine et animale : dessins de Charles Le Brun gravés pour la Chalcographie du Musée Napoléon en 1806*, RMN, Paris, 2000.

> *'Many works have been written on Expression, but a greater number on Physiognomy - that is, on the recognition of character through the study of the permanent form of the features. With this latter subject I am not here concerned. The older treatises, which I have consulted, have been of little or no service to me. The famous 'Conférences' of the painter Le Brun, published in 1667, is the best known ancient work, and contains some good remarks.'*

However, in the Introduction to his book (p4), Darwin is scathing about Le Brun's remarks in 1667 in describing the expression of fright, when he states

> *'I have thought the fore-going sentences worth quoting, as specimens of the surprising nonsense which has been written on the subject.'*

The next surge in the art came in the 18th century with the publication by Johann Kaspar Lavater of *Physiognomische Fragmente zur Beförderung der Menschenkenntnis und Menschenliebe* (between1775 and 1778).[99] Lavater's innovation was that physiognomy related to the specific character traits of individuals, rather than general types. 'Each man is an individual self, with as little ability to become another self as to become an angel,' he wrote. Thus he concentrated on an individual's specific combination of facial features and attached specific character traits to them. Further, he concentrated his attention on features he called 'defined and definable' rather than those that are moveable and accidental. He distinguished between what is superficial in the character - the passions and accidental determinations of the individual - and the original self. The former he supposed to be indicated by the moveable and muscular parts of the countenance, the latter by the firm and bony. In order to form an opinion of the character from the face, he required to see the face at rest - in sleep or in an unconscious state.[100] Lavater's technique involved a detailed examination of the face especially the eyes, brows, mouth, and nose. A nose

---

99  http://archive.org/stream/prosewritersofge00hedg#page/179/mode/1up

100  Frederic H Hedge (1849) *Prose Writers of Germany*; Carey and Hart - Philadelphia p. 187 - 205

slightly bending upwards, for instance, pointed to a contemptuous attitude and led to the expression 'stuck-up' which derives from this time. Lavater's work was enthusiastically received throughout Europe and marked the beginning of a new sense of individual personal identity rather than a collective social identity rooted in being a member of a particular class, group or sex.[101]

One famous disciple of Lavater was Captain Robert FitzRoy of the Beagle. His conviction about the utility of the system almost cost Charles Darwin his place on board the *Beagle*. As Darwin wrote in his autobiography

*'Afterwards on becoming very intimate with FitzRoy, I heard that I had run a very narrow risk of being rejected, on account of the shape of my nose! He was an ardent disciple of Lavater, and was convinced that he could judge a man's character by the outline of his features; and he doubted whether anyone with my nose could possess sufficient energy and determination for the voyage. But I think he was afterwards well-satisfied that my nose had spoken falsely.'*

Physiognomy, throughout the 18th and 19th centuries underpinned ideals of what constituted human physical perfection and what was base and ugly. This provided a spurious foundation for many prejudices - social, criminal and racial. Cesare Lombroso (1835 -1909), deemed by many the father of criminology, propounded a theory of anthropological criminology. This held that criminality was inherited, and that someone 'born criminal' could be identified by physical (congenital) defects, which confirmed a criminal as savage or atavistic. He wrote that criminal behaviour could be predicted in people with ape-like features.

In the U.S.A, the physician James W. Redfield published his *Comparative Physiognomy or Resemblances Between Men and Animals* in 1852. This document is liberally illustrated with caricatures designed to support the underpinning thesis. Chapters link appearance and character of different

---

101 J. Arianne Baggerman, Rudolf M. Dekker; Michael James Mascuch (2011) ; *Controlling Time and Shaping the Self: Developments in Autobiographical Writing Since the Sixteenth Century.* BRILL. p. 250–.ISBN 90-04-19500-9.

nationalities or races or religions with particular animals, e.g. Germans with lions, Chinamen with hogs, Yankees with bears, Jews with goats and the Irish with dogs. It is a document of its time and, rather than being a serious academic study, provides an important record of prevailing social prejudices that were rooted in racism, and stereotyping.

As an Irishman, chapter 31 was of particular interest to me. It opens thus -

---

*We have lingered on the verge of one part of our subject, longing for the eloquence which it would seem calculated to inspire, and find that we are likely never to go on unless we content us with plain English, like that which has already served us. That subject is the resemblance between the Irish man and the dog; and the eloquence which we craved (without knowing exactly what we were waiting for) is "Irish eloquence". This is so prominent a trait of Irish character, that if the resemblance alluded to exists, it must be characteristic of the dog. And so it is.'*

---

How about these for examples of racial stereotypes:

1.   *'Has not the Irishman pathos also to express his bereavement? and does he not hold his ' wakes,' in which he rivals the dog in wailing, as at other times he rivals him in debate and oratory' ?*

2.   *'We speak now of the 'common run' of Irish, and they are like the 'common run' of dogs that 'take after them,' and that are thieves and vagabonds without qualification.'*

3.   *'Compare the Irishman and the dog in respect to barking, snarling, howling, begging, fawning, flattering, back biting, quarrelling, blustering, scenting, seizing, hanging on, teasing, rollicking, and whatever other traits you may discover in either, and you will be convinced that there is a wonderful resemblance.'*

4.   *'Bloody Irishman' is a term applicable to the Irish in general, but particularly to that variety that resembles the bulldog. 'Kill' is a word attached to half the places in Ireland — Kildare, Kilkenny, Killarney, Kilkerny (sic), etc.'*

And what about this gem....

5.  *'Among the Irish, the commonality take to dirt-digging more naturally than to anything else; they are dirty in their persons, and admit their pigs in the mud-cabins which they themselves occupy. They are good servants if you deal harshly with them, as a master does with his dog ; but the moment you are disposed to be familiar with them they are all over you, jumping against you, and laying their dirty paws upon your clean clothes, as if you were no better than they. You are loved by them quite as well, and they are quite as happy, if you teach them good manners : but the true way to restore to them that sensibility, delicacy, sense of propriety, tender affection, and exquisite susceptibility of enjoyment, which is their rightful inheritance from their ancestors, is, to treat them as if they were possessed of these qualities, and thereby to set them the example. The man who wounds the feelings of his dog, will soon have a dog as hard and ungenerous as himself; but the man who treats his dog as he should, will have a faithful servant, who will say, "Go on, master, I will follow thee to the last gasp, with truth and loyalty."'*

In the 18th century, Franz Joseph Gall (1758-1828) held that behaviour had a neurological rather than a philosophical basis. This was centred on the brain and as the skull takes its shape from the brain; the surface of the skull can be read as an accurate index of psychological aptitudes and tendencies. The pseudo-science of phrenology was built upon this foundation. For a time this became a serious pursuit for some scientists. Indeed it rapidly eclipsed physiognomy. Redfield was piqued by the sidelining of his ancient 'science' by this new upstart. Indeed, he devoted his preface to railing against the pretentions of phrenology at the expense of physiognomy. Phrenology flamed briefly (less than 50 years) and quickly became discredited and with it the popularity of physiognomy began to wane.

Physiognomy like phrenology is now regarded as a pseudo-science and mainly of historical interest. However, the desire to make snap judgements about people from their appearance seems hard-wired into us. This may be a reflection of the need for a snap judgement about a person that might protect us from harm and avoid a dangerous encounter.

Sarah Waldorf,[102] in the *Getty Iris* blog (2012) wrote 'even though the term 'physiognomy' no longer resonates, the assumption of physical appearance as moral indicator lives on. Homer Simpson must be ugly, because he is stupid. When Dorothy asks the good 'white' witch in The Wizard of Oz why she's so beautiful, she replies, 'Why, only bad witches are ugly.' Though our consumer-driven world has increasingly substituted clothing and material possessions as signifiers of character, we continue to label our fellow humans as 'thick-headed,' and people get stopped on the street because they 'look suspicious.'

Physiognomy may be dead as an 'art' or a 'science' but it lives on in all of us as an ingrained behaviour. As a species we are all about 'first impressions' - especially about making good ones, even if counterfeit.

Arthur Schopenhauer (1788 -1860)[103] summed it up well....

*'It is also a fact that in private life everyone criticises the physiognomy of those he comes across, first of all secretly trying to discern their intellectual and moral character from their features...............In private, people always proceed upon the principle that a man is what he looks; and the principle is a right one, only the difficulty lies in its application. For though the art of applying the principle is partly innate and may be partly gained by experience, no one is a master of it, and even the most experienced is not infallible. But for all that, whatever Figaro may say, it is not the face which deceives; it is we who deceive ourselves in reading in it what is not there.'*

---

102  http://blogs.getty.edu/iris/physiognomy-the-beautiful-pseudoscience/

103  The Essays of Arthur Schopenhauer; Religion, a Dialogue, Etc. [Kindle Edition] By: Arthur Schopenhauer, T. Bailey (Thomas Bailey) Saunders

# CHAPTER 9

## The Third Amnesty

I t was a rule in the cities of Vietnam, particularly Ho Chi Minh city and Hanoi, at least when I was there in 2000, and apparently is still so, that if you wanted to cross the road you stepped off the kerb and launched yourself into the traffic flow, walking steadily and purposefully, in as straight a line as possible, to the other side. None of this 'Look right, look left and then look right again' *'Safe Cross Code'* nonsense drummed into us in Ireland since childhood. The fact that the Vietnamese, ostensibly, drive on the right rather than left would seriously undermine this injunction anyway. Vietnamese cities are full of kamikaze motorcyclists, cyclists, and an increasing number of cars, whose drivers are incapable of dealing with the 'unexpected'. The 'expected' is that you will stride across the road ignoring all other users, as Vietnamese pedestrians do; the 'unexpected' is that you will dither, look everywhere and skip and swerve as you try to avoid traffic. The former strategy will, in general, see you safely across the road; the latter will, invariably, see you in hospital or the morgue. The rule seems to be that if everyone does what they are expected to do then traffic will adjust to avoid you. However, it is worth bearing in mind that there is always an exception to rules, which is what makes crossing the road in Vietnam heart-stoppingly exciting every time.

Traffic in Vietnam is truly mad. While there are rules for road use, in practice, it seems that there are no rules. Cities teem with vehicles – motorbikes, bicycles, motorbikes, pedicabs, motorbikes, cars, motorbikes, vans, motorbikes, buses, motorbikes, trucks and motorbikes. And did I mention motorbikes?

In June 2016 it was reported that there were 8.5 million motorbikes in Ho Chi Minh City. This is an interesting statistic considering that the reported population of the city in 2016 was 8.426 million. However, more than 1 million motorbikes registered in other provinces are used to travel around the city and it is certain that all of the registered bikes are not in working order all of the time. A similar situation exists in Hanoi, the slightly smaller capital and, because of its traffic, one of the most polluted cities in Asia.

The freedom of movement provided by motorbikes, and their manoeuvrability in the traffic chaos that typifies these cities, makes them the mode of transport of choice of most people. In Vietnam, about 95 percent of registered vehicles are motorbikes or scooters. Their relatively low cost, and the ease with which they allow riders negotiate narrow streets and the tiny alleyways that typify Vietnamese municipalities, as well as park near their destination, partly explains their popularity.

Unlike much of the rest of the world, where a family car is seen as a necessity, in Vietnam the 'family motorbike' or scooter is the norm. It is not unusual to see a family of three or four – two adults and two children - being transported by motorbike, often with the mother shading herself from the sun with an umbrella. Motorbike taxis are common and instead of expensive vans, motorbikes are used to transport insane, teetering, huge loads of raw materials, manufactured goods or agricultural produce that completely dwarf the rider and vehicle. I once saw a man and his wife transport three fully grown pigs on a Honda 50 – one strapped upside-down on each side and one strapped to the rear luggage rack. The wife's comfort was severely diminished by the fact that she had to open her legs to an extreme angle to accommodate the width of the pigs strapped along each side of the saddle.

A drive of some 90km north-west of Ho Chi Minh City brings you close to the Cambodian border and the 'Holy See' in the province of Tay

Ninh. No! The Pope hasn't relocated from Rome; rather, this Holy See belongs to Caodaism.

On the way from Ho Chi Minh City you drive through the town of Trang Ban. This was the site of the infamous Pulitzer Prize-winning photograph, taken by Associated Press photographer Nick Ut, of a badly burned and naked nine-year-old girl, Kim Phuc, following a napalm attack by South Vietnamese warplanes.

In order to appreciate the structure of the Holy See, or Great Temple, it is necessary to have some basic knowledge of the rather complex Cao Dai beliefs.

Cao Dai is a relatively new syncretistic[104] religion, founded in Vietnam that was revealed to a number of founding 'mediums' through spiritualist séances. It was formally established, and legally recognised – its first time - in 1926.

There are two main Gods, the 'Highest Lord'[105] and the 'Holy Mother'[106]. They represent respectively the *Yang* and *Yin* forces. *Cao Đài* is revered as the Supreme Being of both Heaven and Earth and as the Father of all beings. While Caodaism stresses equality among men and women, ordained women may not attain the two highest positions - the Legislative Cardinal (*Hộ Pháp*) and the Pope (*Giáo-Tông*). This was revealed by *Cao Đài* himself, who proclaimed that, as *Yang* represents the ordaining, positive and expansive activity of the male creator and *Yin* represents the feminine, nurturing and restorative mother of humanity, *Yin* could not dominate *Yang* spiritually without chaos ensuing.

Organisationally, the church has a politico-religious basis sharing similarities with a state and with the Catholic Church. Caodaist hierarchy and

---

104 A syncretistic religion involves the blending of two or more existing religious belief systems into a new system

105 *Cao Đài Tiên Ông Đại Bồ Tát Ma-ha-tát*

106 *Đức Phật Mẫu*

clergy mimic the Catholic Church in that, as well as a Pope, there are Cardinals, Bishops, Priests, student Priests (no limit) Sub-dignitaries (village religious chiefs) and Followers.

The words *Cao Đài* in Vietnamese mean 'High Palace' or the place where God resides viz. the Kingdom of Heaven. The words are also used to designate the Supreme Being himself, whose full title is *'Cao Đài Tiên Ông Đại Bồ Tát Ma-ha-tát'* ('The Highest Power of the Ancient Immortal and Great Bodhisattva').

The official full name of the religion is more complex - Đại Đạo Tam Kỳ Phổ Độ, which means 'the third Great Universal Religious Amnesty (or Revelation)'.The first revelations were given to Dipankara Buddha, the sages and Phuc Hy (Fu Xi)[107] and the second to Gautama Buddha, Lao Tzu, Confucius and Jesus. These prophets who received the will of God, and founded their respective religions – Buddhism, Taoism and Christianity, were charged with serving and educating humanity. Due to the human frailty of these common men, the will of God was, inadvertently, misinterpreted, forgotten or corrupted and the religions they founded are seen by Caodaists as being culture and age bound and applicable only to restricted ethnicities. A primary aim of Caodaism is to unite all these religions.

The third revelation was intended to establish and evolve a great new faith for the salvation of living beings before the destruction of the universe. This third revalation supercedes and corrects misunderstandings of the first two.

Caodaists believe that God now speaks to humanity directly through mediumship and spiritualistic séances. The Legislative Body of Cao Dai, led by the *Hộ Pháp* or the Legislative Cardinal has the duty of communicating with divine beings. Revelation from the divine is aided through the use of the *'corbeille a bec'* or beaked basket.[108] This consists of a bamboo basket

107 The originator of the I Ching – the basis for divination practices used for centuries across the Far East.

108 Known in English as a planchette

and a wooden pointer which, under divine influence, indicates which letters should be picked out to reveal the message from *Cao Đài*. These messages provide the cornerstones of Cao Dai scripture and provide for the continuing development of the religion.

Cao Dai, as a syncretistic religion, has borrowed heavily from Taoism, Buddhism and Confuscianism but also draws from Geniism,[109] Judaism, Christianity and Islam.

Caodaists worship a single god, superior spirits and ancestors. They believe in nonviolence,[110] karma[111] and reincarnation. Morally, adherents are instructed in their responsibilities to self, family, society and all of humanity; philosophically, the religion preaches contempt of honours, riches, and luxury, and values the role of servitude in the quest for tranquillity of spirit. Cao Dai draws its ethical precepts from Confucianism, its theories of karma and reincarnation from Buddhism and its spiritualist and occult practices from Taoism. These three founding religions form the basis for the three enclaves within Caodiasm.

Cao Dai is governed by two powers:

1. The invisible heavenly council made up of the founders of five religions: Shakyamuni (Buddhism), Lao Tzu (Taoism), Confucius (Confucianism), Jesus Christ (Christianity), Jiang Ziya (Geniism)

---

109 This is an indigenous religion of Vietnam. Genies, as spirits, have had great accomplishments in serving humanity. Genies are higher than humans but less than gods and are responsible for the well-being of individuals and groups, who may interact with them through prayer. As a religion it has similarities with Japanese Shintoism.

110 Paradoxically, for an avowedly non violent organisation, Cao Dai had a private army, formed in 1938, that defended the effectively semiautonomous 'state' they had developed in the Mekong Delta. During the Second World War, Cao Dai supported the Japanese against the French in the hope of independence after the war – but after the Japanese were defeated, the French returned. Thereafter, Cao Dai was an effective force in national politics; first supporting, then opposing, Premier Ngo Dinh Diem. In 1955, under military pressure, the Cao Dai yielded their independence to Diem. Pham Cong Tac, Interim Pope of the Cao Dai, fled to Cambodia in February 1956 and South Vietnamese forces seized control of Tay Ninh.

111 One's future reincarnated life, or lives, is greatly influenced by our actions in this one. Good deeds can advance us towards Nirvana (heaven) bad deeds can set us back in our progression.

2.  The earthly power made up of an Executive Body headed by the Pope who is in charge of the administration of the Religion and its missionary activities, and a Legislative Body headed by the *Hộ Pháp* (the Legislative Cardinal who is the Protector of Laws and Justice) who is responsible for legislation, jurisdiction and communication with God or Divine Beings

Caodaism sets rules for adherents who are expected to

- Pray at least once per day, at 6 am, noon, 6 pm, and/or midnight, either at a temple or a home altar

- Eat a vegetarian diet at least ten days each month and avoid killing living beings

- Cultivate Confucian duties (obedience between king and citizen, father and child, husband and wife), and five virtues (humanity, obligation, civility, knowledge, reliability)

- Practice good and avoid evil

Adherents are bound by the following precepts

- do not kill

- do not steal

- do not commit adultery

- do not get drunk

- do not sin by word

The *Giáo-Tông* or Supreme Pontiff is the titular head of the Cao Dai Church. The *Giáo-Tông* is not considered to be a living person but rather the sanctified spirit of the philosopher-saint, Ly Thai Bach.[112] Interestingly, Le Van Trung, the first great Cao Dai leader only served as *Quyen Giao Tong* or 'Interim Pope'.

---

112 The Pope is reputed to be the Spirit of the poet Li Tai Pe (Vietnamese, Ly-thai-Bach), who lived during the Tong Dynasty.

Despite this, the process for selecting a pope is outlined in Cao Dai scripture and is reminiscent of the selection of the Dali Lama. He is selected in a special ceremony attended by various members of the Church hierarchy and led by the three Enclave Cardinals representing the three branches of Caodaism viz. Taoism, Buddhism and Confucianism. This sacerdotal body visits temples and meets the faithful at a time when the former *Giáo-Tông* has died. It is charged with finding the child who carries a special mark signifying that he is the *Giáo-Tông*. This mark consists of a blinding light that radiates from the child to the Enclave Cardinals. Once the *Giáo-Tông* is found, he is proclaimed Supreme Pontiff and his enthronement begins. This has yet to happen.

After Le Van Trung died in 1936, leadership duties and the role of Interim Pope was assumed by the then *Hộ Pháp* - Phạm Công Tắc. It was Phạm Công Tắc, who wrote the scriptures for Caodaism and who gave the order to build the Holy See. With the exception of decoration, the building was all but finished by 1940.

Following the exile of Phạm Công Tắc and other leaders to the island of Nosy Lava near Madagascar in 1941, together with the wars within Vietnam with the Japanese, the Viet Minh, and the French, the official opening was delayed until 1955. Following reunification of Vietnam in 1975, Cao Dai was repressed by the communist government in Hanoi. It was legally recognised, for the second time, in 1997. Currently the position of Interim Pope is vacant, and has been since the death of Phạm Công Tắc in May 1959.

The Great Temple is situated within a 100 hectare compound which is surrounded by a fence. There are 12 gates, the main gate and eleven auxiliary gates. The main gate, which is topped on each side by a statue of a blue, yellow, black and pink painted dragon - each facing the symbols of Cao Diasm, set on a lotus - normally remains closed. It is only opened to admit dignitaries and public personalities. Access to the public is through one of the auxiliary gates.

Behind the gate are three towers dedicated to deceased leaders of Cao Dai, who are now regarded as divines, namely i) His Holiness Phạm Công Tắc, Chief of the Legislative Body and Interim Pope, who unveils the mystery of the invisible and is the maintainer of the rules and laws of the religion; ii) Thượng Phẩm Cao Quỳnh Cư, leader of the Spiritual Realm, who aids and directs souls in the process of spiritual and heavenly evolution; and iii) Thượng Sanh Cao Hoài Sang, the Leader of the Temporal Realm, for souls experiencing purgatory before being elevated. All souls must be guided by the Thuong Sanh in order to be able to cross over from the temporal realm and abyss of suffering.

As well as the Great Temple, the complex houses administrative offices, residences for officials and adepts, and a hospital of traditional Vietnamese herbal medicine, statues, grandstands and pillars.

The Great Temple is highly decorated and, architecturally, is a combination of Neo-Gothic, Baroque and Oriental design, combining the features of a Catholic cathedral and a Buddhist temple. It is 140m long and 40m wide. Its four towers echo this mix of styles, the two at the front of the building, resembling typical Christian bell towers, hold statues of the first male (on the right) and female (on the left) leaders of CaoDai. The domed tower in the middle of the building is topped with the statue of a Chinese unicorn. The fourth tower displays statues of three gods of Hinduism – Brahma, Vishnu and Shiva. Above the doorway there is a statue of Lao Tzu carrying Jesus Christ on his shoulders: in turn, Christ supports Confucius and Buddha, symbolizing the eclectic and unifying nature of the Cao Dai faith.

Within the main entrance there is a picture of the three saints signing an agreement with God – these are Victor Hugo (the French poet, novelist and dramatist) writing in French, Sun Yat Sen (founding father of the Republic of China), who is holding the ink and Nguyễn Bỉnh Khiêm (a Vietnamese administrator, educator, poet, sage), who is writing the same words as Victor Hugo but in Chinese.

The interior of the temple consists of a colonnaded hall and a sanctuary. The main hall is divided into nine different levels, a step and a pair of columns delineating each level. The pink columns are decorated with black dragons and snakes that spiral towards the ceiling. These levels represent the stages of spiritual ascension to heaven. The domed ceiling is also divided into nine parts and is painted as a night sky full of stars to symbolise heaven. Two blue painted pulpits (similar to the minbar in a mosque) are situated between the columns in the main hall. The one on the right is for males and the one on the left for females.

The back of the temple is the sanctuary, which holds the main altar. Eight plaster columns, entwined with multicoloured dragons, support a dome. Under this dome is a large star-speckled blue globe on which is painted the Divine Eye, the official symbol of Caodaism. The eye is the left eye and represents God. Symbolically it serves as a reminder that God witnesses everything, everywhere, eternally. There are fifty depictions of the Divine Eye in the Holy See; these are of five different shapes, with each shape holding a separate spiritual meaning. The eye on the globe is painted above a depiction of the constellation Ursa Major and the North Star. The eye on the façade is has 35 rays of light and represents the three major religions and five main religious doctrines of the world. Other depictions of the Divine Eye show sixteen rays of light. Nine of these, like the nine levels inside the temple, represent the levels of heaven and radiate upwards. The remaining seven downward radiating rays represent seven human passions that need to be controlled. Painted into the pupil of each of the eyes is the *Yang* and *Yin* symbol for male and female. The parallel between the Divine Eye, the Eye of Providence on the reverse of the Great Seal of the United States (and shown on the American one Dollar bill) and the symbol for Freemasonry, and Christian and Judaic iconography all reinforce the eclecticism of Cao Dai.

In front of the globe are seven thrones. The largest of these is reserved for the Cao Dai pope, a position that remains vacant.. The next three thrones are for the Cardinals responsible for the Legislative Council. Between these three thrones is coiled a great brown cobra, which represents the seven human passions (jealousy, lust, anger, sadness, beatitude, joy and love). The seven heads form part of the *Hộ Pháp*'s throne, the tails curl around the other two thrones. The passions of Jealousy, Lust, Anger and Sadness are the heads that form the feet and armrests of the throne. During a ceremony, when the *Hộ Pháp* is sitting down, his hands and feet press down on these heads to subdue these passions. Behind him, the heads representing Beatitude, Joy and Universal Love rise up, forming the back of the throne. The remaining thrones are reserved for the Cardinals, who represent the three branches of Cao Dai and are represented by the colours yellow, red and blue.

The temple's enormous windows, emblazoned as they are with the Divine Eye and lotus flowers, let in the muted light.

Visitors, who are welcome at any of the services, must remove their shoes before entering the Holy See and make their way to the balcony from which they may watch and photograph proceedings.

The service, called the mass, is simple, choreographed and colourful. Female worshippers enter through the left door and male worshippers through the right. They process up the Temple to where they sit in rows on the level appropriate to each individual - women on the left and men on the right. The number of years they have been members will determine which of the nine levels they will occupy.

Most of the worshippers are lay members and wear pure white robes. Men, with the rank of priest or higher wear a smock over their white robe that reflects their spiritual allegiance – yellow, for Buddhism and virtue; blue, for Tao and pacifism and red, for Confucianism and authority. All three branches wear headpieces, rather like a Bishop's Mitre but square rather than pointed on top, and, like a mitre, with long ribbons hanging down the back. Bishops and cardinals have the Divine Eye emblazoned on their headpieces. Ordinary members of the clergy may marry and raise families. Those above the rank of priest are not allowed to marry and must remain celibate and vegetarian in order to commit their total energies to the religious life. This is, in ways, similar to the Eastern Orthodox Church.

The mass starts with the offering of incense. A small orchestra of ten musicians and a choir of twenty youths lead the service with hymns. This is followed with prayers, including the canticle to the glory of God (recited in unison), and three more canticles in honour of the three saints Confucius, Lao Tzu, and Buddha. Every time a gong sounds the worshippers touch their joined hands to their foreheads and bow in unison from their seated position. This continues for a time. The service then continues with the occasional beating of a gong and clackers whilst a clergyman recites a canticle. On a cymbal clash, the congregation stands and turns so that the male and female worshippers face each other. Prayers continue during this time. On the clash of a cymbal, the faithful turn back to face the altar and sit again. After more prayers and music the mass ends and worshipers turn and file out of the Temple.

Although watched by many tourists, particularly at the noon mass, the ceremony is peaceful and solemn and a joy to watch. I only wish I had as much understanding of the religion when I observed the mass in Tay Ninh as I do now. Then, although I enjoyed it, my memory is of a riot of colour and imagery, but with little perception of what it symbolised or what was intended.

# CHAPTER 10

## When we were Ophiophagus

I will eat anything. Well, almost anything. I have a particular aversion to broccoli, Brussels sprouts, spinach and okra. Fortunately, I have recently found a scientific explanation as to why I dislike the first three; my aversion to the fourth is pure prejudice.

Everyone has five basic tastes – sweetness, sourness, savouriness,[113] saltiness and bitterness. It seems that scientists have discovered a gene, memorably (not) called TAS2R38 that controls sensitivity to bitter tastes. This gene is responsible for the manufacture of a protein that binds with a chemical called phenylthiocarbamide (PTC),[114] which results in nerve fibres attached to taste receptors in the taste buds sending signals to the brain indicating that there is a bitter taste. Salty and sour tastes are determined through ion channels that enervate the appropriate nerve to the brain; sweet, savoury and bitter are, however, determined by taste receptors. Taste receptors in humans are divided into two families: Type 1 where three genes control sweet tastes and Type 2 where about twenty six genes control bitter tastes. Savoury taste is a combination of particular Type 1 and Type 2 receptors.

The ability to taste PTC is often treated as a dominant genetic trait. PTC tasting is largely determined by a single gene, TAS2R38, with two common alleles. The allele for tasting is mostly dominant over the allele for non-tasting. This has resulted in people being classed as supertasters,

---

113 Also known as umami - it has been described as brothy or meaty.

114 also known as phenylthiourea (PTU)

who can't abide these vegetables, and non-tasters, who love them. Recent studies have shown that this basic Mendelian model is too simplistic. It now appears that there are other genes or environmental factors that influence PTC tasting. This results in a continuous range of PTC tasting ability, not an absolute separation into tasters and non-tasters. This may well account for the fact that I like cabbage and cauliflower but detest broccoli and Brussels sprouts.

While PTC is not usually found in the human diet, very similar chemicals such as glucosinolates and isothiocyanates are found in brassicas such as Brussels sprouts and cabbages and it is most likely that it is these that are causing the bitter reaction.

The bitter taste may be alleviated to some extent by seasoning. Salt helps to block the bitter taste of foods, so a pinch of salt or a dash of soy sauce may well help. Given that chefs are generally reputed to be in the 'supertaster' category, this might go some way to explain their love of seasoning. Frequently you hear TV chefs berate amateur cooks or trainees that something is not seasoned enough and often when I eat in restaurants I find the food too salty, and wonder if the chef actually tasted it before serving it.

None of this, however, explains my aversion to Okra, also known as lady's fingers or gumbo. Okra I have heard described, accurately in my view, as vegetable snot. I have tasted it in the past and it did nothing for me. It had a mild taste that wasn't good, it wasn't bad, it just ...wasn't. It has the texture and crunch of green beans or green pepper (but not the taste) and is reputed to have a taste similar to aubergine or asparagus[115] (but I never detected it) – so I just eat green beans, green peppers and asparagus, as they don't have the slime that fills the okra pod. As a vegetable it is ephemeral, and remains edible for only a matter of days. Old okra pods are hard, fibrous, woody and even more unpleasant.

---

115 Asparagus taints your urine with a unique smell. This scared the Bejaysus out of me the first time I noticed it and I feared I had picked up a terminal disease. Now, I just take it as confirmation that my internal organs, and my kidneys in particular, are working effectively.

Is the appellation of vegetable snot accurate, you may ask? Well, it produces a water-soluble acidic polysaccharide more generally known as mucilage. This is somewhat different to the glycoprotein-based mucus produced by animals. So it is not animal snot, but vegetable snot seems a more than fair description. An effusion of this vegetable snot, when chopping these little green devil's pods, is one of the most unappealing aspects of their use. Your chopping board and knives look like the entire family has had a gigantic nasal eruption, all at the same time. I have to admit that it is this spew of sticky slime that continues to prevent me from trying any of the myriad recipes that purport to transform this hideous vegetable into the food of the gods. What they say to me is, if you fry okra slices to the edge of cremation and if you pair it with flavourful and tasty ingredients, or an incandescent hot-sauce, you will enjoy your meal, as these ingredients will smother both the taste and texture of the slimy seedpod. I really couldn't be bothered.

Recently scientists have tested okra slime as a vector for delivering drugs nasally.[116] It is almost a case of using vegetable snot to replace animal snot in order to dose animals. The fact that it sticks in the nasal cavity, and that goats (the animals it was tested on) don't have fingers, is a bonus.

When we were in Vietnam in 2000 and travelling from the Cao Dai Temple to the Cu Chi tunnels we stopped at a small restaurant for lunch. It was run by a Khmer woman who had escaped from Cambodia in the 1970s, either to escape Lon Nol's anti-communist forces or the Pol Pot's subsequent Khmer Rouge rule. I never found out which. The fixed menu for VND 40,000,[117] less than €2.00 at the time, was excellent value. We were offered the speciality of the house, sautéed snake, which Mary and I had. The snake we were informed by the owner was captured just 200

---

116 Sharma, N., Kulkarni G.T., and Sharma, A. (2013) Development of *Abelmoschus esculentus* (Okra)-Based Mucoadhesive Gel for Nasal Delivery of Rizatriptan Benzoate: Tropical Journal of Pharmaceutical Research April 2013; 12 (2): 149-153

117 Vietnamese đồng: VND26,863 was worth €1.00 (as of 30ᵗʰ March 2017)

metres from the restaurant on the banks of the Saigon River. There was something clandestine about the whispered offer of this speciality and it was only later that I discovered that hunting snakes without a permit was illegal. Whether the owner had a permit is moot and it is highly possible it was obtained from an illegal snake-catcher. She explained that it was a king cobra (*Ophiophagus hannah*), which can grow up to 5.7 metres and yield up to 7kg of meat, and is the longest venomous snake in the world.

The king cobra is not a member of the *Naja* genus (the 'true cobras'), but is the sole member of the *Ophiophagus* genus. As this name suggests it preys on other snakes and sometimes on lizards and rodents. Its most common prey is the rat snake. For this reason, it is often found close to human settlements, where rats abound.

The king cobra is a dangerous snake but appears docile and avoids humans where possible. This is just as well, as its venom is potent and can kill. Indeed in August 2014 it was reported in the international media that a chef from Guangdong Province in southern China was killed by a cobra that bit him 20 minutes after he cut its head off, when he picked it up to throw away. Even the chopped up bits of snake can move for a considerable period of time after being severed.

The snake we were served had a delicate flavour. The meat was finely chopped and fried in oil with ginger, chilli and turmeric and maybe a couple of other spices. These were the flavours we could discern but, friendly though she was, the cook was unwilling to reveal her recipe. We ate it loaded onto rice crackers, and we enjoyed it. It was not an unpleasant experience, but I wouldn't go out of my way to try it again. There are so many other tasty dishes in Asia that I still need to try that it causes little distress for me to drop this particular culinary delight back to the bottom of my 'must try' list.

# CHAPTER 11

# Vodun, Santeria and Candomblé

From the 15th to the 19th century, millions of people were trafficked from their homes in Africa, around the globe, to be sold into slavery. The greatest part of this obscenity was manifested in the transatlantic slave trade, which saw some 20 million people being shipped to the Americas and the Caribbean. The area on the coast of the Bight of Benin (which includes modern day Togo, Benin and Nigeria west of the Niger Delta) was so involved in this trade that it became infamous as 'The Slave Coast'. Over these four centuries, some twenty percent of the total number of enslaved Africans departed from these shores alone.

This barbaric trade, now perversely viewed by some as the first great attempt at 'globalisation', involving as it did five continents (Europe, Africa, North and South America and Asia), was purely economic in its intent.

European trinkets, cheap jewellery and weapons were traded for people captured by African slave traders. Following purchase, these poor souls were loaded on to the slave ships. Typically, the ships had open platforms below deck in the hold. These were arranged in tiers on which the slaves would lie. The slaves were usually ankle chained in groups, or coffles, with the coffle, rather than the individual being secured to the platform. The availability of space limited the number of slaves that could be transported. More slaves could be carried if they were forced to lie on their sides rather than their backs and if the space between the tiers of platforms was minimised. Poor or no sanitation, little light and poor ventilation meant that slave ships stank – they could be smelled before they were seen – and disease was rife. The more tightly the slaves were packed the greater the loss in transit. On average, some 15% of the slaves died in transit.

When the slave ships reached their destination in the Caribbean or Americas, the slaves were traded to middlemen or plantation and mine owners and the emptied ships were then filled with sugar, cotton, indigo, coffee and tobacco for sale back in Europe.

Slave trading also took place northwards and eastwards across the Sahara from centres such as Timbuktu and Bilma to ports such as Carthage and Alexandria on the Mediterranean, Zeila in the Gulf of Aden and Zanzibar in the Indian Ocean. Arab slavers exported captives to Egypt and the Middle East, to Pakistan and India, and even as far away as Japan.

The only way this trade could be justified and consciences could be salved, both by Christians[118] and by Muslims[119] was to consider the status of enslaved people a manifestation of their inherent wickedness or that they be considered to be no more than an intelligent beast that could then be regarded as chattel. This denigration of the humanity of the slave allowed those involved in the slave trade to regard themselves as superior in every way and provided the insidious basis for the racism that still persists in much of the so-called First World.

People living in the countries bordering the Bight of Benin have had a deep rooted belief system going back millennia. This not merely encompasses religion (in the sense of belief in a god or gods) but embodies all aspects of culture including philosophy of life and living, medicine, art, language, music and dance. This system of interlocking beliefs is known

---

118 St Augustine The City of God, 19:15 believed it to be the natural consequence of sin ...'The prime cause, then, of slavery is sin, which brings man under the dominion of his fellow'

119 The principle of knowing that all things belong to God is essential to purification and growth. One of the five pillars of Islam, zakāt (charity or alms giving) is obligatory for all Muslims who are able to do so. It is the personal responsibility of each Muslim to ease the economic hardship of others and to strive towards eliminating inequality. The Quran provides for emancipation of a slave as a means of religious atonement for sins.

as Vodun, pronounced vodǔ (or in the West, Voodoo) and means 'spirit' in both the Fon and Ewe languages. It has roots that may go back more than 6,000 years in Africa.

Vodun belief centres on spirits and deities that govern and protect the Earth. This includes major deities that govern the forces of nature and human society, as well as individual spirits of rocks, trees and streams and spirits of dead ancestors who live amongst us. Vodun priests and priestesses act as intermediaries between the spirit world and the living world.

In this belief system, all creation is considered divine. This is the bedrock of the belief in the efficacy of using 'fetishes' and herbal remedies for both physical and spiritual healing, for invigoration and for rejuvenation.

In 2003 I visited the Akodessewa fetish market (*Marché des Féticheurs*), the biggest fetish market in the world in Lomé, the capital of Togo. Myriad dried animals and dried bits of animals, bones, skins and glands were piled on serried rows of trestle tables – a grey, dusty and foetid mass, festering under the tropical sun. Here you could find a tangle of antelope skulls and horns; dried cobra and other snake skins; monkey hands and monkey feet; hyaena heads, a few leopard heads, hippo skulls, baboon bits and dried dogs; tortoises and elephant bones; varied vertebrae including some from whales; dried tails of a variety of animals; dried bats, vultures and wooden dolls.

None of these fetishes is effective until a Vodun priest, through ceremonies of blessing and incantation, channels the spirit within them to intercede with the god. Sometimes, in order to be effective, use of the fetish may involve it being crushed and consumed by the supplicant.

All fetishes have to be passed through certain ceremonies to imbue them with the energy of a deity or spirit, or to release the energy of the spirit that is already in them. The power locked up in fetishes may be used for either good or evil purposes. If the effect of invoking a particular spirit results in an evil outcome then this is to be expected, as this is the nature of that spirit and the reason it was invoked. Evil is recognised simply as the negative reflection of good.

Tourists and locals mix freely in the fetish market. The locals indulge in the serious business of buying fetishes and remedies that will address imperatives in their own or their families' lives. Tourists are there, at best, to gain an understanding of this religion and, at worst, to gawk. Locals understand this and offer explanations and experiences tailored to the gullibility and visible wealth of these potential clients.

A self-proclaimed priest we met at the market tried to explain the use of some of the sad desiccated limbs and bones on display. Whatever desperation he saw in my face led him to explain only those fetishes that could be used to seduce members of the opposite sex, act as a natural Viagra to promote and maintain an erection or to ward off evil spirits. He suggested that ground and dried bat mixed into a potion would encourage the mother and father of a 'stiffy' in any man.

He led us into his small shack to witness a ceremony. Here he rang a small bell, got me to repeat my name three times and uttered a few incantations. Having blessed them, we were presented with six fetishes, consisting of a couple of nuts, some seeds and a twig, to ensure good luck, attract a lover, impose your will on your daily fate and of course to promote the inevitable 'stiffy' through judicious use of the twig. I was not sure how to use the fetishes, whether they should be consumed or just kept. The priest didn't bother to explain this to us. However, having thanked him, and as I got up to leave, he explained that these items would cost the equivalent of US$80. To say I was aghast would be an exaggeration. I simply burst out laughing and said no thanks. They asked me what money I had on me (I had a paltry CFA 1500 – about US$25. This clearly wasn't enough. They grabbed back the fetishes and shoved me out of the 'temple' banging my head on the low door lintel as I was propelled back into the market. Having witnessed my ignominy, my two companions paid the requested donation for their fetishes. I did not detect, nor was I informed of any change in their luck or improvement in their amorous activities during the rest of the trip. Equally, I didn't notice any diminution in mine.

I learnt two things from this encounter. Firstly the Vodun priest saw me as an economic opportunity rather than a believer and the 'ceremony' that was put on was a show intended to give me the impression of participation rather than the actuality. Because this was a sham, and as there was no real intercession sought from the spirits, the priest was secure in the knowledge that he wasn't compromising his belief. Secondly, irrespective of the dubious nature of the ceremony, the repeated naming of the fetishes as pertaining to me and the possibility that they were actually being blessed was treated in both a disrespectful and casual fashion by me. I participated willingly in the ceremony, when I could easily have refused, so I should have made an appropriate effort to pay for what I got. I didn't, and the regret I still feel may well be a manifestation of my ignorance and my deprecation of the fetishes that I was offered. I saw and valued them as the rude and simple objects they were rather then appreciating them for the spiritual talismans they would become, once they were blessed. My lack of belief contrasts vividly with the strong inbred belief of the people who have lived in this region for centuries. Ah well! Live and learn.

The slaves who were transported to the Americas and the Caribbean[120] brought with them their culture and these religious beliefs.

At first, these were a matter of curiosity and fascination to their new masters, but rapidly they became a source of fear. This resulted in a prohibition on traditional religious practices and a concerted attempt to 'Christianise' slaves by their masters. Slaves who disobeyed this prohibition were liable to extreme punishment, ranging from beatings and imprisonment

---

120 African slaves were first brought to the new world by Spanish settlers in 1501 – i.e. Santo Domingo; now the capital of the Dominican Republic. In 1581 Spanish residents imported African slaves into Florida; and in 1619, British settlers brought African slaves into the Virginia Colony.

for possession of fetishes to mutilation, sexual disfigurement, flaying alive, burying alive and hanging for more overt expression of traditional belief.

Many masters, having bought new slaves, would have them baptised into Christianity as rapidly as possible. This was particularly prevalent in Catholic areas of South America, the Caribbean and Louisiana in North America.[121] In the southern colonies of North America, similar efforts were made to 'Christianise' their slaves. Indeed in the French slave areas the infamous *Code Noir* explicitly forbade the practice of all African religions and specified in its Articles that

- *Slaves must be baptized in the Roman Catholic Church*

- *Public exercise of any religion other than Roman Catholicism was prohibited; masters who allowed or tolerated it by their slaves could also be punished*

- *Only Catholic marriages would be recognized*

In America, a distinguishing feature of who could be a slave appeared to be not being a Christian at the time of capture or sale. However, converting to Christianity was not an escape from bondage. The Slave Codes (many derived from earlier British slave codes and informed by the codes of the State of Virginia) of slave owning states established a set of laws that defined a slave and regulated slavery. For example

Act III of Virginia, in 1667, indicated that conversion to Christianity was more for the peace of mind of the master than the spiritual or temporal benefit of the slave ...

*...it is enacted that baptism does not alter the condition to the person as to his bondage or freedom; masters freed from this doubt may more carefully propagate Christianity by permitting slaves to be admitted to that sacrament.*

---

121 It wasn't until 1776 that the Second Continental Congress declared a new, independent nation: the United States of America.

Another Act of Virginia in 1705 decreed...

*...All servants imported and brought into the Country... who were not Christians in their native Country... shall be accounted and be slaves. All Negro, mulatto and Indian slaves within this dominion... shall be held to be real estate.*

The efforts of slave owners to Christianise their slaves did not eliminate traditional beliefs, it simply drove them underground. Slaves practiced Catholicism or other forms of Christian worship openly in front of their masters. However, many would then gather secretly to worship in the old way. Work songs disguised prayers to the spirits, and veneration of Christian saints was a disguise for intercession to traditional gods. Over time, the religious traditions of Catholicism, ancestor worship, animism, tribal shamanism and elements of Islam fused into new syncretic religions that are exemplified in Vodou in Haiti and New Orleans in North America, Santeria in Cuba, Puerto Rico, Dominican Republic, Panama, Colombia, Venezuela, and North America and Candomblé, primarily practised in Brazil but also to some extent in Argentina, Uruguay, Paraguay, and Venezuela. All of these religions share a common origin but each has a distinctiveness that sets it apart, albeit slightly, from the other.

Vodou, a major religion in Haiti, has often, particularly in the western culture, been referred to incorrectly as Voodoo. Through the influence of horror movies, it has falsely become associated with 'zombies' – the fictional reanimation of human corpses - and 'voodoo dolls', neither of which are part of Vodou. While it links West African Vodun with Catholicism it also has many influences from the native Taíno Indians and the Congolese tradition of *kanga* that ties body and soul together. According to Vodou, the soul consists of two aspects, the *gros bon ange* and the *ti bon ange*. The *gros bon ange*, or the 'big good angel,' is the life force shared by all humans and is responsible for the basic biological functions, such as the flow of blood through the body and breathing. It enters the body at birth and leaves at death when it floats back to the *Gran Met*, or pool of life force. The *ti bon ange*, or 'little good angel' is the part of the soul that contains the individual qualities of a person, such as personality, character and willpower. The *ti bon ange* leaves the body during sleep so that the person experiences dreams. As the *ti bon ange* is not necessary to keep the body functioning, a person can continue to exist without it. For this reason, the *ti bon ange* can leave the body during rituals for spirit possessions, whereupon when a spirit or *loa* takes possession of a priest. However, as the priest's *ti bon ange* floats free, if unprotected, it could be harmed or stolen.

Vodouists believe in a Supreme Creator, *Bondye* (from the French *Bon Dieu*, meaning 'good God'). *Bondye* is a distant and unknowable being and does not intercede in human affairs. Worship is, therefore, directed at sub-servient spirits called *loa*. Each *loa*, of which there are many, is responsible for a particular aspect of life. A person doesn't choose which *loa* to serve. These *loa* are often revealed in a reading with a priest, in a ceremony or in a dream, and are linked to their nature or destiny.

A Vodou house is organized as an extended family, with a hierarchy and all the obligations that brings. As well as the *loa*, adherents serve the spirits of their own blood ancestors. Believers seek to achieve harmony with their own individual nature and with the world around them.

Vodouists revere death. It is seen as a transition from life to the after-life. Some believe that, after death, the spirit is trapped in a temporary rest-ing place for a year and a day. Once a ceremony has been held, the soul of the deceased leaves its resting place, and can occupy trees or even become a hushed voice on the wind.

Priests, are referred to as '*Houngans*', and priestesses as '*Manbos*'. They are responsible for preserving the rituals and the songs; and for maintaining the relationship between the spirits and the community.

A Vodou service consists of prayer and song. It includes a litany and verses in honour of all the European and African saints and *loa* honoured by the house. As the songs are sung, adherents believe that spirits come and take possession of individuals and speak and act through them. Only the family of those possessed is benefited.

Animals sacrifice forms part of some rituals. The sacrifice commonly involves chickens, but pigs, goats and bulls may also be sacrificed. The intent of sacrifice, based on the fact that blood is the essence of life and vigour, is the transfusion of the life of the sacrificed animal to re-enervate the *loa*. This is often demonstrated symbolically, when the priest possessed by the *loa* is given the blood to drink.

On a household level, adherents may set out tables for their ancestors, and the *loa* they serve, with pictures or statues, perfumes, candles, flowers, foods, and other symbols and objects.

In 1791, slaves in Haiti rebelled against their 'owners'. Led by Toussaint L'Ouverture,[122] a former slave, this was the only successful slave revolt in modern history. The rebellion continued until 1803 and saw the death of 100,000 blacks and a quarter that number of whites. However, not only did it bring about the end of slavery but also French control over the colony.

Some white planters fled with their slaves from Haiti to the United States to avoid the death and destruction of property that accompanied the rebellion. They settled in Louisiana, where a new version of Vodun, called Louisiana or New Orleans Voodoo, evolved from the Vodun practices they brought, and combined with the religious and magical beliefs brought by the slaves who were transported directly to this region from Senegal, the Gambia, The Congo and Benin in the late 16th Century.

Voodoo Hoodoo differs from Vodou in its emphasis upon *gris-gris*, Voodoo queens, use of Hoodoo paraphernalia, and veneration of *Dambal-*

---

122 Toussaint was a fervent Catholic and opposed to Vodou. Revolts were a regular feature of the slave plantations from the first one on the island of Hispaniola (now comprises the Dominican Republic and Haiti) in 1522 up until the early 19th century, when slavery was abolished in the UK and the USA.

*lah Wedo*[123] or *Li Grande Zombi*. New Orleans Voodoo Hoodoo is a blending of religious and magical elements.

The incorporation of *gris gris* stems, to some extent, from the Muslim tradition of some of the slaves, where leather pouches or amulets made by marabouts (religious leaders) were worn around the neck, and contained either stitched or written extracts from the Quran. They were intended to provide some benefit, such as healing illness, protection from evil, success in romance, relief from infertility; or they might contain lethal powders that could be used to poison enemies. The use of *gris gris* was common among slaves, both in Louisiana and in Haiti. It is believed by some that *gris gris* played a role in the Haitian slave rebellion.

The *gris gris* is, essentially, a portable charm, prayer or spell. While its physical manifestation may be a bag, doll, or powder, it is the actual act and the magic involved in the creation of the charm that is the *gris gris*, rather than the charm itself. The *gris gris* can be worn as an amulet or carried as a *gris gri*s bag; it may be named and formed into a doll; it may consist of sacred words written in magic ink; or consist of a powder made from combinations of minerals, herbs, graveyard dust, roots, or bones which, when added to water, may be drunk as a potion or may be added to a bath, or concocted into a lethal poison that could be thrown into the path or face of an enemy.

Voodoo dolls may be an expression of sympathetic and contagious magic.[124] Sympathetic magic, results in the creation of a doll that has a likeness of the person for whom the *gris gris* is intended. It is based on the principle that 'like produces like.' For instance, whatever happens to an image of someone will also happen to them. Contagious magic always involves

---

123 Damballa is one of the most important of all the *loa*. Damballa is the creator of the cosmos, of all life and rules the mind and intellect. Damballa is depicted as the great serpent spirit. By shedding his skin, Damballa created all the waters on the earth. In Vodun, Damballa is often syncretized with Saint Patrick, who banished snakes from Ireland. In this way slaves could worship St Patrick, as a proxy for Damballa, without raising the suspicion of their masters that they were practicing a forbidden religion.

124 http://voodoohoodoospellbook.blogspot.ie

incorporating something belonging to the person for whom the *gris gris* is intended, such a fingernail clippings, hair, item of clothing etc. This is based on the belief that there is a permanent relationship between an individual and any part of his or her body. The personal item provides a magical link from the physical to the spiritual world of the person; thus, the *gris gris* is believed to influence that person's life in a very specific way. As a consequence, believers must take special precautions with their hair, fingernails, teeth, clothes, and faeces to avoid them being misused. Anyone obtaining samples of these intimate, personal items could perform magic on them that would cause the person they came from to be adversely affected. For instance, someone could use your fingernail clippings in a magical ritual that would cause you to love them, or to fall ill and die. How much these beliefs are still practiced is anyone's guess. There is no doubt that books and movies have hyped these practices and it is obvious from internet searches that so called adepts offer to trade such objects, hexes, curses and spells for monetary gain. The efficacy of these internet claims remains unproven.

Unlike Vodun, which doesn't distinguish between good and evil, seeing them simply as aspects of particular spirits, New Orleans Voodoo believes in evil magic – left-handed Voodoo or Hoodoo, and good, or white magic – called *juju* (*joujou* from the French for toy) and is performed to capture supernatural powers into an object.

Hoodoo is the folk magic component of the religion. In some places it is practiced without the ceremonial religious aspects of Voodoo. Such people were known as left-handed people. Hoodoo was seen as unholy and the 'dark side'.

Evil magic includes curses (*mojo*) and the use of *gris gris* dolls with evil intent such as revenge, to cause illness or bad luck.[125]

---

125  A self proclaimed internet voodoo high priest provides a menu of black magic spells that he will cast for clients with the following results - break relationships; destroy marriage; cause separation or divorce; control someone's mind for sex; cause alcohol abuse, substance abuse, violence and unhealthy sex; cause accidents, illness and emotional imbalance; induce fear; deprivation of sleep; depression; provoking suicide; block a woman's ability to conceive; rape of women in dreams by the spirits, where the orgasm is real; kill people.

*Gris gris*, or gray gray (from the French), signifies that these charms can be a mix of both black and white magic. When used for white magic, they may be worn or they may be hung on a wall or above a door. When used for black magic, they may be left on a doorstep as a warning.

Another syncretic religion that developed as a result of the Atlantic slave trade is Santeria, which is still a primary religion of mestizo[126] and black working class Cubans. Indeed, strolling around Havana in 2010 and glancing through opened windows, it was not unusual to see shrines in homes displaying pictures of Catholic saints and crosses together with other statues not belonging to Catholicism (but later identified as orichás or semi-divine beings), photographs of family members (later discovered to be ancestors), offerings of tobacco, food and drink, candles and sundry random objects such as stones[127] in shallow bowls, or crude clay heads, reminiscent of African masks. At first view this may be taken to represent devotion to Catholicism, but in fact it represents the fusion of West African, mainly Yoruba,[128] tribal beliefs with the Catholicism brought by the Spanish, when they colonised Cuba, and which evolved into a new religion containing elements of its progenitors.

Once you are aware of it, signs of Santeria are obvious almost everywhere – discarded herbs on street corners, strange artefacts in windows and adherents dressed, from head to toe, in gleaming white. Once we started looking, we found evidence of it in Havana, in Trinidad, in Sancti Spiritus, in Santa Clara and in Cienfuegos.

Santeria has long been shrouded in secrecy. Slaves hid the practice from their masters and Spanish rulers, who were predominantly white Catholics, and latterly from the religious intolerance of Castro's Communist government. This is somewhat surprising as rumours hold that Cas-

---

126 A person of combined European and Amerindian descent

127 representing different *orichás* or saints

128 Nigeria

tro practiced Santeria rituals. Indeed, Santeria followers believed their gods were on Fidel Castro's side ever since a white dove landed on his shoulder during a victory speech in Havana after his 1959 revolution. This led them to believe that he was ordained to be the leader of the country. In recent years the practice of Santeria has become less furtive.

The word *Santeria* derives from Spanish and means the worship of saints. The religion has no scriptures, holy books or written doctrine but owes its continued existence to the passing down of the belief through the generations as part of oral tradition.

Believers worship the spirit gods of *Olodumare*[129] (God) and the *Orichás*. Santeria is a monotheistic religion but, like Catholicism, this single God has three representations and three names viz. *Olodumare, Olofi,* and *Olorun. Olodumare* is the Supreme Being, the Creator of all things. *Olorun* is another manifestation of God, visible to us as the sun. *Olorun* is the owner of Heaven. *Olofi,* the third manifestation of God, communicates with the orichás, teaching them what humans need to know to lead healthy, moral, and respectful lives. Believers do not communicate with *Olodumare* or any of his representations directly, but indirectly through the intercession of the *orichás*.

The *orichás* are believed to be semi-divine beings – they have a duality of existence, being living things as well as spirits. Each *orichá* is thought to express a particular aspect of human existence. The *orichás* are considered to have the same needs as other living beings, but they also have the spiritual power to bring good luck or, if improperly treated, misfortune.

Believers nurture personal relationships with particular *orichás*. If they add a new relationship with an *orichá* then, as a precaution to prevent ill fortune descending on the worshipper, they need to appease the existing one - largely by feeding them with the blood of a sacrificial animal. The

---

129 *Olodumare* derives from Eledumare, which is the name given to one of the three representations of God in the Yoruba (from Southwester Nigeria) pantheon

*orichás*, although they are powerful spirits, are not immortal. They depend on nourishment from this sacrificial blood to survive. These sacrifices also open channels that allow believers connect with their personal saints.

The *orichás* were syncretised with Catholic saints to hide the worship of old gods from slave owners. Thus *Babalú-Ayé*, the *oricha* of the sick, is represented by Saint Lazarus; *Shangó*, who embodies justice and strength and is associated with thunder, lightning and fire is represented by Saint Barbara; *Ochún* - the Yoruba goddess of the river and love is represented by *la Virgen de la Caridad del Cobre* (Our Lady of Charity), the patroness of Cuba; and *Osanyin*, the spirit of herbal medicines, is represented by St Joseph.

One evening, when we were walking along the Malecón in Havana, Atlantic waves broke against the rocks and crashed over the sea wall, drenching the street and anyone unfortunate to be close to the wall. A local Santeria initiate explained that this was an expression of the wrath of *Yemayá*, the sea goddess and mother of the *orichás*. *Yemayá* is syncretised with the Virgin of Regla, the patroness of Regla in Havana.

Santeria priests are known as *Santeros* if they are male, and *Santeras* if they are female. Priests will summon *orichás* through music, dance, and ceremonies in which offerings of food, rum, and animal blood are made. These rituals generally take place in a house-temple, also known as an *ilé*. *Ilés* are the homes of the initiated priests and priestesses. *Ilé* shrines are built, by the priests and priestess, to the different *orichás*. Animal sacrifice is central to Santeria. The animal is sacrificed as food, rather than for any obscure mystical purpose, both for the *orichás* and for the congregation. Sacrifices are performed for saint's days, when people are being initiated into Santeria, being ordained as priests, or following birth, marriage, and death. They are also used for healing.

The animal is killed by cutting the carotid arteries. Sacrificial animals include chickens (the most common), pigeons, doves, ducks, guinea pigs, goats, sheep, and turtles. Animals are cooked and eaten following all Santeria rituals (except healing and death rites, where the intent is that the sickness passes into the dead animal).

In an example of 'parallel religiosity', a similar syncretic religion of Yoruba and Catholic origin, called Candomblé (which broadly translates as dance in honour of the gods) developed in north-eastern coastal cities of Brazil, particularly in Salvador da Bahia, and extended to parts of Argentina, Uruguay, Paraguay and Venezuela. People who practice the religion are known as *'povo do santo'* (people of the saint).

It is a spiritist religion that worships a complex pantheon of deities or guardian spirits, the *orixás*. It has named its patron deities (*orixás* or *santos*) with Yoruban names of gods (*Obatala, Oxala, Shango, Ogun, Oshossi,* and *Exu*) and goddesses (*Yemanja, Oxum, and Yansan*), several of which it shares with Santeria. In common with Voodoo and Santeria, Candomblé shares the belief in a supreme creator God who stands above the *orixá*. This Creator God is *Olorun*. Like with Santeria, believers in Candomblé communicate with the supreme God through the intercession of the intermediate spirits, the *orixás*. Candomblé practitioners believe that each individual has his or her own personal *orixá,* who acts both as a protector and a controller of destiny.

Candomblé temples are called houses (*casas*), or yards (*terreiros*). Each family owns and manages one house. Most Candomblé houses are small, independently owned and managed by priests. Inside the temple are the altars to the *orixás. Casas* have indoor and outdoor spaces, with special areas reserved for the gods. Worshippers wear clean, generally white clothes and splash water on themselves, before they enter the temple, to purify themselves from the contamination of the world.

Women are very important in Candomblé. In religious roles, women perform animal sacrifices and cowry shell divination rituals for individual supplicants, and are in charge of the training of priests and leading religious ceremonies. In recent times some male priests have started leading ceremonies and some have also become mediums.

Candomblé priesthood is organized into symbolic *families,* although the members need not be related. In most Candomblé houses the head of the *family* is always a woman, the *mãe-de-santo* (mother-of-saint), assisted by a male priest the *pai-de-santo* (father-of-saint). In a growing number of cases the *pai-de-santo* may act as head priest. Initiation into Candomblé may take seven or more years.

The Candomblé ritual has two parts: the first is the 'preparation', attended only by priests and initiates, which may start up to a week before a major ceremony. The second part is the main event, a public 'mass', followed by an evening of banqueting that ends near midnight.

In the preparatory part, animals are slaughtered. Some parts of the animals are reserved for sacrifice to the *orixás* and the rest are prepared for the banquet of the worshippers.

On the day of the ceremony, starting in the early morning, cowry shell divinations take place, with the shells being tossed and the pattern they make being read to foretell the future. Sacrifices are offered to the desired *orixás.*

Music and dance are central to Candomblé ceremonies, as the dances enable worshippers to become possessed by the *orixás.* In the public part of the ceremony, women – sometimes referred to as *filhas de santo* or 'daughters of the saint', or mediums – sing hymns and perform ritual dances that culminate with the dancer entering into a trance-like state. This is intended to invoke the spirit and allow a single patron deity possesses the dancer's body, whereupon the dancer performs dances symbolic of the *orixá* possessing her. The pai-*de-santo*, or male priest, then leads in the singing of hymns associated with that *orixá*. During the trance, followers may interact with, and consult with, the deity.

To free the dancer from the *orixás*, the hymns are sung in reverse, starting with the last hymn. Finally the spirits are released. The ceremony ends with a banquet.

While practice of Candomblé was furtive and secret in the past, this is not the case today. If you know what to look for, signs are readily discernible, particularly in Salvador da Bahia. A clearly visible expression of the belief in Candomblé are the frothy full length dresses, stuffed with crinolines and decorated with strings of plastic or glass beads, belts and headdresses worn by female believers. On Fridays, the believers wear white in honour of *Oxalá*, the god of creation. *Oxalá* is the son of *Olorum*, the supreme god. He is in control of procreation and eats goat, white pigeon and white maize, which are sacrificed to him during ceremonies. It's a day of purification. Initiates sing and dance for hours, summoning their *orixás* to cross over from the spirit world and possess the chosen.

One of the most popular *orixás,* venerated in an annual beach festival in Bahia,[130] is *Lemanja*, goddess of the sea (known as *Yemayá* in Santeria), who symbolizes motherly love. The ceremony begins at daybreak, with mediums singing and dancing to summon the goddess in order to gain insights into the year to come. Offerings that are most frequently made consist of flowers and beauty products (perfume, jewellery, combs, lipsticks, and mirrors), sweets and petitions. Placed in large baskets these are carried to boats by local fishermen and taken out to the sea. The beach is a riot of colour and movement, crowded as it is with worshipers variously dressed entirely in white, or in blue, or red, the colours associated with *Lemanjá*. Afterwards a massive street party ensues.

---

130 Held on the 2nd February each year

Interestingly, and pointing to the syncretic basis of the religion, *Lemanjá* is celebrated by Candomblé on the same day that the Catholic Church has dedicated to veneration of Our Lady of Seafaring (*Nossa Senhora dos Navegantes*).

*Lemanjá* is not only offered sacrifices on this specific day, but throughout the whole year you can see people bringing gifts to the beach for her. We watched such devotion from a beach-side café in Salvador. A small group of women worshippers, some dressed in red and others in white, sought favour by tossing offerings carved with their petition into the tide. Tossing the offering into the incoming tide is intended to bring benefit to you, tossing it into the ebbing tide is intended to remove problems. If only it were so simple, we would all be able to live stress-free and problem-free lives. The jaded cynic in me sees these practices as interesting mumbo jumbo, but to the faithful they see all the positives in their lives being the result of the intercession of their *orixás*. It is interesting to speculate as to which of us leads the more fulfilled and content life.

# CHAPTER 12

*St. John the Baptist, Evil Spirits and Coca Cola*

L ocated downtown in Mexico City are the ruins of the capital of the Mexica (Aztec) empire – *Tenochititlan* (1325 – 1521 AD). Here, the Mexica ruler, *Moctezuma Xocoyotzin*,[131] held court from his 100 room palace.

*Moctezuma* believed the prophecy that *Co Acatl Topiltzin Quetzalcoatl*,[132] the fair skinned, bearded, Toltec[133] ruler-god would return from the east and reclaim the kingdom. The news, delivered by messengers in 1519, that fair skinned, blue eyed, and bearded strangers, armour glistening in the sunlight, accompanied by prancing 'man-beasts',[134] had descended from giant floating towers in the sea to the east, convinced *Moctezuma* that the prophecy had been fulfilled.

Ever since *Moctezuma* bowed down to Hernán Cotréz and his tiny force of 550 soldiers and sailors, the history of Mexico changed utterly. By the time the Aztecs found out that the *conquistadores* had feet of clay and were mere men, like themselves, it was far too late. Superior weaponry, technology and tactics ensured the downfall of all the tribes of Mexico.

---

131 Meaning - *Moctezuma* the honoured young son. The Aztecs did not use regal numbers to distinguish their kings. Historians refer to him as *Moctezuma II* to distinguish him from *Motecuhzoma Ilhuicamina (meaning Old Moctezuma)*, who is referred to as *Moctezuma I*.

132 Translates as 'Our Prince One-Reed Feathered Serpent'

133 10th century ruler of the Toltecs who controlled the Valley of Mexico long before the Aztecs arrived.

134 Hernán Cotréz's 16 cavalry men and their horses

South of the Valley of Mexico is the State of Chiapas. This is a largely mountainous region with two areas of flat land – the Central Depression (*Depresión Central*) and the Pacific Coastal Plains. The first is sandwiched between the arc of the Northern Mountains, Central Highlands (*Montañas Centrales*) and the Eastern Mountains on one side and, running north-west-southeast, the chain of the *Sierra Madre de Chiapas* on the other. The second forms a narrow flat strip between the *Sierra Madre* and the Pacific Ocean. The south-eastern part of the State is covered by the dense Lacandon rainforest, which stretches into Guatemala.

Prior to the arrival of the Spanish, this challenging environment was inhabited by a variety of indigenous groups, such as the Zoques[135] together with a number of different Maya groups that included the Lacandon Ch'ol[136] and the Tzotzil. By the time of the Spanish conquests, Chiapas was divided between the Zoques to the west and the Tzotzil Maya to the east.

In 1524, Luis Marín arrived at Chamula and, despite an initial friendly reception, was met with armed resistance when he tried to enter the province. The Chamula Tzotzil gathered on a high ridge, inaccessible to Marín's cavalry, and shot arrows and hurled rocks, spears and boiling water mixed with lime on the would-be conquerors below. During a tropical downpour, the defenders abandoned their defensive positions in the nearby fortified town of Chamula and left it to the Spanish. A scorched earth policy meant that local supplies and food were denied to the attackers. Disappointed with the lack of spoils and the resistance of the natives, Chamula was given by Marín to Bernal Diaz along with the right to pillage and impress slaves, and by 1528 it had been incorporated into the *Villa de San Cristóbal* district.

Fellow travellers of the *conquistadores* at this time were monks and priests of the Dominican Order. The Dominicans saw the evangelisation of the native population as a sacred duty and were intolerant of mistreat-

135 The predecessors of the Olmecs

136 Now extinct as an ethnic group

ment of them by the Spanish conquerors. They showed their intolerance of such activities by refusing confession or other sacraments, and even went so far as to incarcerate and excommunicate a number of influential people in order to reinforce this disapproval. In tandem with this social agenda, the Dominicans set about systematically destroying Mayan temples and idols and sought ways to combine traditional beliefs with Christian scripture. Unsurprisingly, this led to a syncretic form of worship that borrows from both traditional indigenous belief and Catholicism – a position more tolerated by the older church than the modern one.

Located about 10 km from *San Cristóbal de las Casas* (or *Jovel* in Tzotzil) and some 2200m above sea level, the town of Chamula was founded in 1524, almost immediately after the conquest of the Chamula Tzotzil. Its three districts (San Juan, San Pedro and San Sebastian) are located in a valley that folklore holds to have been chosen by Saint John the Baptist (*San Juan Baptist*) himself. San Juan Chamula is the principal town of the 80,000 Tzotzils who live in this area. They are a fiercely independent people, forming a closed community that is resistant to both change and outside interference.

After the colonial period, ladinos[137] made a concerted land grab for territory that, intrinsically, belonged to the indigenous Tzotzils and which had been held by the colonial church and Spanish crown. In the years following independence, the State of Chiapas government granted day-to-day control over indigenous affairs to the Catholic Church.[138] In carrying out its civil roles for the State, the Church was permitted to use civil force, if necessary. Exploitation of indigenous labour, in the form of a 'head tax' and expropriation of land, was protested peacefully and through due process by the indigenous people for many years. With the overthrowing of the Government of Mexico City in 1855 by the Liberals, the new Government

---

137 Descendents of the Spanish colonists

138 https://www.researchgate.net/publication/274698147

embarked on a series of reforms that saw the nationalisation of church lands, the undermining of the authority of religious courts and the abolition of civil enforcement of religious taxes. This resulted in the War of Reform in central Mexico throughout 1860, and ended with a Liberal victory in January 1861. Support for the prevailing conservative position saw the European powers, especially the French, attempt to establish a European Catholic monarchy in Mexico – an effort that ended in failure in 1867.

This national upheaval had a replicate in the State of Chiapas, but here it was fought by local factions. The power of the Catholic Church and its clergy was on the wane everywhere. At this time, as well as telling people not to pay religious taxes, the Government encouraged the native peoples to abandon the church entirely and to practice Catholicism without the priests and their 'temples'. The success of these exhortations was immediate and widespread. In 1867, people from Chamula, among others, began venerating a set of magical 'talking stones.' Falling taxes in the region and attempts to bury the new religion led to the erroneously labelled 'Caste War' of 1869. Chamulas attacked and killed several ladinos, but it appears that the killing was never indiscriminate and was often an excuse to gain satisfaction for previous slights, rather than a true rebellion.

Several thousand Chamulas, under the leadership of Fernández de Galindo, approached[139] San Cristobal at dusk and under a white flag with Galindo offering himself, his wife, and some others in exchange for leaders of the new religion imprisoned by the ladino authorities. The exchange was made and the Chamulas retired. The authorities immediately arrested Galindo

Several hundred Chamulas camped outside San Cristobal, but did not engage in any hostilities. However, the ladinos used their presence to stir up fear of a major rebellion and, within a week, a heavily armed force of 300 troops marched from the lowlands and attacked and killed 300 Chamulas in

---

139 Frequently described as 'attacked'

a 'glorious battle' on the 21st of June. The Chamulas, who were armed with digging sticks and machetes, didn't stand a chance. Indeed, the forty three ladinos who died in the skirmish were reported to be local men ogling the spectacle, who got mown down by their own side's artillery. Galindo, who had been under arrest at the time of the 'glorious battle', was executed on the 26th June.

On the 30th June a force of 1000 ladinos attacked Chamula itself. It killed another 300 Chamulas whilst suffering minor injuries to eleven of its own men. Jan Rus (1983)[140] in his excellent essay, which informs much of this account, provides the description of the 'battle' as recorded by one ladino soldier, Pedro José Montesinos, thus....

*When we first spied Chamula, hundreds of them were scattered in disordered groups on the hillsides, and before we were in rifle distance all, women and children as well as men, knelt on their bare knees to beg forgiveness. In spite of the humble position they took to show submission, however, the government forces continued to advance, and they, undoubtedly hoping they would be granted the mercy they begged with tears of sorrow, remained on their knees. At a little less than 200 metres, the soldiers opened fire on their compact masses – and despite the carnage done to them by the bullets, despite their cries for mercy, continued firing for some time.'*

A further attack against refugees from this slaughter on the 7th July left another 200 men, women and children dead, for the loss of four ladinos. In mopping up actions, many Chamulas were persuaded to join the army to better demonstrate their loyalty to their masters. On the 13th of November some 250 indigenous lance-bearers killed a further sixty Chamulas, and on April 18th 1870 thirty two Chamulas were killed, and a final group of thirty six were killed on the 27th July. This brought to a close the 'Caste War'. Far from being a famous rebellion, this is better regarded as a squalid exercise

---

140 Rus, J (1983) 'Whose Caste War? Indians, Ladinos and the 'Caste War' of 1869' in Essays on the History of Ethnic Relations; University of Nebraska Press; Linclon and London

in ethnic cleansing by a privileged elite. Undoubtedly, this sordid experience coloured the view that the Chamulas have of outsiders and of the dominant Catholic Church. Their insularity, their resistance to change and the development of their own unique syncretic religious practices have roots deep in their experience with the evolving Mexican state.

We visited San Juan Chamula on the 7th July 2001. As we stopped above the village, Alex, our guide, explained that this was one of the most closed Mayan groups. They had all but rejected Catholicism in favour of worship of 'Our Father the Sun'. In their pantheon, St. John the Baptist is exalted. They don't really rate Jesus as they feel that, because he was baptised by St. John, he is inferior to him. Thus the only Catholic sacrament they accept is baptism – and this is their only requirement for the services of a Catholic priest.

In this society, men are pre-eminent. Women always follow behind men, women don't vote and women do the menial jobs. Marriages are arranged by the parents and formalised on the payment of a dowry. Girls marry at 13 or 14 years of age and the average family size is seven children, although it is not unusual to have thirteen or fourteen. Each community is identifiable by the colour of, and the design on, the clothes they wear. People from different communities do not intermarry and each community adheres strictly to its own beliefs and traditions; anyone who attempts to change belief, particularly religious belief, risks expulsion from their community.

Chamulas take their religion very seriously. It is the basis of social cohesion. Successful proselytising, mainly by American evangelist missionaries (Pentecostal, Baptist, Mormons, Jehovah's Witnesses, Episcopalians etc.) and Catholic lay catechists, has turned numbers of Chamulas from the 'true faith', with consequent dire social repercussions. Their land has been sequestered and they have been evicted from their houses, exiled from their villages and expelled from Chamula territory. The Chiapas-based Evangelical Commission in Defence of Human Rights (CEDEH)[141] has calculated that, over the past 30 years, municipal authorities have expelled some 30,000 evangelicals. Most of these end up in poor conditions in shanties adjacent to San Cristobal, where, subsequently, they are marginalised by the local ladinos.

As we looked down on the town, we could see activity in the fields around us. Some were terraced to make the best use of the available water and to conserve the soil. They are all cultivated by hand. The Maya don't use oxen or horses, or, god forbid, machinery. Given that the majority are small-holdings – *edijos* – this is entirely feasible. The main crops are corn, alfalfa, onions, potatoes, cabbage, lettuce, broccoli, radishes, squashes and beans. Fruits, such as tomato, strawberries, blackberries, prickly pear (cactus fruit), banana, mango and papaya are grown also. Crops are often paired. Corn and beans (*maíz y frijoles*) are known as 'best friends' because they are frequently grown together, the beans growing up the corn stems. Squashes of different sorts are also grown with the corn.

Beans and tacos are a mainstay of the local diet. The corn is ground and mixed with ground limestone to provide the calcium supplement needed once children are weaned. Additional flavour may be added by sprinkling the taco with ground cucumber seeds. Once children stop taking their mother's milk, milk of any sort never again features in their diet. Chicken is commonly eaten, and an occasional turkey may even make its way into the pot.

Large numbers of black fleeced sheep roamed everywhere; although not very fast as the front foot was tethered to the hind leg. They are sacred to the Chamula and only exploited for their wool. Lamb and mutton never get eaten.

---

141 Annual Report on International Religious Freedom, 2004 ; Report submitted to the Committee on Foreign Relations of the US senate and the Committee on International Relations of the US House of Representatives (edited by the state Department (US)); htpp://www.access.gpo.gov/congress/senate

Typically, men and women dress in the traditional black wool fleece to overcome the prevailing highland climate, which is dominated by cold and damp weather throughout the year. The men wear long black or white ponchos and jeans, and top it off with straw Stetsons, tribal hats or baseball caps. The women wear coarse spun black wool skirts (one size fits all). During festivals to honour patron saints, the dress is more colourful. Men are garbed in 'chujes' or long sleeved unbuttoned woollen coats tied with a strip of animal skin – generally chamois. Men of authority (women cannot hold official positions) swap this for a white wool coat tied with a buckled belt. Women wear traditional *huipils*, made from two or three rectangular pieces of fabric woven on the backstrap loom, which are then stitched together, leaving openings for the head and arms. These are wonderfully brocaded and embroidered. The *huipils* are adorned with red, yellow and green, symbolising Saint Peter, Saint John the Baptist and Saint Sebastian. Women never wear hats. They cover their heads with black *mochibals* – shawls that can be tied at the front with red tassels and worn over the shoulders or on the head.

Chamula and its surrounding indigenous communities have a considerable amount of autonomy from the State. They are largely self-governing, with their own administration, judges, schools, police force and a small prison.[142]

Travelling into the town from the south, we stopped at the burnt out ruins of the old *Iglesia de San Sabastián*. Just as we arrived, a funeral party entered the churchyard. It was led by musicians (accordion and guitars). The dead are never brought into a church – only Mayan style crosses representing them are. The deceased's cross in this case was black, indicating that s/he was an old person. White crosses are used for children, and in between youth and old age blue and green crosses are preferred. Although the deceased was headed for a better afterlife, the mourners felt the loss badly

---

142 The cells are semi-open to expose the miscreants to public shame. If women are imprisoned they are incarcerated in completely enclosed rooms away from public view.

and were openly weeping and wailing. Reverence for their deceased continues after burial and many of the graves were well kept, weed and litter free and clothed with pine needles. This was in contrast to a small number of graves that had no one to care for them.

We drove into the town, an uninspiring collection of single storey adobe, wood and breeze block buildings; parked up and made our way to the main square that houses the *Cathedral of San Juan Bautista*. This is the centre of social and religious life.

Photography of buildings and people – but only with their permission - is permitted in the town and square. Photography inside the church is completely forbidden, and any attempt to sneak a shot will be met by severe punishment, including arrest, should you be so churlish as to try, and then get caught. Women will often cover their head and face with their shawls if they think they are going to be included in a photograph. Mothers will always cover babies, as there is a belief that the fragile soul of infants, which frequently wander from the body, may be confused, blinded and unable to return, should the infant be photographed. We are outsiders and should respect local tradition. The value of a sneaky snap is debased by the hurt it causes to those who want their privacy honoured. Unless you are from the surrounding region, you are a foreigner. As you are not even from the country, you are referred to as an '*Allemagne*' or German, after the foreign overseers of the large lowland farms and plantations where the Chamula and Zinacantan Maya sometimes seek work. The use of this French epithet probably reflects the French influence during the time of Maximilian and the Second Franco-Mexican War (1862 – 1867).

As a reflection of conflict between Church and State, all church structures that existed in 1992 were declared, in law, national patrimony – bringing them into the ownership of the state. Thus the cathedral in San Juan Chamula is national property, not the property of the Catholic Church who built it some 200 years ago. This separation of the secular and the religious is further exemplified in public schools, where religious instruction is prohibited. Both of these strictures have permitted both the development and practice of the type of syncretic religion found in this area. All religious instruction is delivered by the family and the community, and its practice is facilitated in a state owned property – the cathedral.

The Maya believe that First Father, or creator, propped up the sky with huge ceiba trees. These were placed at north, south, east, west and centre of the world. Mayan crosses, normally painted green, are symbols of the ceiba tree. There are many Mayan crosses in San Juan, marking each barrio. When they were being converted by the Dominicans following colonisation, the Maya adapted the story of Jesus and his crucifixion. They believed that there was an Old Jesus and a Young Jesus – possibly a corruption of what they were being taught about the holy trinity – reduced to God the father and God the son. One day the Old Jesus and the Young Jesus happened upon a tall tree, which had, near the top, a bee hive full of wax. Young Jesus climbed the tree, and dropped the wax down to Old Jesus, who promptly started moulding a wax army. Young Jesus continued to drop the wax, even though Old Jesus had enough. This angered Old Jesus to the extent that he got his wax army to bite through the trunk of the tree, resulting in Young Jesus falling to his death. After this the Old Jesus went to his mother, Mary, who told him to go to a nearby mountain top. There he found an umbilical cord hanging from the sky, which he climbed and which took him to heaven, whereupon he became the sun. His mother, the Virgin Mary became the moon. Larger crosses in Chamula represent the sun and are considered male, while the smaller ones represent the moon and are considered female. When male children are born, the umbilical cord is placed on top of a cross to the sun. In contrast, the umbilical cord of a female infant is buried to ensure continuing fertility.

The cathedral dominates the square. Its façade is painted white and outlined in turquoise and blue. The tripartite arch over the brown painted main door has the inner and outer elements painted green and the middle element painted blue. Each arch is decorated with recessed reliefs of alternating multicoloured circles painted in white, yellow, blue, pink or green, interspersed with depictions of four petaled ceiba flowers painted in the same colours. The door to the cathedral is guarded by a village appointed policeman, armed with a hardwood truncheon. As an outsider, you are required to pay a small fee to gain entrance, and must, as a mark of respect, remove your hat. Interestingly, one visitor noted on his website that, although hats were forbidden, it was permitted to enter smoking a cigarette and carrying a can of beer!

Inside the cathedral, which is built in the typical Spanish style, the atmosphere and layout is completely different to any ordinary Catholic church. Inside the door, in a cordoned off area, is the baptismal font. This is the only area to which Catholic priests are given access when they, once every 20 days or so, are invited to perform baptisms. Clearly, this is not a position the Catholic Church appreciates, but it is caught in the dilemma of refusing to officiate and condemn souls to Limbo, or perform the sacrament and hope that, in time, the authority of the church will be accepted. The fact that they no longer own the building puts them in a weak position. The last mass, and the last priest here, was in 1968.

The church is devoid of pews. The floor is completely covered with fresh pine needles and the air is perfumed with the aroma of smouldering copal[143] and live sacrificial chickens, legs tied together, cluck as they await their fate. Near the main altar, or where the altar would be in normal Catholic churches, three hangings descend from the ceiling. The highest of these depicts St. John and the one depicting Jesus is hung in a subservient position. All around the walls are glass cases containing statues of different saints – each labelled with the name of its occupant. The saints are dressed in traditional clothing, which have mirrors sewn onto them. This permits

---

143 Resin from the *copal* tree (*Protium copal*)

155

supplicants to gaze at themselves as they petition their special saint. Various explanations are used for the presence of the mirrors, from being thought to deflect bad thoughts, to warding off the evil eye, or that during prayer as the soul leaves the body the mirror helps guide it back.

Our guide, Alex, informed us that the Chamulas believe that because the central tenet of Christianity is that Christ died on the cross he is, therefore, useless. However, St. John the Baptist and the other saints are thought to still be alive and are, therefore, of practical use.

Worshippers have favourite saints with whom they interact. On busy days when a number of worshippers are present it may require a long wait before you can access your personal favourite saint. Praying in this religion is an entirely individual event, not a communal activity. Chamulas pour out their cares and woes to their chosen saint. They light many candles, as offerings, and stick these to the floor spread out in front of the appropriate statue. Most are white but black, gold, yellow and red candles are also used. The arrangement and colours of the candles convey a message to the chosen saint. Communication with the saint also involves more audible entreaty, including tearful chanting, singing and talking in the Tzotzil language. Once they have finished communing with the saint they offer Pox[144] (pronounced posh), Coca Cola or Pepsi Cola to the saint. First they pour a libation on to the floor; then they drink some themselves. The drink makes them belch – a habit they encourage – and with this they burp up the evil spirits that caused their problems. These can then be ejected through the open mouth. When compared with the availability of pox, the use of Cola is a relatively recent ceremonial embellishment that shows the ability of syncretic religions to adapt and adopt new ideas and artefacts. This may also have been influenced by the fact that children, as well as adults, participate in these worships, and it is better to have a child burp from the gaseous effects of Coca Cola or Pepsi Cola than collapse in a drunken stupor from

---

144 Also known as aguardiente, pox is liquor made of corn, sugar cane and wheat. The word translates from Tzotzil as 'medicine,' cane liquor, or cure. It contains up to 40% alcohol.

over-indulgence in pox. Nonetheless, as the drinking of pox is regarded as an essential element of the ritual, drunkenness is tolerated as a normal side effect. It is not unusual, therefore, to see people collapsed insensibly in public places. The normalcy of this is highlighted by the numbers of people who will pass by without giving the inebriate a second glance.

The church is not only a place of worship but also a place of healing. In this society, the shaman and midwives (both known as *curanderos*) have very high status. If a woman has difficulty with childbirth, every effort is made to save the woman as she can have more children. In serious cases of spiritual or physical discomfort the supplicant is generally accompanied in the church by a *curandero*. Part of the ancient animist belief of the Maya is that spirits reside in all living things. The role of the *curandero* is to channel energy in order to draw out bad energy and replenish diminished good energy. Near every statue of a saint in the church are several pottery figures of animals, alongside which are small dishes of smouldering copal. The clay animals represent the *ch'ulel* or the animal representative of the spirit of people. The Tzotzil discern two souls in the human body. One, the *ch'ulel*, transcends a human's life; the other, *wayhel*, ties them to an animal outside their body. Animals and trees have a *ch'ulel* soul. The *wayhel* soul belongs only to human beings.[145]

In performing a ceremony, the *curandero* rubs a live chicken over the sufferer's body. When he feels that the evil has transferred from the patient to the chicken, he stretches the chicken's neck and kills it. The chicken, now containing the evil, is buried to prevent anyone else becoming infected.

A similar ceremony is used to trap the evil from those cursed by the evil eye. In this case an egg, or bag of eggs, is substituted for the chicken. The ceremony follows a similar path of transference, with the evil eventually being trapped within the egg shell. There were many people present

---

145 Austin, Alfredo López (1997). Tamoanchan, Tlalocan. – Places of Mist; Transl. by Ortiz de Montellano; page 147. Colorado: University Press

while we were in the church, and ceremonies of this type as well as invocations to the saints took place all around us.

Care of the saints is very important. People volunteer to become '*major domos*' and will pay to look after a particular saint for a year. This is a costly process, so individuals are enrolled at a young age to allow potential *major domos* save and collect the necessary funds, mainly through donations. *Major domos* rent special houses for the year, where items pertaining to the saint are stored and an altar is available for individual worship. *Major domos* finance pox for worshipers of that particular saint and supply incense and fireworks for celebrations. At the end of his year of duty, the *major domo* boxes up all the material pertaining to his saint and, in the church, hands it over to his successor. The *major domo* then vacates the rented accommodation and returns home.

San Juan Chamula is a unique and memorable place. A history of repression, persecution and proselytising has resulted in a people who have adapted what was acceptable from their oppressors and would be saviours, and married it with traditions and beliefs that they had held for centuries. They interpreted and interpolated Mayan and Christian beliefs and, where they found reasonable similarity or resonance, melded them into a new, syncretic, belief. Best of all they found a religious reason for the consumption of strong alcohol and even managed to build in a benediction for excessive consumption - you get drunk because you are trying to expel evil and become better. I wonder if I tried this as an excuse with Mary, my wife, whether she would accept it. Chance would be a fine thing!

*Photographs*

# Chapter Two

Penguins of the World

EMPEROR

KING

GENTOO

CHINSTRAP

ADÉLIE

NORTHERN
ROCKHOPPER
SOUTHERN

SNARES

ERECT-CRESTED

FIORDLAND

MACARONI

ROYAL

LITTLE
(OR FAIRY)

YELLOW-EYED

MAGELLANIC

AFRICAN

HUMBOLDT

GALÁPAGOS

D.J.Douglas 2017.

*Penguin Species of the World*

*Two Kings and a Gentoo*

*Gentoo emerging from the water*

*The Plancius in South Georgia*

# Chapter Three

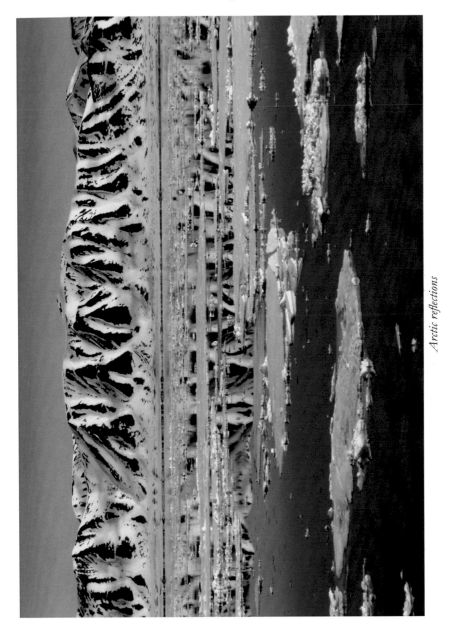

*Arctic reflections*

*Humpback Whale, mother and calf*

*Minke Whale in Neko Harbour, Antarctic Peninsula*

*On the Zodiacs in Arctic Svalbard*

*Finding our way back through the Arctic ice to the Plancius*

# Chapter Four

*Battling Elephant Seals, South Georgia*

*Fur Seal Pup*

*Leopard Seal and Plancius, Neko Harbour, Antarctic Peninsula*

# Chapter Six

*Displaying your beast before it is immolated during the Fire Dragon Festival*

*Firework breathing dragon during the Fire Dragon Festival in Leishang*

*Bridge over the river, Xijiang Miao Village, Guizhou*

*Silver Miao Girl*

*Longhorn Miao, China*

*Miao girl*

# Chapter Seven

*Red chilli shaped coffin, Ghana*

# Chapter Nine

*Cao Dai, Mass*

# Chapter Eleven

*Marché des Féticheurs, Lome, Togo*

# Chapter Thirteen

*Fairy chimney dwelling, Cappadocia, Turkey*

*The Monastery Petra. People near the door give it scale*

# Chapter Fourteen

*Catching Sea Kraits, Sabah, Borneo*

# Chapter Sixteen

*Tree climbing goats, Morocco*

# Chapter Nineteen

*Harpy Eagle*

# Chapter Twenty

*Kaka, an endemic bird from New Zealand*

*Kea, another endemic bird from New Zealand*

# Chapters Twenty One and Twenty Two

*Jumping salt water crocodile, Adelaide River, Australia*

*Across: Singsing, Wamut Village, Papua New Guinea*

*Nuku Hiva, dancers at the giant banyan*

# Chapter Twenty Three

*Mudman, New Guinea*

*Children in village beside the Karawari River, Papua New Guinea*

*Fashionable headgear beside the Karawari River, Papua New Guinea*

*Huli Wigmen, Papua New Guinea*

*Melpa women preparing for a Singsing, Papua New Guinea*

*Megapode egg collector and betel nut chewer, Rabaul, New Britain, Papua New Guinea*

# Chapter Twenty Four

*Secretary bird, South Africa*

*Elephants warning us off*

*Lions feasting on a wildebeest*

# CHAPTER 13

## Hewn from the Rock

## Part 1- Lalibela

The habitual use of fire by Neanderthal and modern humans is believed to date back some 400,000 years. Prior to that, for at least 1.5 million years, there is evidence that human ancestors, opportunistically enhanced their lives, by exploiting and controlling fires created by natural means, such as combustion of dry fuel due to the heat of the sun or lightning.[146] It may well be that exploiting the bounty provided by injury and death of animals and the roasted and toasted vegetable material that is consequential to natural fires imbued in early man a taste for charred animals and plants and that this provided the impetus to cook food. We can only speculate.[147] And we can also speculate that the process of chipping of stone to provide edged tools gave rise to sparks; and the shaping and scoring of wood to hold these points, through friction, caused some charring and smouldering and the production of embers, all of which, over time, resulted in the creative leap of imagination that allowed primitive man start to make and control his own fires.

As men began to hunt more and started targeting bigger and bigger prey animals, they needed to organise into cooperative groups in order to

---

146 J. A. J. Gowlett (2016) The discovery of fire by humans: a long and convoluted process. Downloaded from http://rstb.royalsocietypublishing.org/ on May 24, 2017

147 Charles Lamb (1775 – 1834), in his *Essays of Elia*, speculated on the origin of our fondness for cooked pork in the essay 'A Dissertation Upon Roast Pig'; http://www.bartleby.com/380/prose/491.html

be successful. This resulted in the development of the earliest communities. Evidence exists of members of such communities gathering around a communal hearth for heat, to cook and to socialise. Records indicate that the use of stone hearths goes back some 750,000 years.

To combat variable weather conditions, people started making clothes out of animal skins and building simple shelters of branches and sod, or tents from hides. In some cases, the bones and tusks of mammoths were used. Traces of some of these structures have been inferred from post holes preserved in the soil. Some shelters were nearly 15m long, like the 400,000 year-old shelter from *Terra Amata* in France.

Another major form of shelter was also to be found in caves. The conquest of fire gave early man the means to drive away, and keep away, any other animals that might have been inhabiting the cave, and also provided the means of heating them through the cold periods that prevailed at this time.

There is evidence that man may have made windbreaks by piling rocks on top of each other to make walls. These could have been covered with branches, vegetation, or animal skin to make rude shelters. However, it is not until about 7000 years ago that we begin to see man actually constructing buildings. The earliest of these appears to be the Barnenez Tumulus, near Plouezoc'h in Brittany (France). This Neolithic structure dates from 4800 BC. It is currently considered to be the oldest building in the world. However, the tumulus was not built for living in but as a tomb for the dead.

The earliest recorded man made European settlement can be found at Skara Brae in the Orkney Islands. This Neolithic settlement was built sometime around 3180 BC. It consists of eight clustered stone built houses. Built somewhat later, around 2500 BC, in the Indus valley near Lankana, in Sindh (Pakistan), is what is reputed to be the world's earliest city *Mohenjo Daro* (which translates as the *Mound of the Dead Men*). Laid out in a regular grid pattern, it consists of a central marketplace surrounded with two assembly halls, public baths and one and two storey houses, built from a combination of fired and mortared and sun dried brick. Water was supplied to the city from a number of wells and wastewater drained away through a series of covered drains.

All of these early buildings, and most of those that were to follow, were built from the ground up. Common materials included wood, wattle and daub,[148] adobe,[149] stone and rock, and fired or sun dried and mortared brick. Buildings made from wood, wattles or vegetation did not last as long as those made from the other materials and their existence has often to be inferred from traces left in the soil, such as post holes. This is typically the case with structures such as Bronze and Iron Age houses.

In a departure from the common tendency to erect dwellings and monuments from the ground up, there are several cases where the most magnificent creations were excavated entirely from bedrock. The most well known of these, that I have visited, include the tombs in the Valley of the Kings and the Valley of the Queens, in Egypt, and also the magnificent massive rock temples at Abu Simbel in southern Egypt, near the border with Sudan that were carved out of the mountain by the Pharaoh Ramses II to commemorate the battle of Kadesh, and as a monument to himself and his consort, Queen Nefertari. As these have been filmed and written about many times elsewhere, I do not intend to describe them here. However, less well known, but equally magnificent, are three other rock hewn masterpieces – Lalibela in Ethiopia, Petra in Jordan and the troglodyte villages and churches of Göreme in Cappadocia, Turkey, which I think deserve a much wider audience than they have had heretofore.

The holiest city in Ethiopia is Aksum, which also holds the distinction of being one of the oldest continuously inhabited places in Africa and is a

---

148 Wattle is a woven lattice of wooden strips which is then daubed with a sticky material usually made of some combination of wet soil, clay, sand, animal dung and straw.

149 An adobe brick is made of earth mixed with water and an organic material such as straw or dung.

place where some believe that the Ark of the Covenant currently resides. Second to Aksum, and a place of pilgrimage, is Lalibela, a town in the Amhara Region of northern Ethiopia, some 645km from Addis Ababa, that is famous for its monolithic rock-cut churches.

When he inherited the kingdom from his brother, Gebre Mesqel Lalibela (1181 – 1221) AD moved the capital further south to a sloped, elevated site, approachable from the valley floor below only by steeply ascending paths. At this time the capital was known as *Roha*. The choice of the site was inspired. Its elevation made it easily defensible. Its ready supply of water from an artesian aquifer, whose source lay a distance away in the Lasta Mountain range, gave it the ability to withstand any prolonged siege. The complex and sophisticated water distribution system, designed by Abba Libanos, ensured a consistent supply to the city and its churches.

It is said that the town of Lalibela was created to act as a 'New Jerusalem', following the halting of pilgrimages to the holy land as Moslem conquest spread through North Africa. The most important feature of Lalibela is not the town, now reduced to a mere village, but the 11 Ethiopian Orthodox Christian churches it contains. The churches were not constructed in the usual way from the ground up but in reverse from the ground down. This meant that the first part of each church to be completed was its roof, and thereafter the builders dug down into the solid red basaltic scoriae to initially chisel out huge monolithic blocks up to 11 metres high. Once the blocks were cut into and isolated from the bedrock, decorations, windows and doors were marked and the block was hollowed out to form aisles, vaults and naves as well as supporting columns. Drainage ditches, passages catacombs, crypts, grottoes and galleries were hewn into the bedrock to connect them all.

Local legend holds that it took some 40,000 workers almost a quarter of a century to carve the eleven churches from the bedrock. Archaeologists still find this difficult to believe considering the rudimentary tools that were available to the carvers. It was a prodigious task that must have resulted in an enormous amount of spoil – yet there is no trace in the area of the huge quantity of stone that would have had to be removed. This has led to 'Ancient Alien' adherents speculating that the builders had extraterrestrial help and the advantage of advanced extraterrestrial technology. The legends that angels continued the work at night, when the human workmen rested, has only added fuel to this speculation. Indeed adherents to this belief are unwilling to agree that ancient cultures had the intelligence, means and time to achieve many of the ancient architectural wonders that dot our planet. My counterargument is that manned flight has only been around for about a century and space flight is in its infancy. Over that period we did not need any 'alien' intervention to support its development.

The easiest way to visualise what the free standing churches look like is to consider excavating a huge hole in bedrock and then dropping into it a fully completed church whose roof is level with the surrounding ground, making it impossible to see from any distance. Four of the churches[150] are completely free standing only being attached to the surrounding rock by their stepped and layered bases. The remaining churches were carved from rock faces, back into the cliffs and, with the exception of only one church, remain attached to the bedrock by their floors.

Access to the churches is generally by means of a descending staircase and interconnecting walkways and tunnels between them. The resident priest for each church can normally be seen sitting or standing in the shade of the doorway dressed in colourful brocaded robes, holding either a prayer staff or a silver processional cross.

The biggest church in Lalibela is *Biete Medhane Alem* (the House of the Saviour of the World), which at 33.5 metres long by 23.5 metres wide and 11.5 metres high is the largest rock-hewn church in the world, and is part of the Northern Group of churches. The exterior of the building is surround-

---

150  Biete Medhane Alem, Biete Ghenetta Mariam, Biete Amanuel, and Biete Ghiorgis

ed by 34 large, rectangular, columns that support the extended eaves. Inside there is a barrel-vaulted nave and five aisles. Thirty eight columns support the gabled roof. *Beta Medhane Alem* is the home of the Lalibela cross which is made from seven kilograms of gold.

Connected by a tunnel to *Biete Medhane Alem* is a large underground courtyard containing three churches, *Biete Ghenetta Mariam* (the House of Mary), *Biete Meskel* (the House of the Cross) and *Biete Golgotha Mikael* (the House of Golgotha Mikael). Behind *Biete Mariam* is *Biete Denagel* (the House of Virgins)

*Biete Maryam*, dedicated to the Virgin Mary, is small but exquisitely designed and decorated. It is the only church that has porches extending off it, and above the western one you can see a carved bas-relief of St George fighting the dragon. It is believed to be the oldest of the churches, and is said to replicate the Tombs of Adam and Christ. This is the most popular church among pilgrims. To the left of the door, which is set on the right of the building, are three windows, the middle one containing an 'X' and the two flanking it containing carved swastikas. Unlike the swastikas used by the Nazi, these are the negative form, running in the opposite direction. Inside the church the upper walls and ceilings are painted with frescoes, and the columns, capital and arches are covered with carved details. One of the stone pillars, which is covered with drapery, is said to have the secrets of the buildings' construction carved into it by King Lalibela. Only priests may lift the coverings and look at the inscriptions.

*Biete Denagel*, a grotto church lacking windows, is located behind and to the south of *Biete Ghenetta Mariam*. It is the least striking of the churches in Lalibela.

Across the courtyard and carved into the northern wall is the tiny *Biete Meskel* (the House of the Cross). Four pillars, inside the church, divide the gallery into two aisles spanned by arcades. Seven life size saints, all carved in bas relief, together with a number of paintings, one depicting St. George slaying the dragon, adorn the wall.

*Biete Golgotha Mikael* is in the western face of the cliff. According to legend, anyone who enters this church will go to heaven, as it is the final resting place of king Lalibela, containing his tomb and personal treasures. The church is known for the crosses carved in relief into the stone, as well as a recumbent figure of Christ and a number of vibrant wall hangings. This church, unfortunately, is closed to women.

South east of this group, and reached through a tunnel, is the Eastern group of churches. The first of these, *Biete Amanuel* (the House of Emmanuel), is probably the most finely carved of the churches, with its alternating projecting and recessed layered façade mimicking the alternating layers of recessed timber beams and projecting plastered stone, or limestone blocks, seen in Ethiopia's late Axumite churches. It was, reputedly, the private church of the royal family. It is connected to *Biete Qeddus Mercoreus* by a subterranean tunnel (closed to the public), containing, interred in its walls, the remains of pilgrims.

*Biete Qeddus Mercoreus* (House of St. Mercorius), although now a church, may have had a more sinister origin. The discovery of ankle shackles suggests that it may once have been the municipal prison. A large portion of this building has collapsed and has been replaced with brick walls. What remains of the interior contains some interesting frescoes and wall hangings representing scenes from the New Testament. A pitch black, stygian, tunnel, said to represent hell, leads to *Biete Gabriel-Rufael.*

Lalibela's wife, Meskel Kebra, was obviously as adept at multitasking as her modern counterparts. With the help of a small group of willing angels, she added rock carving to her curriculum vitae, and is said to have carved out the little church of *Biete Abba Libanos* (House of Abbot Libanos) in a single night. In typical female fashion, she added her own design features as this church, uniquely amongst those at Lalibela, remains attached to the stratum by its roof and floor, but is free from the rock on the sides and back.

Another circular church, *Biete Lehem* (House of Holy Bread), was inaccessible when we were there and appeared to have been heavily weathered, with little detail remaining carved into the outside walls. It was surrounded by scaffolding and protected by a temporary roof to prevent further erosive damage.

The last church in the southern group, *Biete Gabriel-Rufael* (House of the angels Gabriel and Raphael), actually provides the main entrance to the group. In contrast to the other churches, which are accessed by tunnels and underground passages, this church is accessed from the top via a narrow walkway high over the trench that encloses the building. Its atypical orientation and irregular floor plan hints at an earlier secular use, and some believe that it may have originally been a fortified royal palace. In contrast to the tunnel leading from here to *Biete Qeddus Mercoreus*, which is said to represent hell, the entrance to this twin church, flanked by two narrow columns of rock, is known as the 'Way to Heaven'. The doorway in the imposing façade gives access to *Biete Gabriel*, while a second interior doorway leads to *Biete Rufael*. In contrast to the grandeur of the façade, both of these are quite small churches.

In the fairly recent past, a portion of *Biete Rufael's* roof collapsed and was rebuilt. In recognition of its weakened structure, religious services are now restricted to Biete Gabriel.

To the west of the southern group is an eleventh church, *Biete Ghiorgis* (House of Saint George). Although it is connected by a system of trenches to the south eastern group, it lies some 350 metres apart from both it and also the northern group. It was the last church to be built, but is also the most iconic.

The story goes that King Lalibela planned to name it after himself, but St George, one of the most important Saints to Ethiopians, visited him in a dream and asked '*Where is my house?*' Lalibela heeded this spiritual intervention and renamed this remarkable church after Saint George, the dragon slayer.

The shape of this church is completely different from the other ten. It was excavated from the bedrock, 12 metres deep, as a huge monolith that stood free in the middle of a 25 metre by 25 metre pit. The stone masons then incised the cruciform outline of the church and its stepped pedestal. They then continued to chip away the exterior façade, shaping while burrowing inwards to excavate the interior of the building. This effort resulted in the creation of three west-facing doorways, nine 'blind' lower level windows and an upper row of twelve windows. The solid roof of the church was carved in relief to depict a series of three Greek crosses set one inside the other. Entry from ground level to the sunken courtyard, 12 metres below, is gained through a descending trench and tunnel. The courtyard contains a small baptismal pool. The vertical walls of the pit, within which the church lies, contain some troglodyte dwellings for the priests, as well as a number of tombs.

Inside the church, a curtain shields the 'Holy of Holies' from both worshipers and visitors, and in one of its cruciform arms rests a replica of the Ark of the Covenant.

Unfortunately, Ethiopia, the most populous landlocked country in the world, is currently best known for its famines, drought, ethnic violence and human rights crises. These, rightly, should be condemned but in so doing we should not forget its four million years of human prehistory, the majesty of its medieval architecture and culture, its magnificent and varied tribes, its 9 world heritage sites and the friendliness of its people. After all, to some extent, we are all Ethiopian. Some 200,000 years ago in the Middle Paleolithic era *Homo sapiens,* the first anatomically modern human, appeared in the Omo valley.[151] Then, about 40,000 years later *Homo sapiens idaltu* was present the Middle Awash in Ethiopia. He is considered by many to be our immediate ancestor.

---

151  Recent research at a site in Jebel Irhough in Morocco dated fire heated flint tools and associated human remains at between 300,000 – 350,000 years old, indicating that human life began a hundred thousand years earlier than previously believed.

# Part 2 - Petra

Four thousand kilometres due north of Ethiopia in the desert of the modern Hachemite Kingdom of Jordan is *Ain Mousa* – the 'Spring of Moses'. Arab tradition holds that it was here that the prophet Moses ('*Musa*' in Arabic) struck a rock with his staff causing water to flow. Nearby ran the great south to north road between Arabia and Syria,[152] which crosses an east-west running natural fault through which *Wadi Musa* flows before draining into the Great Rift Valley south of the Dead Sea. This fault line provided a route to nomadic people and traders - providing access from the high desert, in the east, to the Mediterranean port of Gaza, in the west. It was one of the most important trading routes in pre-Christian times. Some two thousand years ago, a loose grouping of nomadic Arab tribes and families led by a king, and known as the Nabateans, were responsible for much of the trade on this route.

The main trading commodity was frankincense. Sometimes known by the Medieval Latin name of *olibanum,* the English version is derived from Old French '*franc encens'* (meaning pure incense). It is an aromatic resin produced by trees of the genus *Boswellia* by scoring the bark and allowing the resin to seep out and harden. It can then be scraped off the tree. When burnt over charcoal it emits a fragrant odour, and, throughout history, it formed part of sacred ritual in the Ancient Egyptian, Judaic and Christian traditions.

The most important of the four species of tree used for frankincense production was, and still is, *Boswellia sacra.* This tree is native to Ethiopia, northern Somalia, south-western Oman, and southern Yemen. Extending from Somalia, North Africa and the Arabian Peninsula to China and India, there are archaeological and historical records of frankincense use and trading going back some 5,000 years. Indeed, such was its value in ancient times that it was one of the precious gifts, along with gold and myrrh, re-

152 Today it comprises the King's Highway

putedly brought by the Three Magi when they visited Jesus in the stable in Bethlehem.

Frankincense resin is edible. It was chewed in both Asia and Africa as an aid to digestion and as a traditional medicine that promoted healthy skin; its oil has been used as a treatment for scorpion stings.

The Nabateans also traded in myrrh[153]– a resin collected from the tree *Commiphora myrrha* in a similar manner to frankincense. This gum was used as a perfume and formed a major ingredient, along with natron[154] (mined in the *Wadi El Natrun*), in the Egyptian process of mummification. Myrrh has been used throughout history as a perfume, incense, and as a medicine.

Other plant resins that were traded, and that formed important components of ancient perfume manufacture, included Arabian balsam and labdanum. These were exported to the Orient, particularly India and China, where they were exchanged for silks and spices - such as pepper, cassia, cinnamon and ginger - as well as the rare blue dye indigo, which was extracted from the plant *Indigofera tinctoria*. Bitumen, metals and dyes were traded with Egypt to be used in the process of mummification.

The Nabateans located the hub of their trading effort in an area adjacent to *Ain Musa,* comprising canyons, cliffs, towering rocks and plateaus. This area had the dual advantages of being a natural fortress and being ideally located to control, to their economic benefit, the commercial routes that passed through it. A major advantage of this location was that it afforded the Nabateans the opportunity to use its natural features to facilitate them harvest water from the *Wadi Musa*; by constructing dams and drains and to store it in cisterns. The Nabateans were consummate water engineers and their skill allowed them collect and store water resulting from the intermittent, but violent, rainstorms and flash floods that were a feature

---

153  Produced in Saudi Arabia, Oman, Yemen, Somalia, Eritrea and eastern Ethiopia

154  Used for thousands of years as a cleaning product for the home and the body. Blended with oil, it made an early form of soap. It is found in saline lake beds in dry and desert conditions. It is a naturally occurring mixture of sodium carbonate decahydrate, sodium bicarbonate and small quantities of sodium chloride and sodium sulphate.

of their desert environment. Their skill in water engineering permitted the Nabateans to thrive in this harsh land; it provided them with a vital commodity that drew people to their new settlement, particularly when there were periods of prolonged drought; and it provided a critical new source of revenue. The Nabateans half carved and half built a new capital city in this spot, a city that grew rapidly to a population of between 10,000 and 20,000. Whatever the Nabateans called it (sources variously use *Raqmu, Reqem, Pel, Sela* or *Seir*) it is known to us today as Petra, or the Rose Red City, and it is now, rightly, recognised as one of the new Seven Wonders of the World.

The Nabateans carved the city's major buildings and tombs directly from the rock face of the multilayered and multicoloured cliffs in the area. To date, some 3,000 temples, tombs, and dwellings have been identified. It is estimated that much of the city still remains buried and what we see represents about 20% of the total. Nonetheless, even that small amount is hugely impressive. Masons used picks, hammers, mallets and chisels to carve into the relatively soft multicoloured[155] sandstone to sculpt these buildings and tombs directly into the rock. This was an enormous task.

Not all the buildings were cut from the rock, some were partly cut from the rock and the rest were brick built; and some were entirely free standing and brick built in the way of the time. However, the most magnificent buildings that remain are all hewn from the rock. Architecturally, the Nabateans borrowed their style from outside influences that include Assyrian, Egyptian, Hellenistic and Roman sources.

Petra, located, as it was at a junction of major trade roads, prospered for centuries. Petra acted as a reloading depot, providing access to one route that crossed the Negev Desert and led to the port of Gaza, with a second leading through Damascus and on to Mesopotamia in the east and Phoenicia in the west. The continuous passage of camel caravans, ferrying

---

155 Red, white, pink and yellow – Edward Lear's (of 'Limerick' fame) servant and cook Giorgio Kokali, when he visited Petra with him described the colours as 'a world of chocolate, ham, curry powder and salmon'

prosaic and precious cargoes back and forth to and from India, the Orient and Arabia, Greece, Rome, Egypt, and Syria underpinned the enviable wealth of the citizens of Petra.

Petra provided shelter and water – but not for free. Each caravan, some consisting of up to 2,500 camels, paid a fee for these services and a duty was also imposed on the goods they carried. This resulted in Petra becoming one of the richest cities in the ancient world. So rich was it that it attracted the attention of the Romans, who took it over in AD 106. It continued as a trading centre for another 100 years but then rapidly declined, as trade routes west to the Red Sea and the Nile gained favour with the Romans. The decline had begun before the Roman occupation of the city, but accelerated under their rule. A major earthquake in AD 363 destroyed many of the buildings and damaged the critical water conservation and management system leaving Petra as an irrelevant backwater in the region.

'Rediscovered' by a Swiss traveller, Johann Ludwig Burckhardt, in 1812, Petra remained a curiosity until after the First World War. In 1929, it was surveyed and excavated by a four person international team. Its uniqueness and global importance was recognised in December 1985 when it was designated a World Heritage Site.

Ancient camel caravans approached Petra either from the high plateau to the north or from the south across the plain of Petra – passing around *Jabal Haroun*, reputedly the burial place of the brother of Moses, Aaron. Today, visitors approach from the east through a wide valley called the *Bab as-Siq* (Gateway to the *Siq*), leading to a dim, deep gorge, narrowing in places to 3 metres and winding its way 1.2 kilometres to open out and reveal the sun splashed façade of Petra's most exquisite and elaborate rock-cut building known as *Al Khazneh* - the Treasury.

The *Siq* is a natural geological fault, between 91 and 182metres deep,[156] ripped into the rock by enormous tectonic forces. Over time, wind and

156  300 – 600 ft deep

197

water has worn its multi-coloured surface smooth. A large dam near the entrance to the *Siq* replicates that of the Nabateans centuries earlier, but now re-routes the water from the *Wadi Musa*.

Carved into the walls of the *Siq* are votive niches containing *baetyli*,[157] or sacred stones, that were symbols of the gods and were, supposedly, endowed with life. Along the *Siq* are a number of underground chambers, believed to have housed the guards who defended this entrance to Petra. Over part of the route, visitors walk on the 2,000 year old cobblestone road - in places rutted by the chariot and wagon wheels of the ancient traffic that used to pass through, to and from the city.

Along the both sides of the *Siq,* it is possible to distinguish structures that brought water from the spring in Wadi Musa into the city. On the left hand side (as you enter the *Siq* through the remnants of a monumental arch destroyed by an earthquake in 1896), these consist of a covered channel, and on right hand side, they consist of clay water pipes. The clay pipes have tapered ends, a significant structural feature that only re-emerged in modern water engineering within the last two hundred years.

The ingenuity of the Nabateans as water engineers is further demonstrated as you progress along the Street of Facades in Petra, as the water pipe that was running at road height in the *Siq* now appears far above. Although the road drops considerably over the last kilometre the Nabateans kept the drop in the height of the water pipes gradual. This ensured that sufficient water pressure remained within the city centre. The inclusion of sequential particle settling systems helped purify and make the water potable.

Hundreds of underground water cisterns, and piping designed to cope with the maximum spring supply rate, provided for the drinking and hygiene needs of the population, with enough left over to cater for the requirements of the transient camel caravans.

Immediately, upon exiting the *Siq,* you are confronted by the magnificent *Al Khazneh*. The Khazneh, or Treasury, is a stunning building. It

---

157 Singular- *baetylus*

almost beggars description. While it is easy to say what it looks likes, it is impossible to convey the impressions it makes on each person who sees it. The mood of the structure changes on a daily and a seasonal basis with the passage of the sun. Nothing can prepare you for the grandeur of this achievement. The building is incised into the multicoloured sandstone. Its carved facade is adorned with the columns, capitals and pediments of classical Western architecture that seem entirely out of place in the barren, rugged desert landscape of southern Jordan. It is a stunning counterpoint to the rest of the region which, historically, has been inhabited by nomadic, flock-tending, Bedouin and simple farmers, who left little evidence in the landscape of their passage – except, perhaps, for the hundreds of bullet holes they shot in the giant urn carved above the doorway of *Al Khazneh*, as they wishfully hoped to dislodge riches they believed hidden within the carvings. Inside there is an enormous central chamber and two side chambers, forming three huge box shaped rooms.

Although a must visit destination for anyone visiting Jordan, in global terms, relatively few people have visited *Al Khazneh*. Many people have seen images of it but do not recognise it for what it is. For many, it is a cinematic fantasy; they only know it as entrance to the temple that housed the Holy Grail in the 1989 film *Indiana Jones and the Last Crusade*.

Turning left, on leaving the Treasury, you come to the Street of Facades. This leads down into the city proper, but beyond the Treasury it is lined with the large tombs of the deceased rich. Originally all of these had impressively carved facades – but many have now been damaged by the ravages of time, storms, wind and water – to the extent that some are filled with mud from floods. The most impressive tombs are the so called 'Royal Tombs'.

High on the side of the mountain is the Urn Tomb reputed, depending on your source, to be the resting place of either King Malchus II or Aretas IV. Accessed by a series of flights of steps, this tomb has an imposing façade, and to the side of the front courtyard is a line of columns.

The roof of this tomb is spectacular. The exposed beds and micro-beds of individually coloured sandstone have been folded and transected to create a natural kaleidoscope of colour that surely exceeds the ability of even the most lauded abstract artist. Next to it is the Silk Tomb – named from the rich and varied colours of the stone into which it was carved.

Two other large tombs include the Corinthian Tomb, which has an ornate carved façade similar to that of the Treasury, and the extremely wide three storied Palace Tomb. The smaller tombs of the ordinary citizens of the city dot the canyon walls.

Further along the road to the left is the large rock cut theatre. Although damaged over the centuries, it is still an impressive feat of construction. It is backed by the remains of the tombs that survived the construction of the tiered seats of the amphitheatre. The best way to see the theatre is to climb the rock face on the opposite side of the road to get a panoramic view.

Beyond the Theatre, the canyon widens to reveal what is left of the Nymphaeum and The Colonnaded Street. The Nymphaeum was a public fountain built in the 2nd century AD and fed by water channelled from the *Siq*. It, like the colonnaded street, was largely destroyed by floods over the last millennium. A large, 450 year old, pistachio tree marks its location. The Colonnaded Street, paved with ancient flagstones, runs through the centre of Petra. Although severely damaged in the past, the remains of some of the columns and the flagstones hint at its former majesty. Today, tourists, donkeys and camels echo the traffic of Petra in its heyday. The street terminates in an Arched Gate consisting of two smaller arches flanking a larger central one.

Given that the afternoon was progressing fast, Mary and I hired a pair of donkeys to take us up the steep path and steps to the *Deir*, or Monastery, on top of the mountain a couple of kilometres away. The donkeys knew the way, having travelled it many times, so along with their handlers they set out on the trot up the side of the mountain, requiring only the occasional slap on the arse from their running handlers to encourage them to keep up the pace. The narrow track only allowed for the donkeys to travel single file. Donkeys go wherever they want to. Mine brushed a rather large German hausfrau off the path and, only for the fact that I grabbed her by the arm and swung her around the donkey's arse she would have experienced free fall down the side of the mountain. The donkeys bounded up the hill and we arrived at the courtyard in front of the *Deir* eighteen minutes after we started. In places, the slope was almost 60° making it a hairy ride. While we were in danger of slipping off their backs, the donkeys took it all in their stride. The ride up had tested the limit of Mary's courage and she elected to walk back down. I paid the profusely sweating donkey handlers, who had run the whole way with their charges, the agreed fee of 75 dinars, as they had more than lived up to their promise to get us to the *Deir* in 20 minutes. I sweetened the deal by buying each of them a cold soda from an enterprising vendor who had lugged the beverages and an ice box to his small stall in this isolated spot. Interestingly, the speed of our ascent was put into perspective when we noted that our brisk descent by foot took us all of forty minutes.

In many respects, I feel that the *Deir* is the outstanding monument left by the Nabateans. It was constructed sometime during the first century BC and the first century AD. It got its name, apparently, from the adjacent cave, known as the Hermit's Cell, and is one of the largest monuments in Petra. The interior is huge, carved deep into the mountain, and is lit only by the light that comes in through the eight metre high doorway. Whether it was excavated as a temple to the god *Obodas*,[158] or a tomb for close relatives of the god/king is unclear; but its purpose is now secondary to its unique architectural beauty. It is an outstandingly serene building and well worth the arse numbing donkey ride. The sublime views from the *Deir* plateau are an added bonus.

---

158  Obodas I, who defeated both the Hasmoneans and the Greeks, was king of the Nabataeans from 96 BC to 85 BC. After his death, he was worshipped as a god.

# Part 3 – Cappadocia

Thirteen hundred kilometres due north brings you to the centre of Cappadocia in Turkey. Southwest of Kayseri, and located in central Anatolia in the heartland of modern Turkey, are the remnants of the ancient kingdom of Cappadocia. Derived from ancient Persian, '*katpatukya*' means the 'Land of Beautiful Horses'. Now largely a tourism designation, the name reflects a traditional Christian description for the area. It is a region of natural beauty distinguished by its bizarre landscape of so called 'fairy chimneys' and troglodyte dwellings, and its rich cultural and historical heritage stretching from the Chalcolithic or Copper age (some 3500 to 1700 BC) that preceded the Bronze Age.

Geographically, the area consists of plains, rolling hills, and a plateau rising over 1000m that is dotted with volcanic peaks. The area is bounded by the Taurus Mountains in the south, which separate it from the Mediterranean Sea and, to the north, by The Black Sea coastal ranges that separate it from Pontus and the Black Sea. The historical regions of Lycaonia and Galatia provide its western boundary and the upper Euphrates River defines its eastern limits. Its inland location and high altitude provide a climate defined by dry, hot, summers and snowy, cold winters.

Some thirty million years ago, eruption of three volcanoes,[159] whose peaks now dominate Cappadocia, blanketed the land with mud and ash. Over time, the ash was compacted into a solid, but soft, rock called tuff. Deposits of tuff, lava and basalt provided the raw material for Cappadocia's unique landscape. Earthquakes and erosion over millions of years sculpted valleys and gorges and the myriad of weirdly shaped rock formations that typify the region. The most memorable formations are the so-called 'fairy chimneys', for which the region is so famous. These appear to have been formed when lava covering the tuff split along pre-existing cracks and formed isolated pinnacles. Where the tuff deposits were worn away by water and wind they left

159 Erciyes, Hasan and Melendiz Dağları

cone-shaped white chimneys topped with a cap of harder, darker rock. Eventually the soft body of the chimney will erode away and will collapse and eventually be reduced to dust. Some of these 'fairy chimneys' reach a height of forty metres. In some areas, and particularly in 'Love Valley', they create a surreal landscape reminiscent of a graveyard of shallowly buried but priapic giants, who are completely covered except for their tumescent penises, which penetrate the soil and point skyward, each flaunting his petrified manhood in place of a headstone.

The tuff is extremely soft and easily carved. Throughout the ages, people took advantage of this and burrowed into the surface of rock faces and into the bases of the fairy chimneys themselves to make individual homes, places of worship and in some cases multi-storeyed towns.

It was mid April and our expectation, foolishly as it turned out, of bright blue spring days and abundant wildflowers accompanying us, while we travelled in Cappadocia, was cruelly dashed by dull grey, cloud laden skies and cold and wet weather. A walking holiday in Cappadocia, in the snow and the rain does not obliterate the magic of the place, but it is blurred somewhat when you have to stagger along blinded by near blizzard conditions.

We left the village of Selime after breakfast and entered the 14km long Ihlara valley that runs from Selime to Ihlara village. The Melendiz River runs through the valley, and the bordering canyon is honeycombed with troglodyte dwellings and churches cut into the rock by Cappadocian Greeks during the Byzantine period. It is reported that there are some four thousand dwellings and one hundred and five churches in the valley that catered to a population, at the peak of occupancy, of eighty thousand people.

A steep ascent brought us to Selime monastery - a magnificent rock-hewn structure comprising three churches, a huge kitchen with a chimney, camel stables and the remnants of troglodyte dwellings. The interiors of the churches were much more complex than those of Petra, where most of the artistry resides in the facades. Here, with the exception of the churches, the facades were relatively undecorated. Inside, the chambers were carved into separate galleries, with arches and pillars resembling the interior of other free-standing Byzantine churches. Faded frescoes can still be seen in some of the churches, which must have been magnificent in their heyday. The monastery, which dates from the eighth or ninth century, is believed to have taken some two hundred years to build. The largest of the three churches, a cathedral-sized excavation, is believed capable of holding five thousand people.

The school has a two storey central hall and, at first floor level, a whole series of rooms branching off to the sides. Soot staining provides evidence of the primitive heating and lighting system. All the excavations were interconnected by tunnels and underground stairways. Surprisingly, despite the tuff being water absorbent, the interiors are remarkably dry.

After exploring the monastery, we descended into the valley and walked through the poplar forest, accompanied by the music of abundant birdsong and the gush and gurgle of the nearby rushing river. The edge of the riverbank was clothed in a row of pollarded willows - the rods of which are used, among other things, in basket making. Mulberry, oleander, plum and wild cherry trees added to the arboreal variety of our walk. Our interest and curiosity was captured by observing the people and animals working in fields and vineyards we passed.

Although we kept up a stiff pace, as the day was bitterly cold, we paused every now and then to enjoy the scenery, look at birds and observe local farm families at work. After about two and a half hours walking we reached the small riverside village of Belisirma and headed for the welcoming warmth of one of its restaurants. With the exception of a couple of local men, we were the only guests. In high season, this place bustles with visitors.

After defrosting with a cup of steaming tea, we decided to refreeze our innards with a half litre of chilled beer - comfort has many, and often contradictory, manifestations. Kemal, our driver had arrived well ahead of us and was ensconced by the wood-burning stove where he toasted thin slices of potato on its flat, iron surface. Beside him, a steaming kettle provided a continuous supply of boiling water for the many glasses of tea he consumed.

We drove from Belisrima to our pension in Ihlara village at the other end of the valley, and the much anticipated refreshing hot shower. Luck was not with us. The water was heated from solar panels but as we had no sun we were deprived of hot water - or so the story went. The pension was empty except for us, so there was no call for hot water during the time we were in the valley; the explanation probably disguised the actual cause. Even in heavy cloud, most solar panels produce some electricity. The pension was freezing - as were we. We had a small hot meal, a bottle of sickly red wine and went to bed - the one place we were guaranteed some warmth.

The next morning, following an early breakfast, we departed from Ihlara village, and began to walk from there back towards Belisrima. We visited three rock-hewn churches. The first was *Ağaçaltı Kilise* (Church under the Trees), which is famous for its well-preserved fresco ceiling depicting the Ascension. Its dome is decorated with a depiction of Christ accompanied by blue and white painted angles. Also known as the Church of Daniel, a fresco of Daniel in the Lion's Den can be seen opposite the entrance. This church also contains a depiction of the *'Dormition of the Mother of God'* which is the basis of a Great Feast of the Eastern Orthodox, Oriental Orthodox and Eastern Catholic Churches, which is celebrated on August the 15th or, in Armenia, on the Sunday nearest to August 15th. The first fresco shows the dying Mary lying on a bed. Christ and St. John sit on one side to recover her soul; the second, upper fresco, shows Christ, with an angel behind him, as he carries Mary's soul to heaven.

The second church was the *Ptirenllseki* Church, whose faded walls depict the Holy Forty (or the forty martyrs of Sevaste – present day Sivas in Turkey) – Christian Roman soldiers who refused to make a sacrifice to pagan Roman gods and who were martyred in 320 AD by being beaten, stoned and forced to stand naked in a freezing pond overnight; whereupon they perished and their bodies were burned and their ashes thrown into the river. Christians collected whatever remained of them from the water and these relics were distributed throughout the region. The Forty were venerated in Turkey, Albania, Macedonia, Syria, Bulgaria and the Ukraine. There is even a chapel in the 5th century church of Santa Maria Antiqua, in the Roman Forum, consecrated to them.

The third church, the *Kokar Kilise* (variously known as the Fragrant Church, the Odorous Church or the Smelly Church), is adorned with ornate geometrical ceiling crosses and colourful frescoes of the nativity, the crucifixion and the entombment of Christ. The ceiling shows scenes from the Ascension and Pentecost. Its centre shows a large Greek cross and a depiction of the hand of God giving benediction. Each side of the lower parts of the vaulting displays frescoes of the apostles. The church can only be entered through a ruined apse. The original entrance is blocked by an earlier landslide.

Some of the churches show distinct signs of vandalism. Many of the frescoes have had their eyes gouged out. Several explanations have been advanced for this, such as the action of eight century Byzantine iconoclasts,[160] the work of Muslim conquerors, or, the rather fanciful explanation we were given, that vandals thought the eyes were made of pearls and gouged them out.

In the snake church (*Yılanlı Kilise*), so called because it has a fresco of St. George and St. Theodore killing a dragon and a snake, it is said that a man's sins were put in the balance with his good deeds. If his sins out-

---

160 *Blinding was a common punishment in Constantinople*

weighed his good deeds he was fed to the snakes. The paintings, most likely, provide a pictorial metaphor for the devil and hell.

The walk to Belisrima was easy and pleasant. We lunched in the same restaurant in which we had stopped the previous day. After lunch we visited the underground city of *Kaymakli*. Originally known as *Enegup* it is believed that the first people to begin excavating dwellings here were the Phrygians in the 8th to 7th centuries BC. Excavation was expanded by early Christians, who added churches and miles of interconnecting tunnels to the underground city of *Derinkuyu*. The city provided shelter from the Muslim Arabs during the period of the Arab–Byzantine wars (780-1180 AD). After the region fell to the Ottomans, *Kaymakli*, like some other underground cities, provided a refuge from the Turkish Muslim rulers. As late as the 20th century the inhabitants, locally called Cappadocian Greeks, still used the underground cities to escape periodic waves of Ottoman persecution.[161] The houses in the village, which are constructed around some one hundred tunnels but only four floors, are organised around ventilation shafts, and are open to visitors. Some tunnels are still used as stables and cellars. Side tunnels, leading off the main tunnel, provided access to a huge millstone like door that could be rolled across the opening when danger threatened.

The first floor contained a stable, several living rooms and a church; the second floor also contained a church with a baptismal font, and graves for clergy are located adjacent to the church. Some living quarters are also present on this floor; the third floor contains oil or grape presses, kitchens and stores. A large block of andesite (a volcanic rock) displaying several holes, has been shown to have been used for cold copper processing. The fourth floor is given over to storage, indicating that the city supported a considerable population.

Our walk from Cayagil to Goreme, in the afternoon, turned out to be what we had hoped for this trip. Although the tuff slopes were steep and

---

161 *Dawkins, R.M. (1916;. Modern Greek in Asia Minor - A study of dialect of Silly, Cappadocia and Pharasa; Cambridge University Press, p. 16. Retrieved* 01 August *2017*

slippery, making walking difficult in some places, the weather was magnificent, wild flowers were in bloom in abundance, trees were in blossom and scent filled the air. The views were superb.

At Goreme we boarded our bus for the journey to our pension in Uchisar. It commanded superb views of the Goreme valley and Bogdaz Mountain. The next day we hiked through the White valley and the Honey (or Love) Valley. This walk, rightly, is classified as hard, and Mary and I were shattered at the end. It was made more difficult as a result of overnight rain, which turned the tuff dust into a thick muddy sludge, much of which stuck in heavy globules to our boots. Walking in the valley itself was pleasant. As we passed through the gardens of the villagers, we watched them care for their crops. We then walked through the Love Valley, so called because of the myriad 'fairy chimneys that have a distinct and amusing phallic appearance.

Not only did we get to see troglodyte houses and villages in Cappadocia but we also dined in a fairy chimney restaurant next to the Church of the Grapes (also known to some as The Church of St. Nichlitas), located at the beginning of the Red Valley. The fairy chimney, in which the Church of the Grapes is found, is hollowed into a lower level containing the church and an upper level that, presumably, was used as living quarters for clergy. The church was excavated to a square plan and has an apse and a nave with a grave niche. The flat ceiling of the nave is decorated with a cross of geometric figures and bunches of grape. The apse contains frescos of the Madonna and child with the archangels Michael and Gabriel beside them, as well as depictions of the twelve apostles.

Our final two nights in Cappadocia were spent in a cave and fairy chimney hotel – the Peri Pension. This was a friendly, if somewhat small and shabby, establishment just outside Goreme. We were fortunate the first evening in that there was some hot water, which allowed us the comfort of warm showers after our strenuous walks in the pouring rain through the Pancarlick and Red Valleys. The room we were staying in lacked heating, so we huddled shivering in bed throughout the night. We woke to the rain the next morning and found, again, that there was no hot water. By now we had come to expect this level of discomfort and accepted it. Our philosophical approach ensured that we had little expectations of comfort for the second night, and this was amply fulfilled.

Leaving aside the discomfort of the unexpected weather and the Spartan conditions in most of the accommodation we had booked, walking through Cappadocia was a memorable experience. If I ever revisit the area, however, I will rely more on the comfort afforded by the internal combustion engine and drive to the points of interest rather than slog my way through water, mud, snow and rain.

Having visited each of the sites mentioned above, I now find that I have just scratched the surface of what is out there. Travel does indeed broaden the mind and reinforces faith in the intelligence, inventiveness and ingenuity of man down through the generations. What it also shows is that, over time, and in every country, while man has vastly increased his knowledge, it is likely that his intelligence remains the same. What distinguishes different people and different generations is how they have used the knowledge they had and how they built upon it. Some of this has been for good and some has been used for ill.

One of the joys of travel is to discover the physical manifestations of what people have achieved through the intelligent application of their knowledge, sometimes in pursuit of their religious beliefs and sometimes in pursuit of a better way of doing what is necessary for the betterment of their society. While researching into the sites mentioned above, sources indicated other wonders of human endeavour that I have yet to see, and, indeed, some that I missed, through ignorance, when travelling in the area where they were located. These omissions simply provide an excuse to go back to places or to travel to new places. My new 'must see' list now includes:

- The Hypogeum of Ħal-Saflieni – cut into soft globigerina limestone.[162] This is a 5,000 year old Neolithic subterranean necropolis in Paola, Malta.

- Lycian tombs (Turkey) – these date from the 4th century BC, and are carved into limestone cliff faces in the shape of a temple portico, with its entrance at the bottom right.

- The Ajanta Caves – dating from the 2nd century BC to about 650 AD and carved into a horse-shoe shaped basalt cliff in the Aurangabad district of the Maharashtra state of India, and consist of about 30 rock-cut Buddhist monasteries and worship halls. These are richly decorated with frescoes and sculptures.

- Ellora – (also in the Aurangabad district of Maharashtra, India) hewn into a basalt cliff face and dating from about 600 AD, it is one of the largest rock-cut monastery-temple cave complexes in the world. The Kailasa temple, in cave 16, holds the largest single monolithic rock excavation in the world.

I would also love to see some of the hundreds of elaborate rock-cut tombs that were constructed in Israel in ancient times. The earliest of these are Canaanite and date from 3100–2900 BC. However, I remain unwilling to visit the country until there is an agreed and peaceful settlement with the Palestinians. This is not based on religious views but human rights and equality. It is informed by the same philosophy that prevented me visiting South Africa (which I have since visited many times) until apartheid was abolished.

---

162 *Globigerina* is a genus of planktonic Foraminifera (single celled Protists). They have been present in the world's oceans since the Middle Jurassic. Vast areas of the ocean floor are covered with *Globigerina* ooze.

# CHAPTER 14

⚭

# The Two-headed Snakes in the Land Below the Wind

The 7,641 islands that comprise the Philippines lie close to the equator and sit on the Pacific Ring of Fire. This makes them prone to earthquakes and typhoons. Indeed, three of the four worst storms to make landfall in South East Asia in the last 100 years or so hit the Philippines, these were Typhoon Tacloban in 1912, Typhoon Thelma in 1991, and, the worst of all, Typhoon Haiyan in 2013.[163]

To the south west of the southern tip of The Philippines lies Sabah – one of the Malaysian states on the Island of Borneo. Unlike its larger neighbour, Sabah lies just outside the typhoon belt and is characterised by an equatorial climate that never gets too hot (rarely above $30^0$C) or too cold (rarely below $20^0$C, except in the mountains, where it can get cold at night). Sabah is sheltered from the storms that affect many of its neighbours to the north and, for this reason, has become known as the 'Land below the Wind'.

On the 20th and the 21st September 1897 two earthquakes, registering 7.4 and 7.5 respectively on the Richter scale and with an epicentre just off the south-western coast of Mindanao in the Philippines, triggered a volca-

---

163 Cyclone Nargis, with a maximum wind speed of 215 kph, while weaker in strength than Typhoon Haiyan (315 kph wind speed) ravaged the Ayeyarwady Delta region of Myanmar in 2008 killing some 140,000 people and affected about 2.4million others and did US$ 10 billion worth of damage. This is greatly in excess of the 6,300 fatalities attributed to Typhoon Haiyan, although its economic impact is thought to be greater and is estimated at US$ 14 billion.

nic eruption in the northern part of Borneo. This eruption resulted in the formation of three islands which, over time combined, to form *Pulau Tiga*, which translates from Malay as Three Island.

*Pulau Tiga*, is located a thirty minute, 18km speedboat ride from Kuala Penyu on the west coast of Sabah, which is some two hour's drive south of the capital, Kota Kinabalu. Although it has been developed somewhat for tourism (ever since it achieved a modicum of fame as the site of both the UK and USA television game show series '*Survivor*') it receives relatively few visitors, despite marketing itself as '*Survivor Island*'. This is not necessarily a bad thing as it helps preserve much of the true character of the place.

We arrived there in August 2005, when much of the resort was closed down, and stayed in adequate, if somewhat spartan, cabins set back from the sea. Given the places we had already been to in Sarawak and Sabah, this island provided a relaxing interlude. Distinctive features of Tiga, at the highest part of the island (100m), are the so-called mud 'volcanoes'. Here mineral-rich mud, propelled by volcanic gas, bubbles, 'gloops' and farts its way to the surface, or shoots a few feet into the air from deep underground. This is fairly mild stuff, as the last major outpouring of mud was in the early 1960s. The continuing emissions of methane gas, however, add inexorably to the global quantum of greenhouse gases. Varying pools of thicker or thinner mud some short distance from the volcanoes provide 'baths' for those who are taken in by the propaganda that the mud is an excellent treatment for your skin, rather than the basis for amusing photographs demonstrating the child that still remains within us all.

One of the things I look out for on all my trips are snakes. Some people shy away from them but I am drawn to them. I was lucky so far on this trip; I had managed to see four different species as we travelled through Sabah. These included

1.  Oriental Whip Snake (*Ahaetulla prasina*)

    While this is a common snake, it is so well camouflaged that it is difficult to see. Many people who walked with us along the boardwalk into the Orangutan Rehabilitation Centre in Sepilok passed right by it, without noticing it resting on a branch within 50cm of where they passed. I can just imagine how many would have freaked if they had known. We also saw one near the trail as we descended from the 'mud volcanoes' on Pulau Tiga towards the beach to wash.

    These long nosed, bright green snakes have superb eyesight. They feed on frogs and lizards and are active hunters by day and by night. They are aggressive and quick to bite if disturbed and, although they don't produce venom, their saliva is mildly toxic. You know if they intend to strike because they expand their neck, puff up, and reveal the black and white skin between their scales. Some locals believe that they will aim for the eye if they attempt to bite humans but there is no evidence to support this. The one I saw in Sepilok was obliging enough to hang around and provide me with the opportunity to take a couple of photographs.

2.  Mangrove Cat Snake (*Boiga dendrophila*)

    This is a beautiful animal. We were very lucky to see one as we travelled on the Kinabatangan River. It is a large (up to 2.5m) and unmistakable snake. It gets its name from its large, cat like eyes. Its general body colour is black, marked with 35 – 45 bright, but narrow, yellow rings. For this reason it is sometimes called the gold-ringed cat snake. It inhabits lowland forests and mangrove swamps and is generally seen, as was the case for us, coiled up and resting on a branch near the water. It feeds on birds and their eggs, amphibians, lizards and other snakes. It will also eat tree shrews and it has been recorded consuming a chevrotain, or mouse deer.

It is a non-venomous snake but its saliva, like that of the oriental whip snake is suspected of being poisonous. Mostly nocturnal, it is a potentially aggressive snake and if provoked will strike repeatedly so it needs to be treated with caution. Despite this, many people keep them as pets.

3.   Wagler's Pit Viper (*Tropidolaemis wagleri*)

This is, perhaps, the most commonly seen of all pit vipers in Borneo. It is sometimes called the temple viper because of its abundance around the Temple of the Azure Cloud in Penang, Malaysia. Females grow to approximately 1m, while smaller males rarely exceed 75cm. The large head is triangular and the body is thin. Almost entirely arboreal, the prehensile tail makes it an efficient climber of trees. These vipers present a wide variety of colours and patterns, from black or brown with orange and yellow banding to light green with yellow or orange banding, and many variations in between. The times I observed it in Sabah and in Pahang (peninsular Malaysia) the specimens were green with narrow yellow and orange bands. Primarily nocturnal and arboreal, it hunts using sensory pits that lie between the eyes and nostrils on the sides of the head capable of detecting temperature difference. These sensitive pits can distinguish changes of as little as 0.003 Celsius.

These snakes appear quite sluggish during the day, spending most of their time resting on a low branch digesting a previous meal, or resting in anticipation of the night's hunt. They are fairly lazy during the day, remaining motionless for long periods of time. However, should any unwary bird, rodent, or lizard pass or perch close, or if you should inadvertently disturb one as you push through a bush (they seem to prefer bushes to trees) in which it is resting, it will strike quickly. Due to its efficient thermal sensing ability, it does not have to rely on eyesight to detect prey.

The venom of Wagler's pit viper is potentially deadly. However, it does not usually result in human death. Victims experience a strong burning sensation and swelling and necrosis of tissue. Fortunately, antivenin is available. Wagler's pit viper venom is known to contain 4 novel peptides described as Waglerin-1 through to Waglerin-4. Waglerin-1 inhibits transmission across the nerve-muscle junction. Interestingly, a synthetic form of Waglerin-1 was included in several skin creams marketed as wrinkle removers.[164] There is little reliable scientific evidence supporting the efficacy of these products, but I'm sure it is just as plausible as the www.Greensations.com anti-aging wrinkle butter called **Earthworm Complex** ($29.95 a tub at the time of writing) that is made from an extract of earthworm poop known as 'castings'. Reassuringly, the blurb states that the cream doesn't smell like shite[165] (but not necessarily in these exact words).

A short, fairly choppy crossing by speedboat from *Pulau Tiga* brings you to the nearby small rocky outcrop of *Pulau Kalampunian Damit*. Consisting of limestone, sandstone and shale this 40 metre long islet is covered in thick vegetation dominated by Pisonia, or bird-catcher trees (probably *Pisonia umbellifera*) and some figs. What gives it its claim to fame is the fact that it is a breeding site for the highly poisonous yellow-lipped, or banded, sea krait (*Laticauda colubrina*). For this reason, it has become famous as 'Snake Island'. This was the fourth species I had the pleasure of seeing.

Yellow-lipped sea kraits are large, pearly-blue, black banded snakes. Their upper lip is distinctly yellow, hence the name. While there is no obvious neck, the head is slightly distinct from the body. The snout is yellow, and this extends backward above the eye as far as the temporal shields, leaving a dark bar in between. The rest of the head is black. The tail end is flattened

---

164 Syn-ake - developed by the Swedish company Pentapharm Ltd, is used in Aldi's award winning Lacura wrinkle stop cream, Snake Venom Cream by INKANAT and Venomous Wrinkle Serum by Greensations, amongst others.

165 Although one customer review, which was found helpful by 0 of 0 people, stated '*Does not smell so great, however the smell doesn't hang on the body after use which is alright*' (sic).

sideways to provide a paddle for swimming. The tail has a U-shaped yellow marking along the edge that borders a broad black band. In colour, the tail and the head look very similar. For this reason it is sometimes described as the two-headed snake.

These are the only sea snakes whose nostrils are not situated dorsally; theirs are on the side of the snout. Other adaptations they have to live in the sea include valvular nostrils to prevent water getting in; salt glands to prevent build up of excessive salt in the blood; and a special diving adaptation consisting of a rearward extension of the lung, known as the saccular lung, that allows them to dive to depths up to 60m in search of food. This extension expands lung volume by compensating for the limited volume of their tubular lung that is dictated by the body shape of the snake. Research has shown that they also have the ability to absorb 10% or more of their total oxygen demand across skin surfaces.[166] This cutaneous respiration, along with extra oxygen storage in the saccular lung, is a key adaptation permitting long submersion times. It is also believed that the snake can get rid of all its carbon dioxide through its skin.

All sea snakes are most closely related to terrestrial elapids. This is a group of tropical and sub-tropical snakes that comprise the cobra group. All of these have short fangs fixed in the front of the upper jaw (i.e. they are proteroglyphous). They include some of the most poisonous snakes of the world e.g. brown snake, taipan, death adder, cobra, krait, and mamba.

The yellow-lipped sea krait, in common with its relatives, has highly toxic venom which affects both muscle and nerve. Available lethality figures suggest that its venom is at least 10 times more toxic than that of a diamondback rattlesnake.[167] Each snake can produce up to 15 mg of venom

---

166 https://opwall.com/wp-content/uploads/Dabruzzi-et-al-2012-Sea-Krait-metabolic-thermal-sensitivity.pdf

167 Lethal dose is expressed as the LD50. i.e. the amount of the substance that kills 50 percent of a test sample, expressed in milligrams of the substance per kilogram of body weight. The test subjects used were mice and while this gives an indication of lethality it cannot be directly extrapolated to humans.

per bite. In a single bite, a yellow-lipped sea krait can inject more than 12 times the venom required to kill a human.

Yellow-lipped sea kraits are considered feeding specialists. They feed mostly on eels burrowed in sand at the bottom of the sea and in reef crevices. Large females tend to specialise on conger eels, while the smaller males concentrate on moray eels. As well as this, they are known to supplement their diet with typical reef fish such as lizardfishes, damselfishes, clownfishes, sergeants etc. They use their eyes and nostrils to locate and identify prey.

Their elongated bodies and small heads enable them to probe holes, cracks, and crevices in coral reefs as they forage for food. While probing crevices, they are unable to observe any predators that may approach them from behind. As mentioned above, the pattern on the head and on the sides of tail, particularly when it is turning and waving, is very similar. By using this type of mimetic defence, the yellow-lipped sea kraits can fool predators into believing that their tail is their head. Potential predators assume they have lost the element of surprise and back off. This allows the krait to continue to hunt freely. Once prey is spotted, the snake strikes, and its powerful venom attacks the muscles and nerves of the prey, quickly rendering it helpless. The sea krait then swallows its prey whole. Like a number of other snake species, the sea krait is capable of swallowing prey as big as itself. Engorged after a meal, and with its swimming ability impaired the snake, itself, becomes vulnerable to predators such as sharks, especially tiger sharks *(Galeocerda cuvieri)*.

Yellow-lipped sea kraits are unique among sea snakes in that they are amphibious and able to live on land or in the ocean. They are thought to spend as much as 50% of their time on land where they breed, shed their skin, bask and digest food. As they can only drink fresh water, they must come ashore frequently to drink. Unlike other sea snakes that give birth to live young, the sea krait lays eggs and it can only do this on land.

After feeding, it returns to land as quickly as possible to digest its prey in the comfort and in the shelter of rock crevices, or under bushes. It can move easily on land and can even climb trees, but it is much slower here than it is at sea. This leaves it vulnerable to terrestrial predators, particularly the white-bellied sea-eagle (*Haliaetus leucogaster*) and the brahimny kite (*Haliastur indus*), both of which, unsurprisingly, I saw on Snake Island.

When we landed at Snake Island, we scrambled ashore and our guides went searching for snakes. We amused ourselves watching the antics of the abundant hermit crabs that crawled around the tide-line. Mary found the shed skin of a fairly large sea krait (greater than 1metre when we stretched it out) among the rocks. Yellow-lipped sea kraits shed their skin far more often than do land snakes in order to protect themselves from parasites. Sometimes they change skins as often as every fortnight.

One of the guides called to us. He had found a yellow-lipped sea krait in a crevice under the rocks at the edge of the tide. Soon, we found three more. The guide called to me and said 'Hold this'! Instinctively, thinking he wanted me to hold some of his gear while he hunted for a snake, I reached out to help him and to my astonishment found myself holding a one and a half metre sea krait. It felt like a warm, dry, dead fish. I stood mute wondering what to do with it and who I could pass it on to. I knew it was poisonous – all sea snakes are. I did not then realise quite how venomous it really was. However, I was somewhat reassured by the thought that a National Park guide would not deliberately put visitors in danger. What I have since come to realise is that these snakes, while highly venomous, are not highly dangerous. On shore they are docile and would require significant mishandling before they would bite. I must say, I was relieved when the guide took it back. He offered it around but did not get any other takers.

The fact that they can be collected this easily and the fact that they are frequently caught by fishermen in nets has made them vulnerable to human exploitation. They are harvested for their skin, organs and meat. Their meat is smoked and exported to Japan

I have since learned that in New Caledonia, a French overseas territory in the southwest Pacific, they are called *tricot rayé* or striped sweater after their blue and black striped appearance. Children play with them draping them around their necks like striped scarves. This rarely leads to harm. However, there is one recorded case of death by sea krait bite in New Caledonia, and that was of a child.

# CHAPTER 15

## I'll Take Socks

Make no mistake about it, I love India! However, it is a sub-continent that demands patience, forbearance, curiosity, humour and wonder from its visitors. If you lack these then you will be rapidly ground down by the dirt, the smells, the grinding poverty and the third world diseases on display. India and sensory overload are synonymous. I experienced this on my first visit, just after I disembarked at Delhi airport. The first thing to assault me was the heavy, dusty, humus smell that pervaded the airport terminal. Then the heat and humidity delivered a rapid combination of blows that left me gasping and sweating. Inside the terminal, the slow grind of immigration added to my growing testiness after a long and tedious flight.

Outside the terminal, on the bus to my hotel, I stared at the many groups of people who had set up for the night and were sleeping on the ground on traffic islands, roundabouts and in bus shelters. Dogs could be seen everywhere. I saw a naked man hunker down in a basin of water on the roadside verge and soap himself for a basin bath. One woman, squatting beside a pool of rain water, held her sari up to her waist with one hand while she defecated. She waved at us with the other hand, before she proceeded to use it in the rain pool to clean her backside. Such sights were to become commonplace as I travelled through India over the years.

Old Delhi is ramshackle, dusty, and smelly, and teems with people. Families set up home on the sidewalk, where they cook, eat, defecate and sleep, and presumably make love, in the same place. The smell of steaming and festering piss is everywhere; spitting in public is commonplace. Begging abounds. It is conducted by the dispossessed, physically and mentally damaged, by urchins, holy men and professionals. Amputees stagger or, while seated on skateboards, propel themselves towards you seeking alms; other unfortunates lie around exhibiting festering sores and Technicolor skin disorders and, as you pass, cry out either singly, or as an *a capella* chorus, beseeching potential benefactors to drop coins, or notes, into the tin dishes lying beside them. Conditions and diseases, long banished from the first world, still find expression here.

Labour is cheap in India. Manpower shifts enormous burdens; hefted on skinny but strong shoulders; pushed on rickety carts; or strapped in huge piles to bicycles. But man is not the only animal to be put to backbreaking work in India; this fate is shared by countless donkeys, camels, mules, water buffalo, oxen and elephants.

Roads are stuffed with vehicles as well as animals: cars, trucks, buses, bicycles, rickshaws and tractors together with cows, pigs, donkeys, dogs and people. Driving in India is a challenge. On my first short visit I witnessed three separate fatal road accidents. I was horrified; locals looked upon it as a common occurrence. This is not surprising when you consider that the World Health Organisation, in 2013, estimated that there were 231,000 road traffic fatalities in India (85% of which were male). This is almost the equivalent of destroying the entire population of the city of Eindhoven in the Netherlands; or Bordeaux in Frances; or Reno, Nevada, in the USA.

The current Indian Prime Minister, Narendra Modi, expressed great concern over the fact that a person dies on India's roads every four minutes. He promised to bring in new laws to cut the accident rate. Indians are still waiting.

Some 60% of drivers of motorbikes in India wear helmets in compliance with national law. Interestingly, while there is law on wearing crash helmets there is no requirement that they be fastened. The illusion of safety inherent in the assumption that crash helmets protect even if they are not fastened, is shattered by the fact that drivers and passengers of two and three wheeled vehicles top the table, by a considerable margin, in the number of fatalities and injuries.

Many Hindus are fatalistic. These believe that their fate is written by Brahma on their foreheads before they are born or reborn. Such fatalism is a dangerous belief when you are a road user. It assumes that what will be, will be; so it permits some crazy road user decisions to be made. It reminds me of the poster I saw on the Internet, which said 'It is called Karma and it is pronounced *"ha ha, fuck you!"* Judging by some of the lunatic manoeuvres I experienced on India's roads, I find this fairly accurate.[168]

I read some advice on a website[169] that said there is an *'unofficial pecking order for the right-of-way: cows (because they are considered sacred), large trucks, buses, SUVs, cars, mopeds, rickshaws, bicycles, and, lastly, pedestrians – presumably ranked in order of vulnerability. Many motorists play 'chicken' while driving, meaning that they will drive in the middle of the road, challenging oncoming traffic to move aside into the ditch. Try not to get involved in this game, and if your driver does it, just look away and hope for the best!'*

From personal experience, I would add camel carts to the list – ahead of mopeds but behind cars. As we travelled south from Delhi to Agra, along the dual carriageway that is National Highway 2, and which used be the main rout prior to the recent construction of new Yamuna Expressway, we encountered a camel cart coming towards us in the outer lane of what, in any other country, would be deemed our side of the road. Either the camel had some unwritten right of way over our bus, or the farmer in charge of the camel simply didn't care. The latter possibility seems to be

---

168 I have noticed that this is a recurring theme in my writings on India. It has become increasingly obvious to me that road travel in the sub-continent has, psychologically, left me deeply scarred, or, at least, frightened out of my wits.

169 www.internations.org/india-expats/guide/driving-in-india-15620 (accessed 18/04/2016)

the more likely and provided us with an example of karma in action. Nonchalant would describe his attitude and fatalism his philosophy. In his mind it appeared that he believed his future was predestined and that there was little he could do to change it. If he was going to die, then he would die. The fact that we might also be killed would not even have entered his mind, as our futures were also predetermined and if we were to be obliterated in the bloody crash, then it was written already in our individual books of life.

Unfortunately, this incidence wasn't the only one we were to experience whilst driving in India. Any time I permitted myself to look out of the front window of our bus invariably brought from me the exclamation '*Oh Jesus, we are going to be totalled!*' Our driver's fatalism when taking blind corners on the wrong side of the road (if any side of the road in India can be deemed the wrong side), as we passed sundry buses, trucks, cars and tractors, instilled in me a conviction that any hopes I had for the future depended entirely on the good deeds and positive choices that our driver had made in his previous incarnations. The fact that we survived, surely, is proof that he had been good man.

It is not just driver behaviour that is a problem. The Global NCAP organization,[170] in 2013, initiated a testing project in India on five key models that together accounted for around 20% of all new cars sold in the country. Four of the five models failed the UN regulation test and all scored zero at 64km/h, either as a result of poor structure or lack of air bags.

A thirty seven kilometre drive S.S.W of Agra brings you to a long narrow ridge whose fine red sandstone was quarried for Mughal palaces and forts. It was the place where the Sufi holy man, Shaykh Salim Chishti lived in a cave during the 1560's and 70's.

The Emperor, Akbar the Great, had many wives who bore him children, but all had died. Desirous of producing an heir he sought the blessing of Chishti. The holy man foretold the birth of Akbar's three sons. Such was

---

170 New Car Assessment Programmes

Akbar's respect for the saint that he named his first born son Salim (who later became the emperor Jahangir), in honour of Chishti.

Following his victory in the siege of the huge fort at Chittorgarh and then the fort at Ranthambore, Akbar, decided to establish a new capital close to the Chishti's hermitage. This was to be called the 'city of victories' – or Fatehpur Sikri. While the decision to locate the capital here was prompted by reverence for Chishti, Akbar, always a pragmatist, noted the strategic location of the site that placed his armies closer to the Gujarat region – upon which he had set his sights for conquest.

The new walled city was to be built in an area that was previously uninhabited, except for a small village of stonecutters, and took five years to complete.[171] It became the capital in 1571 and throughout the following decade was expanded and modified.

The high ground of the ridge was reserved for the imperial palace complex, with its geometrically arranged pavilions, and religious buildings. The low ground was occupied by the caravanserai, wells, waterworks and garden. The harem, courts, private quarters, library and audience hall are among the many other buildings. Akbar built a magnificent white tomb for Shaykh Salim Chishti within the city.

Fathepur Sikri is a gem of Mughal Architecture. The complex of buildings, all of uniform architectural style, includes one of the largest mosques in India, the Jama Masjid, which is capable of accommodating 10,000 worshipers, and the largest gate in the world (it is said) the Buland Darwaza.

Perched on the ridge, the bright red and buff sandstone construction material highlights the city against the prevailing blue sky. Up close, judicious use of white and black marble relieves the monotony of the rusty appearance of many of the buildings, providing decorative accent to gates, towers and the edges of pools.

---

171 Statues, up to 1,000 years old, have been discovered, suggesting that the area was once an important Jain site.

The city was inscribed as a World Heritage Site by UNESCO in 1986. The inscription states '*The authenticity of the Fatehpur Sikri has been preserved in the palaces, public buildings, mosques, living areas for the court, the army, and the servants of the king.*' The inscription also acknowledges that repair and conservation work carried out to a number of buildings, from the time of British Government in India (early 1800's), has been achieved without changing original structures.

Paintings and painted inscriptions have also been chemically preserved and restored, apparently, to their original condition.

Despite being a major achievement of Mughal design and construction, Fatehpur Sikri had an ephemeral existence as the capital of the Mughal Empire. It was continuously occupied for a mere ten years. The transfer, by Akbar, of his capital to Lahore in 1585, to deal with the challenges posed by the Uzbeks from beyond the Khyber Pass, precipitated the demise of the city and this was compounded by a severe water shortage resulting from the exhaustion of the small, spring-fed lake that supplied the city with water. The area was largely unpopulated before Akbar built the city, and with his move north it returned to that condition.

When Akbar returned to the region in 1598, he set up court in the Red Fort in Agra, where he had begun his reign. He only returned to Fatehpur Sikri for a brief visit in 1601.

After Akbar's death, the city was only sparingly occupied over the next two centuries. It was refurbished in 1719 to host the coronation of Muhammad Shah. Later, the palaces were occupied by the Marathas (a renowned warrior caste) after their victory in the first battle of Delhi in 1737 and subsequently transferred to the British army, which used the fortified complex as a barracks.

In 1899, the 39 year old Lord Curzon was appointed the youngest ever Viceroy of India. Curzon (1859 to 1925), regarded by many as a libidinous, arrogant, egotist had a great interest in Indian culture, if not in the Indian peasantry. The beginning of his administration coincided with a major famine. It is believed that in excess of six million people died. Curzon did little to fight the famine. His attitude reflected that of the British administration in Ireland, half a century earlier, when that country suffered from the great potato famine of 1845 to 1852.

The Chief Poor Law Commissioner during the Irish Famine, Edward Twisleton, testified that...

*'comparatively trifling sums were required for Britain to spare itself the deep disgrace of permitting its miserable fellow subjects to die of starvation.'*

Despite the overwhelming evidence of prolonged distress caused by successive years of potato blight, the underlying philosophy of the relief efforts was that they should be kept to a minimalist level; in fact they actually decreased as the Famine progressed

In a reprise of the attitude that prevailed in Ireland through the Poor Laws and the notorious 'Gregory clause', Curzon also cut back rations that he characterised as 'dangerously high' and stiffened relief eligibility by reinstating the Temple tests (named after Sir Richard Temple) which were introduced during the Southern Indian Famine of 1876 -1878.

Curzon proclaimed that ...

*'any government which imperilled the financial position of India in the interests of prodigal philanthropy would be open to serious criticism; but any government which by indiscriminate alms-giving weakened the fibre and demoralized the self-reliance of the population, would be guilty of a public crime.'*

An arch imperialist, considered by many to be one of colonial India's most effective viceroys, Lord Curzon firmly believed British rule was essential to civilize 'backward' India. Curzon was a prodigious worker. He involved himself in every aspect of administration and governance, although his paternalistic attitude often invoked deep resentment. He launched sweeping modifications in administration, agriculture, education, frontier policy, land rent and industrial development.

Curzon, however, is best remembered for his role in conserving Indian monuments. It was he who signed 'The Ancient Monuments Preservation Act, 1904' into law.[172] The Act provides for the preservation of ancient monuments, for the exercise of control over traffic in antiquities and over excavation in certain places, and for the protection and acquisition in certain cases of ancient monuments and of objects of archaeological, historical or artistic interest.

Lord Curzon visited Fatehpur Sikri in 1899 and it is believed that this stimulated his interest in preserving India's decaying archaeological and architectural heritage. He sponsored a great variety of archaeological surveys and restoration efforts including Agra Fort, the Taj Mahal, the Jain temples at Mount Abu, and the buildings at Fatehpur Sikri.

When we visited the city in 1998 a huge Muslim festival meant that the steeply pitched 42 steps leading to the main gate – the massive 53.63m high and 35 meters wide Buland Darwaza – was teeming with devotees. Below, the muddy puddle riddled road was lined with food and flower stalls. We had great difficulty passing on the road because of the hundreds of ramshackle buses bringing the pilgrims.

Hawkers were everywhere – all refusing to take 'NO!' for an answer. It required patience and good humour not to get annoyed by their persistence. One character wanted to sell me a small, and rather crudely carved, statue of *Ganesha*, the elephant headed Hindu deity, revered as the remover of obstacles. Given my predicament, being slowly dragged along in a sea of humanity, this had the hallmarks of a sensible purchase. The seller wanted

---

172 This Act is still in force in India

400 rupee (about €5) but I had left my wallet safe in my locked bag on our bus, so I didn't have that much money with me. I informed him that all I had in my pocket was INR100, which I pulled out and waved at him.

He looked at me with disbelief and pointed to my other pocket, which he could see was bulging. I told him that this was not money but my socks, which I had pocketed earlier. He clearly didn't believe me. We had left our hotel early that morning and to discourage pre-dawn mosquitoes from feasting on my ankles, I had worn socks – very unfashionably – with my sandals. Once the sun rose and the morning began to heat up I pulled them off and put them in my trouser pocket – not giving them another thought until now. To prove the point to him, I pulled the socks from my pocket and flourished them in front of his disbelieving face.

Immediately he said he would give me the *Ganesha* for both the socks and the 100 rupee. I told him he would have to choose, one or the other. He persisted and given that the 100 rupee was less than €1 and the sweaty socks needed laundering, I gave in and gave him both. Given that I cannot recall seeing anyone other than city businessmen in India wear socks, I wondered what he was going to do with them.

Widely revered by Hindu, Jains and Buddhists as the remover of obstacles, *Ganesha* proved his mettle that day. Brandishing my newly acquired statue, a path opened up for me through the crowd that let me easily make my way back to our bus. He now sits in my study on a bookshelf (as *Ganesha* loves to read and is a patron of learning and letters) facing the main door and visitors as they enter our house. As the god of transitions, he is placed at the doorway of many Hindu temples to keep out the unworthy. Unsurprisingly, I find his presence reassuring.

# CHAPTER 16

# The Oil and the Coffee are Crap!

I n order to get the best from what they eat, as they cannot digest cellulose – a major component of plant cell walls - ruminants, such as cows, goats, sheep, giraffes, yaks, deer, antelope etc. use bacteria and other microbes to ferment the food they swallow. This takes place in a special compartment of their four chambered stomach called the rumen. Here, plant material is processed mechanically and exposed to the organisms than can break down cellulose. Food is then passed to the second chamber, the reticulum, which allows the animal to regurgitate and re-chew the food – a process called *'chewing the cud'*. Finely-divided food is passed to the third chamber, the omasum, for further mechanical processing. Following this the broken down food passes to the fourth chamber or 'true stomach', the abomassum. Here, the digestive enzyme known as lysozyme breaks down the bacteria that passed with the food so as to release nutrients incorporated in their cells.

Rabbits, unlike ruminants are coprophagous. They eat their own shit to get the maximum nutrition out of what they first eat. Part of their hind-gut can break down a proportion of dietary fibre called digestible fibre. This passes out through the anus and is immediately re-eaten by the rabbit so that it can extract the nutrients and vitamins that have been released. Hamsters, guinea pigs, chinchillas and naked mole-rats eat their own droppings to boost the levels of vitamins B and K in their bodies.

We humans lack the ability to digest cellulose; so much of the plant material we eat passes undigested through our gut. We call this dietary fibre and it has an importance in the smooth operation of our digestive tract.

I never thought that we, i.e. humans - or more especially - me would resort to consuming something that was a part of another animal's faeces, but the sad story is I did and, sadly, I still do.

Some fifteen years ago while driving from the desert town of Tata to Tagoudiche, in Morocco; we passed through the Amein Valley on the way to our lunch stop in Tafraoute high in the Anti-Atlas Mountains. We arrived on a Wednesday, and were fortunate to find a Berber market in full swing. It was bustling with merchants attempting to sell their fresh goods and valley locals purchasing their essential supplies. They had come in from the cluster of small villages that dot the valley and lie sheltered in barren land between jagged and wind-eroded granite formation. They belonged to the Cheleuh Berber people, a happy and friendly bunch and we were welcomed to Morocco again and again by each individual we met. We were doubly fortunate as, at this time of the year, there were few tourists to be seen, so strolling through the market was less frenetic than it might otherwise have been. This relaxing and very friendly atmosphere allowed us to indulge in leisurely shopping.

We had arrived in March when the almond (*Prunus dulcis*) and argan (*Argania spinosa*) trees were just coming into flower. We were very familiar with the former species but the argan tree was completely new to us. These are slow growing, long lived, squat, spreading trees of up to 8 to 10 metres high when fully grown.[173] They have a gnarled trunk of hard wood (prized as firewood) and a dipping canopy of small, leathery leaves with small yellow-green flowers.

In the unlikely event of me being attracted to its fruit, the tree is armed with formidable thorns that would deter any rational person from attempting to climb to reach the unpleasant tasting bounty. This, however, is no deterrent to the local goats that easily climb the tree in search of a meal. Indeed, the sight of one, or more, of these trees festooned with feed-

---

173 Some trees are reputed to live up to 250 years

ing goats is one of the iconic sights of this part of Morocco. During the lean months of the year, browsing on the shoots and developing fruit of the argan tree provides the main sustenance for the goats.

Thriving in the calcareous soil of the semi-desert region of southern and south-western Morocco, argan trees have questing roots that dig deep into the dry soil in search of subterranean water. These long roots anchor the trees firmly against the strong winds common in this area and also, by binding the soil, protect against erosion. Physical characteristics, such as tough woody stems and small leaves, maximise water retention.

The fruit of the argan tree can grow up to 4cm long and 3cm wide but, in general, it is about the size of a large olive. Maturation of the fruit takes more than a year. A thick and bitter outer layer of peel encloses a pulpy pericarp within which is a very hard nut. Inside the nut is an almond shaped, oil rich seed.[174] Occasionally, the nut may contain two or even three seeds. It is the peel and the pericarp that the goats eat. The hard nut is indigestible and is excreted from the body with the faeces, or regurgitated with the cud and spat out with other indigestible food items.

The Berber people of this region have long valued the oil that can be recovered from the argan seed. It has been used as a food ingredient and in folk medicine for generations. Traditionally, the nuts were collected, having first passed through the digestive system of a goat. The next stage involved cracking the nut to harvest the seeds. Berber women, in the main, undertook this tedious task. This is achieved by placing the nut on a stone 'anvil' and cracking it with a smaller handheld stone 'hammer'. If the seeds are going to be used for culinary purposes, then they are lightly roasted. Once they have cooled down, they are ground and cold pressed. The unfiltered oil expressed from the process is decanted into storage vessels, left to stand for a couple of weeks, to allow the bulk of sediment settle, and decanted again. Natural argan oil always contains some residue of harmless sedi-

---

174 Each seed may contain up to 60% oil

ment. Unlike olive oil it cannot be used in cooking as it cannot take heat. Its culinary uses include a dressing for couscous and salads, or it may be used straight, like olive oil, as a dip for bread. In tandem with ground roast almonds and honey it forms a thick brown paste called *Amlou*, which is also favoured as a bread dip.

If the oil was to be used in folk medicine or cosmetics, then the stage involving lightly roasting the seeds was omitted.

Traditional methods of production in Morocco are becoming rarer. As the message got out about this 'super product', demand increased and traditional methods of production proved inadequate to this. Better, more industrialised methods of extraction, filtration and packaging were devised, which in turn demand a more efficient method of removing the peel and pericarp than the digestive system of the goat. It also allowed for the greedier side of our nature to expand into a new area of deception. It is reported that double the amount of oil is being exported from Morocco each year than the trees are capable of producing. It is like watered whiskey. The unscrupulous cut their overheads and double their profits by adulterating argan oil with ordinary cooking oil – who will be able to tell the difference anyway?

Argan oil's growing international popularity over the last decade, both as a component of cosmetics and as a healthy dietary supplement, has seen a boom in production and a consequent deterioration of the environment. Increasing wealth in the growing areas has resulted in an increase in the goat population and this, in turn, has seen increased damage to the argan trees, the source of this new prosperity.

We were lucky to taste the traditional stuff in a local home just outside Tafraout. Here they produced a small amount of oil each year for their own use. Small dishes of argan oil and olive oil were served to us with pieces of bread so that we could taste both of the oils and identify the difference. The Argan oil we got did include a little sediment but this didn't detract from its distinctly nutty flavour. It was pleasant and could readily be distinguished from the olive oil. As we were told to expect, it also had a slight musky odour, reminiscent of goat, but this didn't detract from our enjoyment. From the goat's gut to ours – not a bad experience at all.

Our only regret, while in the Amein valley, is that we didn't see any of the local goats in the trees. Later while driving from the coastal town of Essaouira to Marrakesh we came across these famous 'flying goats' clambering through the branches of the roadside argan trees, totally unconcerned about the fate that would befall their turds.

Argan oil is not the only highly regarded product that sees part of its production cycle residing in the bowels of an animal. While in Bali in 2013, Mary and I took a cab to visit Cantik Agriculture in Gianyar. This is a regular stop for tourists who decide to forsake the beach for a day and spend some time seeing a bit more of the island and its people.

On arrival, a guide from the plantation takes you along pebbled paths, through the grounds, and shows you the plants they cultivate, such as cacao, cinnamon, cloves, ginseng, ginger, lemon grass, turmeric, and vanilla, among many others. These plants are used to infuse a kaleidoscope of flavours into the teas and coffees produced by the farm.

At the end of the walk we were taken to a place where we could see the coffee beans being roasted and taste a selection of the coffees and teas they produce. In a cage nearby was a sleeping palm civet (*Paradoxurus hermaphrodites*).

Coffee is not native to Indonesia. It was introduced by Dutch colonists in the early 18th century. Locals were prohibited from picking the coffee cherries and thus their access to coffee, as a beverage, was severely constrained. However, the locals observed that the palm civets , which they called *luwak*, that roamed the coffee plantations also had a taste for the coffee cherries and during the night would feed on the ripe cherries. After consumption, the coffee beans passed, relatively unchanged, in their faeces. Clusters of beans could be found in dung where the civet marked its territory. The enterprising natives collected these beans from the droppings, cleaned them, roasted them and ground them to make coffee for themselves. The fame of this rich and aromatic coffee spread and came to the notice of the Dutch plantation owners, who soon developed a taste for it themselves. Given the novel method of production it quickly became known as lewak coffee.

From the outset, lewak coffee was relatively rare and, as a result, was always more expensive than normal coffee. In an attempt to cash in on this growing fame, some producers kept captive civets and fed them coffee cherries. It was felt that the selection of the strain of cherry and the internal processing the beans underwent in the civet's digestive system accounted for the alleged superiority of the final product. Currently, lewak coffee is the most expensive coffee in the world and can sell for up to €550 a kilogram.

Is it better than any other expensive coffee? This is questionable, as there is little objective evidence to show that it is better than coffee produced by the traditional method. Well, for me the jury is out and doesn't look like coming in with a verdict soon. Aficionados maintain that those who will not admit its superiority have not tried the real thing but have been served an inferior product. Those who have expertise in this area tend to disagree. In fact many experts find it disagreeable. The Washington Post food writer Tim Carman wrote[175] *'It tasted just like...Folgers.[176] Stale. Lifeless. Petrified dinosaur droppings steeped in bathtub water. I couldn't finish it!'*

When I tasted it in Bali, I found it acceptable, but not something I would go out of my way to find. In company with the many people who buy it in the shop in Cantik Agriculture and in shops throughout Bali, I bought a couple of small packets so that I could try it out on my friends.

---

175 *Carman, Tim (4 January 2012). "This Sumatran civet coffee is cra*(sic)*...really terrible". The Washington Post.*

176 The largest-selling ground coffee brand in the United States

Its cost has little to do with its superiority, more to do with its rarity and the willingness of 'foodies' to pay over the odds for a new sensation they can boast about.

Whatever the truth of its taste, one thing is sure; it is a really good story. When I serve from my diminishing supply to my friends, and they say to me 'your coffee is shite!' I can reply, 'You don't know how right you are!' and watch the disgust creep into their expression as I explain to them the origin of their after dinner espresso. This alone makes it worth the cost.

# CHAPTER 17

*The Dutchman and the Man of the Forest*

It was one of those things I shouldn't have done, but bravado compelled me. We were hungry and had stopped for lunch at a rural roadside eatery, somewhere between Sepilok and Sukau in Sabah, Borneo. It was housed in a gloomy wooden hut so dark that we could barely see the two other occupants, who, like us, had taken places at the rickety bar. We ordered *Mee Goreng* with a side of the boiled greens. We never could tell what these vegetables were, and, as they were one of our daily 5, we numbered them sequentially as spinach number 1 through to spinach number 12, representing the twelve varieties of unidentifiable leaf we had consumed so far on this trip. Like most of the meals we had it was very tasty.

On the counter at which we were seated was a small dish of thick black-red condiment. I asked Adi what it was and he said 'Chilli'. 'Oh great', I said. 'I like chilli.' 'It is really hot', responded Adi. 'I like hot chilli', I said. 'No it is really, really, really hot', he replied. Having seen him take a couple of heaped teaspoons of it, and not wanting to appear a wimp, I took a spoonful and popped half of it into my mouth. To say regret was instantaneous would be misleading. However, it did occur within nanoseconds. Floods of tears descended my cheeks, snot streamed out of my nostrils, and I could swear that steam came out of my ears. My scalp was sodden; rivulets meandered from my back and armpits and trickled down my body. My tongue felt as if I had licked the hot plate of the stove and my throat was on fire. I got the hiccups and started refluxing, sending the cause of my discomfort back up my inflamed oesophagus to further corrode my already scorched pharyngeal and oral tissue. I dreaded to think what would be the outcome if I had to void my bowels. The prospect of an incandescent and blistered rectal sphincter was not at all welcome. The obviousness of my discomfort did not invoke sympathy from Mary, or Adi, or our four other companions on this trip. The look on their faces was pellucid confirmation that they thought I was an idiot. I had been warned. I ignored the warning. I should now suffer the consequences in solitary uncomplaining misery.

The next morning we rose at six. I could still feel the effects of yesterday's chilli and purloined extra milk at breakfast to salve the burn. We had spent the night in a lodge close to the Sungai Kinabatangan (Kinabatangan River). The Kinabatangan River flows some 560 kilometres from its source in the Crocker Mountains of southwest Sabah to drain into the Sulu Sea, southeast of the city of Sandakan. Just a few kilometres shorter than the Rajang River in Sarawak, it is the second longest river in Malaysia.

For decades, the upper catchment of the Kinabatangan catchment has been subjected to intense logging and conversion to oil palm plantations. Huge areas of both Sabah and Sarawak have been converted to massive oil palm plantations, changing the ecology from ecologically rich primary or secondary forest to a monotonous monoculture that supports little in the way of wildlife. The twenty or so palm oil mills in the floodplain of the Kinabatangan produce over a million tonnes of effluent every year to further degrade the river.

While we may decry this activity, it has, undoubtedly, brought employment and prosperity to many in Malaysia, but at the cost of disruption of traditional life, appropriation of land and degradation of habitat. The hunger in the west for palm oil, which is used for cooking, margarine, spreads, soap, feed for farm animals, dog food, laundry detergent, lubricants, biofuel, and a myriad of household and industrial products, seems insatiable. Rainforest-rescue[177] has stated that it is so pervasive that it is now a component of as much as half of all supermarket products. Almost half of the palm oil imported into the EU is used as biofuel, a result of the requirement that, in order to reduce greenhouse gas (mainly $CO_2$) emissions, up to 7% of fatty acid methyl ester (FAME), an oil palm product, may be added to diesel. This has resulted in a logical inconsistency that does not appear to bother those in the first world – in that deforestation in tropical areas accounts for 10% of manmade $CO_2$ emissions. Greenpeace claims that the deforestation inflicted on palm oil producing countries produces more greenhouse gases than is removed by their addition to biofuel.

It is testament to our unrelenting quest to purchase things at the cheapest price possible, rather than source products derived from less ecologically damaging but more expensive raw materials, that manufacturers and food producers have clasped this 'wonder' ingredient to their bosoms. In this way, we are complicit and have seriously compromised our authority to decry the destruction of habitat and reduction of biodiversity in these countries. We bleat that governments and authorities (generally labelled 'they') should be doing more, while 'we' (the 'impotent' citizen) continue to do nothing other than enjoy the cheap consumables that are the end products of this destruction. A simple solution is in our hands – read ingredient labels and then make informed choices about what you buy. This is easy to say but inconvenient to do.

In the European Union, as of 2015, all products that contain palm oil have had to state 'Palm Oil' on their packaging.[178] A recent examination of products in my house revealed that a number of the spreads (including the one I use on my bread that claims proof of its efficacy in actively reducing cholesterol) contain palm oil, although the producer, Unilever, states on

---

177  www.rainforest-rescue.org

178  Following a ruling of December 2014, food packaging in the EU is no longer allowed to simply use the generic terms "vegetable fat" or "vegetable oil" in the ingredients list. Food producers must list the vegetable origin (e.g. palm, sunflower or rapeseed) and the phrase "in varying proportions"

the tub that it is committed to 'sustainable palm oil'. This prompted me to check other products and I found that palm oil is an ingredient in the manufactured cookies, chocolates, crackers and cakes I eat.

Is this a bad thing? Well, it may have been in the past when there was little public awareness of the depredation being inflicted on fragile and valuable habitat and indigenous farming and fishing communities, particularly in Malaysia and Indonesia. This led to many conservationists and international wildlife organisations seeking a boycott of palm oil. This position has changed somewhat in recent years. It is now appreciated that, per hectare, oil palm yields are more than four times that of rapeseed, which provides the vivid yellow patchwork of fields that, depending on your opinion, enhances or blights our summer landscape; and requires a tenth of the fertiliser and pesticides needed for soya bean[179] production – plantations of which have resulted in the destruction of swathes of the Amazonian rainforest and other fragile habitats in South America. Once oil palm plantations are established, these trees, like other trees, become important carbon sinks that convert carbon dioxide into oxygen. Notwithstanding this belated beneficial by-product, the effect of such plantations on biodiversity is nothing short of catastrophic.

The policy now adopted by international wildlife organisations is to cut the link between negative environmental impacts and palm oil, rather than seeking the elimination of its production, by promoting 'sustainable' production that provides safeguards for communities and sensitive habitats.

For chocolate lovers, of which I am one, Mondelez International (which owns Cadbury), Nestle, Lindt & Sprungli, Ferrero and Mars have committed to sourcing certified sustainable palm oil. While this may not be a solution to the problems of deforestation and degradation of wetlands and peat lands, it is a start. Manufacturers in developed countries must

---

179 A major component in the feed of almost all commercially produced poultry, pork, cattle and even farmed fish. It is also in the production of biodiesel, paint, ink, wax, and plastic products.

continually be held to account to ensure that actions they take to mitigate the negative effects of raw material production have meaningful and measurable outcomes lest they simply comprise 'greenwashing' that paints over the significant underlying problems.

The part of the river we were to explore in the lower catchment of the Kinabatangan flows through the largest remaining forested floodplain of Sabah. Here, original lowland forest and mangrove swamps have survived, largely because the land is permanently waterlogged and there are few commercially valuable trees. This part of the river provides a rich ecosystem with a remarkable and varied concentration of wildlife. We hoped to travel on the river and see as much of this as we could.

Near the lodge we boarded our small boat and set off in the steely grey morning light to keep appointments with the Dutchman and with the Man of the Forest. We knew that they were both in this area, but we didn't know exactly where, so we kept our eyes peeled from the outset.

Shortly after we had embarked, we spotted a small group of long-tailed macaques in the trees and riverside cliffs opposite our lodge. Before we could get close to them they disappeared, scared off by something in the riverine forest. We searched the trees and high on a fork in one of them we spotted the Dutchman sitting nonchalantly on a branch that gave him an unimpeded view up and down the river. We recognised him immediately because of his huge nose and the rather large pot belly he was lazily scratching. He gazed down on us in an imperious but disinterested way that barely acknowledged our presence. This did not disturb us. Indeed, we hoped he would remain this way for some time.

All around him, at least a dozen females and juveniles jumped from tree to tree, their boisterous activity obviously being what scared off the macaques.

Lest you haven't guessed yet, the Dutchman is a monkey. He gets this name from the Indonesian part of Borneo, where the species is still more widespread, with natives referring to him in Malay as *orang belanda* (which translates as 'Dutchman'), pointing to the similarity of big bellies and large red noses it shared with the aloof Dutch colonists who occupied the now Indonesian part of Borneo (Kalimantan) in the 19th and early 20th century.

Given its most noticeable endowment, its huge nose, it is unsurprising that the scientific name for this creature is *Nasalis larvatus* and that its English name is proboscis monkey. It is so well endowed in this department that it makes 'The Schnozzola' of the late, great, Jimmy Durante seem like a pathetic under developed imitation in comparison. Indeed The Schnoz would have difficulty competing with female proboscis monkeys, not to mention males. The nose, or proboscis, is the outstanding feature of this primate and although big in the female, often in the mature male it hangs lower than the mouth, where it can exceed 10cm (4.0in) in length and may have to be pushed to the side to allow the animal eat.

Proboscis monkeys are endemic to Borneo. This means that they do not occur naturally anywhere else in the world. It is one of the largest monkey species in Asia. Males can reach a body length of 76cm and weigh up to 20kg, while females are smaller reaching up to 62cm and weighing up to 10kg.

The fur on the back of the monkey ranges from bright orange through various shades of brown to brick-red. The fur underneath the body ranges from light-orange, through yellow to grey and the long tail is white. The face, including the prominent nose, is orange-pink in colour.

It is not uncommon to see a large male relaxing on a branch and flaunting his permanently erect, cherry red penis, set atop of his jet black scrotum. This endowment, together with his fleshy and pendulous nose, provides visible signals of his sexual readiness and prowess to any curious females.

Both sexes have bulging pot bellies. This is caused by their folivorous (leaf eating) and frugivorous (fruit eating) habit. They have complex chambered stomachs that rely on symbiotic cellulose digesting bacteria to digest their food.[180] This is a slow process of fermentation, so the contents of a full stomach can account for up to a quarter of the total weight of the monkey. As well as their favoured mangrove leaves, proboscis monkeys will also eat other leaves, shoots, seeds, bark, flowers, non-fleshy unripe fruit and the occasional insect.

Proboscis monkeys have partly webbed feet and hands that make them proficient swimmers. As divers, they leave everything to be desired as they leap up to fifteen metres from trees to hit the water with resounding, slapping belly flops. However they have a very efficient 'doggy paddle' type of stroke when swimming and can swim underwater for a considerable distance. Their proficiency in the water provides some chance of outpacing the saltwater crocodile (*Crocodylus porosus*) and the much endangered false gharial (*Tomistoma schlegeli*) (if it still exists in Sabah) that share these waters and which would regard them as a welcome meal should they catch them. Fragmentation of the forest forces monkeys from the trees in search of food. On land they are vulnerable to predation from the largest cat in Borneo, the Sunda clouded leopard and, despite its endangered and fully protected status, hunting by some native people who still consider them a delicacy. By far the greatest threat to them, however, is the progressive destruction of their habitat.

Troops of proboscis monkeys, consisting of a dominant male and up to ten females and their offspring, wander the tree tops in a continuous search for food. These foraging exercises are led by females, who also share the care of all the youngsters in the troop. The males defend the troop by making loud honking noises amplified, according to some, by their large nose, while at the same time baring their teeth. This is primarily intended

---

180 These bacteria do not occur in other non-colobine monkeys, apes or humans, who cannot efficiently digest cellulose. However highly digestible foods such as ripe sugary fruit is fermented rapidly in their stomach causing a build up of gas and causing the monkey to bloat. This may be fatal. This explains why proboscis monkeys prefer unripe, non-fleshy fruit.

to scare off rival males. Some troops are composed entirely of adolescent bachelors. The monkeys communicate through a range of nasal honks, roars, grunts and squeals.

Having spent some time watching this troop, we headed downriver. The birdwatching was sublime. Among the birds of prey we saw were several brahimny kites (*Haliastur indus*), two Blyth's hawk eagles (*Spizaetus alboniger*), their prominent tall crests and banded tails making them easily identifiable. Added to these two we spotted a crested serpent eagle (*Spilornis cheela*) perched on a tall dead tree. Stork-billed kingfishers (*Pelargopsis capensis*), black-capped kingfisher (*Halcyon pileata*) and banded kingfishers (*Lacedo pulchella*) provided flashes of colour as they flew along the river or perched on a branch overhanging the water. Plumed egrets (*Egretta intermedia*), numerous swifts and swiftlets, the oriental darter (*Anhinga melanogaster*), blue-throated bee-eaters (*Merops viridis*), the tiny blue-crowned hanging parrot (*Loriculus galgulus*), the large black hornbill (*Anthracocerosmalayanus*) and oriental pied hornbill (*Anthracoceros albirostris*) were all spotted beside the river.

As we returned to the lodge for lunch, we passed several more troops of feeding and resting proboscis monkeys. Suddenly, our guide called to us in an excited voice and pointed to the trees on the right riverbank. We stared for a bit at what looked like a very large orange-brown, scruffy ball of fur caught in a fork of branches. As we stared it began to move slowly and as it turned to look at us we saw that it was a large flanged male orangutan. Here was the second anticipated, but unexpected, object of our trip – the Man of the Forest.

This name orangutan has its source in Malay and Indonesian. It derives from two words, '*orang*' meaning person and '*utan*' (a corruption of '*hutan*') meaning forest. In effect orangutan means 'man of the forest'. Its scientific name is *Pongo pygmaeus* and it, like its long-nosed fellow primate, is endemic to the island of Borneo. A second species (the Sumatran orang-

243

utan) *Pongo abelii* is only found on the island of Sumatra. We had seen quite a number of these rare and endangered apes the previous day at the Sepilok Orangutan Rehabilitation Centre. This was set up in 1964 by the wildlife section of the Department of Forestry of the Government of Sabah and is run now by the Wildlife Department of Sabah. The purpose of the centre is to return orphaned, injured or displaced orangutans back to the wild. Having successfully undergone rehabilitation, the orangutans are released into the Kabili-Sepilok Forest, a virgin jungle reserve rich in tropical rainforest and mangrove swamp.

When we were there, seven orangutans turned up for the morning feed – mainly adolescents – while in the afternoon, when there were fewer visitors, two mothers carrying one year old babies made an appearance and, inadvertently, posed for snaps. While these were fun to watch and photograph, and the purpose of the Centre is laudable, I couldn't get over the feeling of a primate enclosure, albeit a very large one, in a zoo. The tangle of ropes strung from the forest and providing aerial access to the feeding platform up a tree, together with the adjacent and crowded visitor viewing platform only reinforced this feeling. I was more taken with the little spiderhunter (*Arachnothera longirostrata*) I saw feeding on banana inflorescences, the flying squirrel high on a tree trunk, and the mottled green pit viper resting in a shrub.

This viewing was different. We had actually encountered this endangered and rare ape free, in the wild. There was nothing contrived about the less than perfect photo opportunities he afforded us. He was perched in this fruiting tree for the sole purpose of guarding a food resource from all comers. Our presence on the river was of little interest to him as he did not perceive any threat from us.

The orangutan is a great ape,[181] in fact the only great ape in Asia and, like all the great apes is tail-less. It is one of our closest relatives and among

---

181 Gorillas, chimpanzees, bonobos and humans are the other great apes.

the most intelligent animals on earth. Sexual dimorphism is marked - males are much larger than females. An adult male orangutan can grow to a height of 1.5 metres. Their arms are much longer than their legs and they can have an arm span reaching 2.5 metres; males can weigh as much as 140kg, females half of this. Orangutans have long, sparse, orange or reddish hair unequally distributed over their bodies. Adult males have deep chests and much longer body hair than female. They have large jaws and flattened noses in concave faces. Mature males develop large cheek pouches, known as flanges that border the face and a pendulous throat sack under the chin. A feature that they share with humans is that they all have distinctive fingerprints.

Orangutans are the largest arboreal animals in the world, usually spending the vast majority of their time in the trees - eating, sleeping, and travelling in the canopy. On rare occasions, when they must, they can travel on the ground supporting themselves on their fists or the palms of their hands. Unlike the African apes, orangutans are not morphologically built to be knuckle-walkers.

They have unique methods of arboreal locomotion. They are tremendously strong and their long arms and mobile shoulder and hip joints are specifically adapted to facilitate brachiation, or hand over hand swinging between branches, and hanging on to tree branches, often upside down. Normally, they move cautiously through large trees by climbing and walking, a process greatly aided by 'quadrumanous scrambling'. This means that all four limbs are adapted to function as hands providing secure grip when stretching between branches and when reaching for fruit. In the case of orangutans, the possession of long curved fingers and toes and an opposable thumb and big toe makes this possible.

Almost every night orangutans construct a new sleeping nest from branches in a tree. Occasionally they may refurbish and reuse an old nest.

Alfred Russell Wallace, in his book *The Malay Archipelago* (1869), disputed the fact that a new nest was built every night, when he described the process of nest-building by the orangutan (he uses the native name of *Mias* interchangeably with Orang and Orangutan throughout this section) thus…

*'This is placed low down, however, on a small tree not more than from twenty to fifty feet from the ground, probably because it is warmer and less exposed to wind than higher up. Each Mias is said to make a fresh one for himself every night; but I should think that is hardly probable, or their remains would be much more abundant; for though I saw several about the coal-mines, there must have been many Orangs about every day, and in a year their deserted nests would become very numerous.*

*The Dyaks[182] say that, when it is very wet, the Mias covers himself over with leaves of pandanus, or large ferns, which has perhaps led to the story of his making a hut in the trees.*

*The Orang does not leave his bed until the sun has well risen and has dried up the dew upon the leaves…'*

Orangutans are primarily frugivorous (some 60% of their diet). However, they will also, if necessary, consume young leaves (25% of their diet), shoots, bark and flowers (approximately 10%). A range of insects such as ants, termites and crickets makes up the remaining 5%.

Among the most solitary of the great apes, males spend much of the time alone in the forest, except for those times when they mate with females. In order to advertise their presence to receptive females or warn away potential male competitors, males can produce a very loud, deep call, known as the long call, which is used to communicate over distance. The presence of enlarged throat sacs causes the long call to resonate. When a male meets a receptive female, they enter into a 'consort' relationship. During this period, lasting several weeks, they live in relative harmony. They also tolerate her previous offspring when they join together in feeding aggregations, as the young stay close to their mother until they reach adolescence.

---

182 Dayak was a catchall term for over 200 riverine and hill-dwelling ethnic subgroups in Borneo.

Adult males, particularly flanged males, are generally intolerant of each other and, if they do meet, they either try to avoid each other or else they fight. Fights are more likely if a sexually receptive female is in the vicinity. Fights, when they occur, are vicious and depending on the protagonists and their relative strength and skill, may last for minutes or up to an hour. Injuries are common and range from scarring on the face, flange or head; to having an eye plucked out; to missing fingers or toes.

Although the females do not form tight social groups and tend to forage in the forest with their offspring, they may establish friendly relationships with other females when their ranges overlap. At those times, when fruit is abundant, males and females may come together in large groups known as 'parties'. Within the party, individuals exhibit great tolerance of each other and are highly social.

Females will not have their first offspring until 15 to 16 years of age, although they become sexually mature earlier, when they have grown fully. Orangutan mothers look after their young for eight years; this, with the exception of single parent humans, is longer than any other animal single parent. During this time, she teaches them where to find the fruits that form much of their diet; shows them how to distinguish when they are ripe and demonstrates how to build a nest – a process that may take three or four years instruction before perfection is achieved.

Males may attain sexual maturity in their teens, but their flanges may not become fully-developed and males may not attain full size until they are in their twenties. Males without flanges are less successful in attracting sexually receptive females than fully mature males with flanges. Such unflanged males may resort to rape (described in the literature by the euphemism - 'forcible copulation') to spread their genes. It is likely that the presence of a dominant flanged male within the range of younger adult males delays the development of both flanges and full body size.

It was clear that the adult male we watched that August morning had nothing more on his mind than feeding and sleeping. After we observed him for some time we headed back to our riverside lodge in Sukau. As we breakfasted, a large saltwater crocodile slid down the bank from under a bush opposite where we were sitting, made its way into the river and swam away downstream towards where we had seen the proboscis monkeys. It was a fitting end to a perfect morning.

# CHAPTER 18

## *Frankenrat*

hile The Gambia may be world famous for its 540 recorded
species of bird, the story of its mammals is not so glorious
and, in common with much of West Africa, many have been
hunted to and, for a significant few, beyond the point of extinction.

The elephant (*Loxodonta africana*), formerly the symbol of The Gambia, is long gone. The last individual, spotted in 1913, was promptly shot.
Other extinctions within the last century include a number of antelopes,
including the buffoon kob (*Kobus kob kob*), the topi (*Damaliscus lunatus jimela*)
and the korrigum hartebeest (*Damaliscus korrigum*) as well as the red river
hog (*Potamochoerus porcus*) and the lion (*Panthera leo*) - to name but some.

From time to time antelopes of several species wander across the border from Senegal, but local hunters pursue them and they are either shot or
chased back from whence they came. Being a big mammal in The Gambia
guarantees a precarious existence.

Despite my lifelong interest in natural history, Mary and I were not
here to search for game animals, we were here to work. We took up resi-
dence in the Bungalow Beach Hotel - colloquially known as the BB. Our
*de luxe* room had a few advertised added extras over the normal rooms,
such as television (with a single watchable channel), in-room safe, towelling
bathrobes and air conditioning, but those that were not advertised included a family of geckos, marauding cockroaches, vampiric mosquitoes and a
couple of colonies of relatively harmless ants.

I love animals, but my tolerance only goes so far. While I am a fan of geckos, I spent some considerable time berating the indolent co-habitants of our quarters for not doing their work and leaving our nocturnal flesh exposed to the blood-sucking depredations of gnats such as the persistent and whining mosquitoes and tiny, stealthy, silent midges.

Spraying the colony of ants, as they ferried their eggs up from the subterranean nest beneath our patio, through tunnels carved into the crumbling wood of the framework of our door, caused me not a thought; smashing the 2 inch long cockroach that had the temerity to invade our bathroom evoked no pang of conscience. I chased the scuttling creature behind the toilet S-bend and into the shower tray where the crunch of its bursting body under the heel of my shoe was satisfying in the extreme. Our room may have been numbered B9 but my feelings towards these invaders of our privacy were anything but benign.

As a reward to myself for saving 'SHE WHO MUST BE OBEYED' from these marauding wild African animals, I treated us both to dinner at the 'Captain's Table' restaurant, just outside the main gate of the BB. Our table was set on an open patio allowing us dine *al fresco* under a shimmering crescent moon. The food was surprisingly good, both in value and taste, the Chilean merlot delicious, and the service excellent.

Bats and birds heading for nocturnal roosts flitted between the several thatched pavilions that make up the bulk of the restaurant. We were located in a courtyard near the entrance so had a good view of all the activity.

Several cats, as seems the norm in The Gambia, wandered the dining area. Presumably they are kept for their mouse and rat hunting proclivity. From what transpired, it was obvious that they had not expected **Franken-rat!**

An enormous rodent, literally the size of a cat, with a long naked tail, ran in the entrance, skated along the passageway; scooted in front of our table; scuttled up the steps and dodged left under the chairs of people beside us, escaping along the wall to a loud exclamation of 'Jeez!' 'Is THAT a RAT?' 'It's huge!' The scratching of its toe-nails on the tiled floor, as it sought an exit, added an interesting tonal counterpoint to the djembe drums throbbing in an adjacent establishment. To say our fellow diners were astonished would be an understatement!

I recognised it at once. It was a Gambian giant pouched rat (*Cricetomys gambiensis*). I had read about them before I came and brought a full description with me in the hope of seeing one. It is not a true rat but is part of a uniquely African branch of muroid rodents. The old adage that 'if it looks like a duck, quacks like a duck and walks like a duck - it is a duck' does not hold true here. While the giant pouched rat looks like a rat, runs like a rat and squeals like a rat - it is not a rat, but it is a rodent.

Two true rat species are present in The Gambia - the African grass rat and the West African shaggy rat – that in comparison to this fellow are mere lightweights. Indeed, the largest rat in Europe is less than half its size and a third of its weight.

Its name derives from the fact that, unlike true rats, (or indeed our domestic rats) it has cheek pouches like a hamster. These biological 'shopping bags' allow it to gather up several kilograms of nuts each night for storage underground. One study has shown that they are capable of transporting 3 kg in two and a half hours.

They are greedy little sods and have been known to stuff their pouches so full of date palm nuts that they are barely able to squeeze through the entrance of their burrows.

The burrows consist of a single long passage with side branches that contain chambers. One of these is reserved for sleeping, the rest are used for food storage. It is an omnivorous animal, feeding on vegetables (such as cassava, beans, sweet potatoes, and other roots), termites, insects, crabs, snails, and other items. Apparently, of all the foods available, it prefers palm fruits and palm kernels.

Gambian giant pouched rats are nocturnal animals. This appears to stem from the fact that they have little tolerance of the intense heat of the African day. They have little body fat so are also susceptible to cold.

In appearance they have coarse, brown fur and a dark ring around the eyes. They are very good climbers and swimmers. However, their eyesight is very poor so they rely heavily on their acute sense of smell and hearing. So acute is their olfactory ability that an organisation called APOPO now trains Gambian pouched rats to detect land mines and, surprisingly, tuberculosis. These trained pouched rats are called HeroRATS and it is possible to adopt one of them to help fund mine clearance efforts. You can choose a name for your HeroRAT and, as the APOPO web site explains: .... 'We will take you through your rat's development and training in real time, through to graduation where you can choose if your rat becomes a fully operational HeroRAT in TB Screening or Landmine Detection. We'll keep you informed of your rat's development along the way, and its REAL WORLD impact through your personalized my APOPO wall, where you'll receive badges as your rat progresses and see what impact your rat is having when it becomes operational.'

Normally considered harmless, they are reputed to make good pets. This used to be the case in the USA where they were imported as pets, but this practice has been banned since 2003 because of an outbreak of monkeypox. While some remain skittish and become aggressive, most, with regular handling and training, become friendly, and remain gentle and easy to handle. They are intelligent and playful. Like dogs they have a tendency to lick their owners and enjoy belly rubs; but like magpies they will also collect shiny objects and other treasures and store them in a hideaway.

Despite the good news on the pet front, all is not rosy in the garden when it comes to the animal in the wild. Some cases of deadly attacks against human babies have been recorded in South Africa.

The International Business Times on the 3rd June 2011 reported[183]

---

*.... 'Huge rats the size of a cat have killed and eaten babies in two separate attacks this week.*
*The attacks happened in slums near Johannesburg and Cape Town of South Africa.*
*A three-year-old girl from the Khayelitsha slum was killed by the giant rat as she slept.*
*Nobody heard a sound, until her 27-year-old mother discovered her daughter -with her eyes gouged out. She was apparently eaten from her eyebrows to her cheeks.*
*In a separate attack, a baby girl from Soweto town was attacked by giant rats. Her teenager mother, who had been out with friends, was arrested on charges of culpable homicide and negligence. The suspected species of the attacks are believed to be the African Giant Pouched Rats, a species native to sub-Saharan Africa.*
*They are the biggest rats (sic) in the world and can grow up to three feet long. Its front teeth can grow over one inch long, and they are nocturnal omnivores, capable of producing up to 50 young per year. The giant rats thrive in squalid towns.'*

---

Gambian rats are considered pests in urban areas, where they infest the sewers. In rural areas they often destroy farm crops and their large burrows can lead to soil desiccation and loss of plant crops. Like us, they enjoy the comforts of shelter and often inhabit barns and other farm buildings, which can result in property damage.

After the rodent's peregrinations through the restaurant, the shocked diners returned to their meals in a more subdued mood.

Suddenly, and not uncommonly in The Gambia, the electricity failed. Diners had sufficient time to nervously contemplate an invasion of battalions of these creatures before the generator kicked in.

The Gambian giant pouched rat has no true predators. Occasionally, a large bird of prey has been recorded as eating one. However, when threatened they band together and provide a formidable defence against potential

---

183  http://www.ibtimes.com/giant-rats-viciously-kill-eat-babies-644603

predators. The biggest predator of Gambian giant pouched rats is human. It is considered a delicacy and it features heavily in the bush meat trade. So popular a source of meat has it become that this has led to a significant drop in the population.

The rat did not feature as one of the meat options on the menu at the 'Captain's Table'.

However, its appearance and performance was both an unexpected and interesting addition to our night's entertainment. For me, at least, it added immeasurably to my dining experience.

We went back to the 'Captain's Table' the next week. Same ambience, same good service, same good food! Unfortunately, there was no repeat floor show. Frankenrat was a no show. Pity! The place wasn't the same without him.

# CHAPTER 19

## ❦

# The Wraith of the Rainforest

T he daughters of the sea god *Thaumas* and the sea nymph *Electra* - *Aello*, and her sister *Ocypete* - each had the body of an eagle and the long haired head of a beautiful woman.[184] Originally seen as the personification of destructive winds, the sisters became better known as the Harpies, whose literal meaning is 'snatchers'. They earned this appellation because of their habit of stealing food from their victims while they are eating: and their role in abducting evildoers and torturing them on their way to *Tartarus*, the bottomless pit, used as a prison for the wicked, where they would be further tortured, judged, and receive divine punishment. The harpies were seen as vicious, cruel and violent. Their name is now used as an insult and to describe cruel, grasping women in general. It is also used to describe one of the largest and most powerful birds of prey in the world.

Towering high above the surrounding trees, where we were standing in the Amazonian rainforest in Peru, was a majestic kapok tree (*Ceiba pentandra*). These trees can grow to a height of more than 70 metres, increasing in length by as much as 4 metres in a single year and their trunks can grow to a diameter of 3 metres or more. Being very tall, the kapok towers over the canopy of the smaller rainforest trees making it susceptible to any strong wind that might blow. Like most rainforest trees, the kapok is shallow root- ed to enable it exploit the nutrients in the rich upper organic layers of forest

---

184 Hesiod, the Greek poet describes two daughters Aello, and Ocypete as long haired and beautiful winged creatures– a description endorsed by contemporary decoration on pottery. Later Roman and Byzantine writers state that there are three sisters Aello, Ocypete and Celaeno and described them as being terrifyingly ugly.

floor soil, so it enhances its stability by developing large buttresses that extend from the trunk and connect with the roots in the ground. Its pink and white flowers emit an unpleasant (to us) odour that is attractive to bats. As the bats flit from tree to tree,when feeding on the nectar produced by these noisome blossoms, they cross pollinate the trees.

Native tribes have found many uses for the kapok tree. Its seeds, leaves, bark and resin are used in a wide variety of medicines, to treat fevers and kidney disorders, as well as digestive and bowel conditions. Kapok floss is harvested from the fruit pods of the tree and used to wrap around the base of the poisonous darts that the natives shoot from their blowguns. The soft, lightweight, wood of the kapok tree is used traditionally to carve dugout canoes,

The kapok we were standing beside marked the location of a rough wood hide perched on a bank above a gully. Below a small stream trickled its way down to the river. We had come here because it held a saltlick habitually used by some of the native mammals. Despite a stay of a couple of hours, we spotted nothing except the occasional bird as it flitted between the branches in front of us. We were wondering why our guide had brought us here, as we were due back in the lodge soon. The reason quickly became apparent when he instructed us to emerge quietly from the hide and look up into the branches of the kapok.

At first we couldn't see anything and then I spotted an enormous black, grey and white bird of prey perched where a branch forked off the trunk about 40 metres up. Immediately, I recognised it as a harpy eagle (*Harpia harpia*). This bird was always on my must see list whenever I visited Central or South America, but this was the first time I had been lucky. On reflection, it was obvious that our guide knew that the bird frequented this particular tree but didn't tell us in case we might be disappointed if it didn't arrive on cue. The view over the salt lick was intended to keep us occupied until it arrived. I was delighted, but a couple of my companions, who weren't sure what it was, were rather underwhelmed. It was only a large bird of prey after all – it wasn't a jaguar or something similarly 'exciting'. I won't tell you their reaction when they saw me lying down beside the trail photographing a crocodile of leaf-cutter ants making their way back to their nest.

One of the world's largest eagles, the harpy eagle, which can weigh up to 9kg, has a body that can measure a metre or more and it has a wingspan of up to 2 metres. Both male and female are alike, although, as is common with birds of prey, the female is somewhat larger than the male. It is armed with a black, viciously hooked, beak and, at 13 cm, its sharp talons are as long as those of a grizzly bear. Its plumage is distinctive – the feathers on its back are slate-black, its underside is mainly white, except for the feathered part of its legs, which are white and striped with black. The unfeathered, scaly lower leg and toes are yellow. The tail is black, with three grey bands on the upper side and three white ones on the underside. A broad black band across the upper breast separates the grey head from the white belly. The pale grey head is crowned with a double crest. All of this makes it a readily distinguishable bird.

Harpy eagles mate for life. Although they may be seen singly, they most commonly occur in pairs or, occasionally, three may be seen together. In this latter case it is generally the parents and a juvenile from their most recent breeding season. When hunting, however, they are solitary with females taking larger prey than the males. Daytime hunters, they use their keen sight to spot prey and may often perch for hours on a branch scanning the forest for signs of life.

Breeding usually takes place in April or May. The birds build a large platform of woven green sticks, usually in the main fork of the tree, some 20 to 40 metres above ground level. This is lined with soft vegetation and fur. The nest is refurbished each year by the resident pair.

Harpy eagles can lay two white eggs, but will only care for the first born – the younger sibling perishing from neglect and starvation. To say that incubation is undertaken by both parents is slightly misleading, as the female does the bulk of the work. It lasts for 56 days. During this time the male hunts for food. The downy chick fledges at 6 to 7 months. After this, and while the juvenile learns to fly, it is fed by its parents once every few days. This may last for another three or four months. The juvenile may remain in the parent's territory for up to a year.

The main prey of harpy eagles consists of tree dwelling mammals and, in particular, sloths – both two toed and three toed. Where we were, it was most likely that the brown throated three-toed sloth (*Bradypus variegatus*) made up the bulk of its diet. The body fur colour of the brown-throated sloth ranges from greyish-brown to beige. Stiff, coarse guard hairs overlie a dense, softer layer of under-fur. The outer hairs have numerous microscopic cracks across their surfaces that are colonised by a number of commensal species of algae, giving the sloth an overall greenish appearance. This helps it blend in with the foliage of the trees where it lives and feeds. Sloth hair also harbours a rich fungal flora so, if taken by a Harpy Eagle, it provides a full meal of meat and two veg.

As well as the brown throated three-toed sloth, the eagle will also take Hoffman's two-toed sloth (*Choloepus hoffmanni*), where their habitats overlap. While they seem to prefer sloths to all other forms of prey, other arboreal species that have occurred in its varied diet include, dusky titi monkeys (*callicebus moloch*) , common squirrel monkeys (*saimiri sciureus*), brown and wedge-capped capuchin monkeys (*cebus paella* and *cebus olivaceus*), monk saki monkeys (*pithecia monachus*), red howler monkeys (*alouatta seniculus*), and white-bellied spider monkeys (*ateles belzebuth*), as well as squirrels, opossums, anteaters, kinkajous, olingos, coatis and tayras. They do not confine themselves solely to arboreal animals but have been known to take armadillos and porcupines, agoutis, coatimundi, capybara, peccaries and brocket deer on the ground. They do not discriminate; as well as mammals they will happily take birds, snakes and other reptiles - as and when the occasion arises. As man intrudes more and more into their habitat and as the destruction of the forest continues apace they have been known, albeit rarely, to kill domestic livestock, including chickens, lambs, goats, and young pigs.

This huge predator can take prey weighing as much as itself, although the majority of its catches are much lighter. Their extremely powerful feet and talons can bring a force of up to $400N/cm^2$ to bear on its prey. This is an enormous force when you consider the main land predators in Peru. The force exerted by the harpy eagle's claws is 83% that of the bite of a jaguar (*Panthera onca*), which can bite straight through the skull of its prey. However, the force exerted by the harpy eagle is 65% greater than the bite force of the puma (*Puma concolor*) which has been known to kill deer, livestock and, sometimes, humans.

Harpy eagles generally hunt from a perch or fly a short distance between perches, near an opening in the forest, above a river, or beside a salt-lick (where many mammals go in search of mineral nutrients), as was the case with the bird we saw. Anything hidden in the foliage is relatively safe, but anything exposed on a branch is dinner. Once prey is spotted, the eagle quickly swoops in, fans its tail as an air brake and grabs the prey. Sensors in the pad of its foot cause the talons to sink in and penetrate the vital organs or the skull if the prey is caught by the head. Death is thought to be instantaneous and the eagle flies on, with barely a pause, to a perch where it will deal with its catch.

On occasion, they may also hunt by flying within or above the canopy, their relatively short and broad wings making them highly manoeuvrable between the branches. This happens most often when they are pursuing other birds in the forest.

Survival of the harpy eagle is threatened by habitat loss due to the expansion of logging, legal and illegal, agriculture and cattle ranching, legal and illegal, and prospecting – also both legal and illegal. Whether the human activity is legal or illegal is irrelevant, the destruction is long lasting and terminal for the species that once inhabited that forest. The current level of habitat loss for this species has resulted in the harpy eagle being classified as 'Near Threatened' by the International Union for Conservation of Nature (IUCN) and as threatened with extinction by CITES.[185]

It would be shameful, as is the case with innumerable species that have disappeared as a result of human ignorance and greed, if the harpy eagle were to disappear completely from the planet. This view, however, might not be shared by the sloths or monkeys – if they can have a view on the subject - to whom it appears suddenly, like a wraith from the rainforest presaging their sudden and violent death.

---

185 The *Convention on International Trade in Endangered Species*

# CHAPTER 20

*The Transmogrification of Aotearoa*

Some 700 years ago, as the two huge double-hulled canoes crested a wave, *Kupe's* wife, *Hine-te-aparangi*, called out *'He Ao, he Aotea, he Aotearoa – It is a cloud, it is a white cloud, it is a long white cloud.'* Thus the land got its name - Aotearoa or 'The Land of the Long White Cloud'.

What, in hindsight, is surprising is the fact that, as these Polynesian explorers circumnavigated the North and South Islands of Aotearoa, there were no human inhabitants anywhere. It is hard to conceive that such an expanse of land had yet to be colonised. This was just before the beginning of fourteenth century.

Elsewhere in the developed world it was a time of turmoil that marked a hiatus between the intellectual and mathematical advances of the Middle Ages and the philosophical, cultural and scientific advances of the Renaissance. The fourteenth century saw the Black Death rampaging throughout Europe; a great famine in its second decade killed millions; the hundred years' war raged for much of the century; the Ming dynasty took over from the Yuan (or Mongol) dynasty, and China, although entering a cultural golden age, became isolationist, expelled foreigners and closed the land route through its borders. On the positive side, Boccaccio wrote the *Decameron*; Dante completed the *Divine Comedy*; Shi Nai'an penned the great classical Chinese novel, the Water Margin; and Giotto finished his masterwork, the fresco cycle in the Scrovegni Chapel in Padua.

Aotearoa was a land of wonder. As well as the absence of human inhabitants there was an almost total absence of land mammals – in fact there were only three, the long-tailed bat, the greater short-tailed bat and the lesser short-tailed bat. Of these, the greater short-tailed bat has been considered extinct since 1967.

The land was heavily forested (closed forest covered up to 90% of the land) and had a unique, highly endemic and abundant avifauna. The early settlers found that the islands, like those they had come from, had no harmful animals such as poisonous snakes, and scorpions and its one venomous insect a poisonous spider – the katipō, or night stinger[186] – was rare and confined to coastal sand dunes. This general lack of mammals led to Aotearoa being described as 'a land without teeth' – a situation that was to change completely with the arrival of man.

On the thirteenth of December 1642, the Great Dutch explorer Abel Tasman caught his first glimpse of the west coast of the larger South Island. Following a clash with the now established Polynesian inhabitants, Tasman was deterred from landing and never set foot ashore. Later a Dutch map maker named it *Nova Zeelandia* after the province Zeeland in the Netherlands. Over the several centuries of settlement since first arriving, the Polynesian settlers had by now developed a distinct and unique culture and described themselves as '*Māori*'.

As with any colonists, the *Māori* endeavoured to exploit the easily accessible assets of the new country and, where necessary, modify the landscape to serve their needs.

The native forests of New Zealand were very vulnerable to fire. Although the early settler population was small, much of the South Island's lowland forest was destroyed by fire, both deliberately and accidentally, within a couple of centuries of initial settlement. Repeated re-burning of

---

186  A relative of the American Black Widow and Australian Redback spiders, katipō are so rare that they are now classified as a threatened species. Only the pea sized female katipō (the male is about a quarter of her size) can bite. Although their bite is highly venomous, there have been no reports of fatalities since the 19th century. It is a non-aggressive spider, occupying a restricted coastal sand dune environment and nearly needs to be trodden upon before it will bite. Due to its increasing rarity (it is currently classified as rarer than the kiwi) it is illegal to collect or deliberately kill them.

these areas prevented the forest from re-establishing. By the time the first European settlers arrived in the mid-nineteenth century 40% of the forests had been replaced by grass, bracken and scrublands. Despite this, when the first Europeans arrived, in 1772, there was still thick, dense forest cover.

European settlers exploited the forests for gum (to make varnish and linoleum) and timber (for repairs to sailing ships, for construction and for export) and used slash and burn methods to clear land for gardening and farming. Policy encouraged land clearance, as settlers lost homesteads they had been granted if they did not clear enough bush. By 1840 forest covered around half of New Zealand. Over the next 150 years, intensive logging reduced the remaining forests by about half. Currently, forestry cover in New Zealand comprises about 25% native forest (most in reserves and parks) and 8% exotic (mainly pine) plantations.

A major challenge for the Polynesian settlers, who had arrived from tropical regions, was the fact that most of their traditional crops would not grow in New Zealand's temperate climate. The only successful transplant was the sweet potato (kumara).[187] Through trial and error a range of edible native plants and berries was discovered although some (such as the kernels of the fruit of karaka[188] and tawa trees[189]) required special preparation and cooking (such as washing, steaming and grinding) to rid them of poison, before they could be consumed. The rhizome and tender palm heads of the cabbage tree (*Cordyline australis*)[190,191] as well as rhizomes of the common

---

187  *Ipomoea batatas*

188  *Corynocarpus laevigatus*

189  *Beilschmiedia tawa*

190  Interestingly, the trunk of the cabbage tree is so fire resistant that early European settlers used it to make chimneys for their huts (http://www.doc.govt.nz/nature/native-plants/cabbage-tree-ti-kouka)

191  In 1987, a parasitic organism called a phytoplasma started to kill off cabbage trees in the North Island. This was spread from tree to tree by a tiny sap-sucking insect, the introduced passion vine hopper. The phytoplasma is native to New Zealand flax, and early last century destroyed the extensive flax swamps of Manawatu, thus contributing to the collapse of the once flourishing flax fibre industry.

bracken fern *(Pteridium esculentum)*[192] became essential items in the Māori diet. The abundance of fish (sea fish and freshwater fish, eels and lampreys) as well as molluscs, crayfish and crabs, ensured a healthy and varied diet.

Due to its long isolation from other landmasses, evolution of animals in New Zealand took a different track to other parts of the world. This is clearly demonstrated by the archaic endemic genus of frogs *Leiopelma*[193] – of which the four remaining species are all either threatened or endangered[194] - and the tuatara *(Sphenodon punctatus)*[195] - the so-called 'living fossil'. While many species of marine mammal, such as whale and dolphin[196] and eight species of seal[197] can be seen around the New Zealand coast, only three indigenous terrestrial mammal species, all bats, are known.

The unique avifauna of New Zealand is a testament to geographic isolation. Seventy percent of all freshwater and terrestrial species are endemic. In the absence of mammals, birds diversified into ecological niches occupied by mammals in other areas of the world. However, given their specialised feeding habits (many had become ground foragers) and the relative lack of natural predators for many of these species, they were partic-

---

192 It is now known that bracken contains a carcinogenic chemical (ptaquiloside), and should not be eaten at all.

193 These frogs differ from other species in that they have no external eardrum; they have round (not slit) eyes; they do not have webbed feet; they don't croak regularly like most frogs and they don't have a tadpole stage.

194 Of the eight introduced frog species only three managed to establish themselves. However, of the remaining three species, the Bell frogs (*Litoria aurea* and *Litoria raniformis*) are also endangered.

195 Tuataras are rare, medium-sized reptiles found only in New Zealand. They are the only surviving members of the order *Sphenodontia*, which was represented by many species during the Mesozoic era. All other species, except for the tuatara, became extinct about 60 million years ago.

196 Hector's dolphins are among the world's smallest marine dolphins – up to 1.5m in length. They are found only in the inshore waters of New Zealand. Two sub-species exist: the South Island Hector's dolphin (*Cephalorhynchus hectori hectori*) which is found around the South Island of New Zealand, and the Māui dolphin *Cephalorhynchus hectori maui*) which is found off the west coast of the North Island. They are the only dolphins in New Zealand with a rounded black dorsal fin. Their bodies are a distinctive grey, with white and black markings and a short snout.

197 New Zealand sea lions are only found in New Zealand and are one of the rarest species of sea lion in the world.

ularly vulnerable to man, to the animals he introduced and to his penchant for habitat destruction and modification.

Early *Māori* bought kiore[198] (Polynesian rats) and kurī (dogs)[199] as a valued source of protein and also, in the case of the kurī, clothing. Easily caught forest birds provided an irresistible and abundant source of succulent flesh. Two of the ground foragers encountered by the settlers were the huge moas (of which there were ten species[200]) and the kiwis (of which there are five species).

The moas were large browsers, and were in turn the prey species of the massive Haast's eagle (*Harpagornis moorei*). Both the moas and the eagle became extinct shortly after the arrival of humans – some sources say within one hundred years. Human hunters killed and ate moas of all ages, as well as feasting on the birds' eggs. Large piles of moa bones can be found at many archaeological sites. The two largest species, *Dinornis robustus* and *Dinornis novaezelandiae*, reached about 3.6m in height and weighed about 230kg – an irresistible source of easily caught fresh meat. Extermination of the moa populations deprived the Haast's eagle of its primary food source, leading to the extinction of that species as well. Loss of its prey species and habitat destruction is also believed to have been the cause of the extinction of Eyles's harrier – an eagle sized bird of prey with a wingspan of almost two metres.

Kiwis fared better than the moa and, although endangered, are strictly protected. These flightless birds, around the size of a domestic chicken, are the smallest of the living ratites (ostriches, emus, rheas, and cassowaries),

---

198 *Rattus exulans*

199 *Canis familiaris* – the Polynesian dog became extinct in New Zealand after the arrival of European settlers when, presumably, they began to interbreed with dogs brought in by the settlers.

200 Authorities seem to differ on the number of moa species – it ranges from 9 to 11. Here I have adopted the number given on p182 of The Hand Guide to the Birds of New Zealand by H Robertson and B Heather (2015) Penguin Random House New Zealand.

and, proportionately, lay the largest egg in relation to body size of any bird in the world. Deforestation and introduced mammals (stoats, dogs, ferrets, possums and cats) remain the main threat to their survival.

By the time of European settlement two hundred years ago, Polynesian rats had already rendered the tuatara extinct on the mainland. As a sit and wait predator, juvenile tuatara which are diurnal (unlike their cannibalistic elders who tend to be nocturnal) are highly vulnerable to rats. The fact that tuataras breed very slowly means that if predation pressure is high losses cannot be made up.

The kiore is implicated in the extinction of Scarlett's shearwater, the South Island snipe, the stout-legged wren, Hodgen's rail, the New Zealand owlet-nightjar and the greater short-tailed bat. It also helped hasten the demise of three of the endemic frog species whose extinction is attributed to rats.

Following initial colonisation, it appears that the *Māori* first exploited the larger game animals – all the moa species, geese, swans, adzebills, takahē, shags, large penguins, New Zealand sea lions and fur seals. As numbers of these prey species declined, they came to rely on shellfish, fish, eels and plants. Indeed, middens show a change in the type of shellfish that were exploited as areas became locally depleted and attention was turned from the larger easily detected species to smaller species.

Thirty seven species of birds became extinct following the arrival of the *Māori* and prior to the arrival of Europeans.

By the time Captain Cook 'rediscovered' New Zealand in 1769 half of the endemic bird species were already extinct. Cook brought with him ship rats which escaped ashore and accelerated the extinction of nine more bird species including piopios, kokakos, huia, New Zealand Merganser, Laughing Owl and others.

Currently, there are eighty eight endemic birds listed in *The Hand Guide to the Birds of New Zealand* (by H Robertson and B Heather (2015)). Twenty five percent of these are cited as being either rare or very rare. Nine native birds are listed as 'critically endangered' on the *2006 IUCN Red List of Threatened Species.*

European mariners released pigs and introduced potatoes to New Zealand in the late eighteenth century. The years following Captain Cook's voyages saw new migrants, mainly Europeans, bring in farm animals and a host of non-native crops. The habit of introducing new species from the colonies into Europe and bringing European species that might have a use into new lands, although an age old practice, was brought to new levels by the middle of the nineteenth century. Acclimatisation Societies that en-couraged the introduction of non-native species sprung up in Britain and Europe and settlers to New Zealand imported the philosophy. The new settlers saw the forests as being devoid of game and the rivers as bereft of fish. The Acclimatisation philosophy gave them a rationale to underpin their attempts to improve on nature's perceived failure. They proposed in-troducing all kinds of familiar species of plants and animals from Europe, as long as they were deemed as being 'innoxious.'

The approach was to address deficiencies in agriculture by introduc-ing farm animals; forestry by introducing economically valuable trees; sport by introducing game animals and birds; domestic animals for pets and song birds for familiarity or to combat insect pests.

This saw the introduction of chickens, geese and ducks, pigeons and doves, cats and dogs, horses, donkeys, cattle, sheep, goats, pigs, bullocks for transport, possums for fur. Rabbits and hares were introduced for shooting but as they became a nuisance stoats, ferrets and weasels were introduced to control them. However, these developed a taste for the more easily caught native birds and rapidly became pests in their own right.

A range of game birds was introduced for sport and included the mallard duck, pheasant, wild turkey, helmeted guineafowl, partridge, quail, and chukor among others. The desire to hunt larger animals saw the introduction of chamois, red deer, fallow deer, rusa deer, sambar, sika deer, moose (introduced, but didn't thrive and it is moot whether there are any left), wapiti, white-tailed deer, pigs and the Himalayan tahr. There are no bag-limits or seasons for hunting large game, largely because several of these are now regarded as pests (red deer, chamois, sika deer and pigs) because of the environmental damage they cause.

Beginning in the 1860s, salmon and trout – both brown and rainbow – were introduced to rivers for angling purposes. The Chinook salmon was introduced into New Zealand rivers on the South Island's east coast more than 100 years ago. Unlike their Alaskan counterparts, fish from New Zealand do not spend as long at sea, three as opposed to four years, and consequently do not grow as big. However at an average weight of 7kg they are the biggest fish in New Zealand freshwater.

Brown trout quickly established in rivers and developed healthy breeding populations. Typically, fish are caught at 1 to 2kg but specimen fish have been caught at 5kg.[201] Rainbow trout were also introduced but are less widespread as there is no natural dispersal. Brown trout are known to sometimes migrate to sea and colonise new waterways.

Twenty-one species of freshwater fish have been introduced to New Zealand and have established self sustaining populations. Brown trout, rainbow trout, brook trout, lake trout, Atlantic salmon, chinook (or quinnat) salmon, sockeye salmon, perch, tench and rudd (in Auckland – Waikato only) are managed as sports fish in New Zealand. The remainder are deemed to pose a significant threat to freshwater biodiversity and legally binding attempts are being made to restrict their distribution. Two species,

---

201 Monster fish are also caught from time to time. The largest I could find in a web search was a 42lb 1 ounce (19kg) monster from the Ohau B hydro canal in South Canterbury.

koi carp and gambusia, were detected in the South Island for the first time in 2000, most likely as the result of illegal introduction. While the Acclimatisation Societies have disappeared, the desire to introduce exotic species, for personal reasons or gain, seems alive and well. Introductions, as always, have unintended consequences. The New Zealand grayling, *Prototroctes oxyrhynchus*, a species that spawned in freshwater but developed to maturity at sea – like the salmon - was found only in lowland rivers and streams and declined significantly post 1860. The last known specimen was caught in the early part of the twentieth century. Deforestation and its effect on river water quality and competition from introduced feral trout most likely contributed to its demise.

The introduction of exotic animals is not the whole story. By 2000 it was estimated that over thirty thousand plant species had been introduced. Of these over two thousand have become naturalised. Gorse and broom, introduced for hedging along with wattles and Hawthorn, are now regarded as major weeds. Auckland has been dubbed the weediest city in the world, with exotic species far outnumbering native plants.

Other introductions by the Acclimatisation societies seem bizarre. When I first landed in New Zealand, I was both surprised and saddened to find that the bulk of the bird species I encountered in urban parks and gardens were the same as I encounter on a daily basis in my back garden in Ireland. Of the top ten garden birds surveyed in New Zealand, European songbirds occupy the top places as follows: 1 - house sparrow; 3 – blackbird; 4 starling; 6 – chaffinch; 8 – greenfinch and 10 – dunnock. As well as these, song thrush, skylark, redpoll, goldfinch, yellowhammer, and rook, together with some Asian and Australian additions, such as the myna and the Australian magpie, are common.

New Zealand may have been one of last countries in the world to be colonised by man, but settlers, both *Māori* and Europeans, in the short time they have been there, have endeavoured to modify it to make it as much a 'home from home' as possible. This is also clear in the architecture of their cities, the sports they play, and how they govern themselves. I really like New Zealand, but it takes effort to experience its truly unique aspects. Fortunately these are still evident in its magnificent geography, the remains of its wonderful indigenous flora and fauna and in the character of its people – both *Māori* and European. While some still cling to the vestiges of a culture they may never have experienced directly, Kiwis are distinct, being inventive, hard working and some of the friendliest and most polite people on earth – especially to visitors.

# CHAPTER 21

$\sim$

# *Australia is Interesting*

Australia is very interesting; Australia is very nice; Australia is unique. Unfortunately, I cannot be more effusive that that. It is possible that my feelings are based on my experience that, in general, anything which is over-hyped is, ultimately, underwhelming. Over-hyping, sadly, infects many reports of those who have spent time in Australia on sun-soaked holidays or visiting relatives – activities, or lack thereof, that, by their very nature, are bound to amplify a feel-good factor.

I feel that European, but especially British and Irish, views of the continent are distorted by the seductive possibility of continuous blue-sky holiday weather that contrasts with the prevailing damp and grey reality of our northern climes. This is unsurprising when it is considered that the bulk of the population, of whom some 92% are of European origin, live within 20km of the ocean, with a significant proportion concentrated in an urban south-eastern arc extending from Brisbane to Adelaide. This is the Australia to which most wannabes aspire, but to me it represents a form of purgatory. Life is much more than sun, sea, stubbies, and shrimps on the barbie. I like weather in all its rich variety; I love seasons. I know that it is possible to find these in places in Australia, but, unfortunately, only in a very limited area. While I enjoy beer, beaches and barbecues, these provide punctuation to my life, not its purpose.

Why do so many people live on the coast? Well, much of Australia's 7.5 million square kilometres is arid and flat. One third of the land is desert and a further third is semi-desert or steppe. The harsh interior is typified by high summer temperatures, little rain and some freezing nights in winter. If you are looking for the middle of nowhere, then outback Australia is the place to look.

The fact that Australia, in recent times, has become one of the most expensive countries on the planet; that property in the urban south-eastern arc is eye-wateringly expensive; that fuel, food and drink prices encourage inertia, dieting and abstemiousness has created the new phenomenon of 'ping-pong poms' - people, especially English, who, attracted by the seductiveness of a then burgeoning economy and the promise of a fun-filled and sun-fuelled party life that contrasted with the grey austerity of Europe, emigrated to Australia only to return home again, home-sick, disillusioned and disappointed. Despite its booming economy, a record 91,737 people left Australia for ever in 2012/13, 48.9% of whom were Australia born. Hannah Ewens of the 'Telegraph', in 2015,[202] reported a recent survey, from Removals Company *MoveHub*, showed that for every one of their customers from across the globe who moves to Australia, three were leaving. The countries they were leaving for in greatest number were the UK, New Zealand and other European countries.

While in Australia, we travelled widely by air and by road. We started by exploring the western cities of Perth and Freemantle before heading to Darwin and the surrounding areas of Katherine and Kakadu. A flight to the centre took us to Alice Springs, the Olgas and Uluru. From there we headed to Cairns to see the solar eclipse of 2012 and to visit Daintree and the Great Barrier Reef, and followed this with stays in Sydney (with a side trip to the Blue Mountains), Canberra, Melbourne, the Great Ocean Road, and a number of wineries and Adelaide. This was barely sufficient to give us a taste of this vast continent/country sufficient to shape some informed impressions; but insufficient to claim that we know the country or its people well.

Perth was a refreshing contrast to the cloying, efficient, conservative, ordered and manicured atmosphere of Singapore, where we had spent a

202 http://www.telegraph.co.uk/expat/expatlife/11723866/Is-the-sun-setting-on-the-Australian-dream.html

few days. While we enjoyed wandering the back streets of Singapore and visiting its parks, temples and brightly illuminated streets at night, it is still too anal for me. Besides, I am not a huge fan of high rise modern architecture and brilliant white buildings made to look like huge lotus blossoms, nor am I enamoured of the cast concrete Merlions dotted around the place that symbolise the city-state. What was interesting was seeing an up-market shop selling Dragon Brand cases of small, white, bird's nests for the exorbitant price of $1100 – something over €700 at today's rate. I previously saw such nests being collected when I was in Sarawak (Malaysia). Locals risked life and limb, generally for a pitiable reward, to climb high on bamboo scaffolding in huge caves in order to dislodge the nests of swiftlets, so that the rich in Asia could enjoy the rather tasteless bird's nest soup they extracted with boiling water from the congealed saliva of these pretty little birds.

A memory of Singapore is that we, and a large majority of the populace, used an umbrella to protect us from torrential rain and, when it was dry, we used umbrellas to protect us from the blistering sun. Walking in Singapore was also rendered unpleasant because of haze caused by large-scale burning in Sumatra and Borneo. This has led to strained relationships between Indonesia, where the land clearance is occurring, and Singapore. Paradoxically, Singaporean capital finances many of the oil palm companies that are responsible for the burning.

Perth's reputation is as an easy-going city, and its sunshine, outdoor, lifestyle is well earned. Having just landed on the continent, our first taste of 'bushland' was King's Park, one of Perth's most popular attractions. Here I got my first sighting of the famous and ubiquitous pink, grey, white and noisy galah (*Cucatua roseicapilla*). Indeed, in the time I spent in Perth and along the Swan River and in Yanchep National Park, I saw over forty species of bird, several of which were new to me. The park contains a very interesting walk called the Boodja Gnarning Walk. Interpretive signs, illustrated with artwork from the *Nyoongar* people, help visitors get the most from a stroll. It breaks into two separate trails known as the *Maarm* (male) track and the *Yorga* (female) track. This is not a limitation in terms of use as both are open to either gender. The tracks highlight the different roles and purposes of the *Nyoongar* men and women who visited this place at different times of the year.

The best way to get to Perth's port of Freemantle is by cruising along the Swan River. This small town has a really nice and vibrant ambience. However, neither Perth nor Freemantle feels unique and a visit feels like putting on a new but familiar costume.

In order to get our first kangaroo and koala fix over, we headed some forty kilometres north of Perth to the small Yanchep National Park. This area of bushland and wetland provides a home to western grey kangaroos, and a walk along its raised boardwalk permits observation of koalas. If this is the 'real' Australian bush, it is very tame and very controlled. With picnic tables, free gas barbecues and long beautifully paved walks and a golf course, it is more theme park than wildlife reserve. At least the laughing kookaburra (*Dacelo novaeguineae*) we saw, unlike the koalas, was free and could leave the park whenever it wanted.

Flying up to Darwin and the Northern Territory was like entering a new world. Some of the oldest occupied sites in Australia can be found here and it was one of the last areas to be colonised by Europeans. This is 'Crocodile Dundee' country, but the grizzled white 'characters' and eccentrics who live here seem apart from the landscape as they attempt to bend it to their will, while over 40,000 years of indigenous Aboriginal occupation had developed a culture that is at one with the land and takes it for what it is.

Darwin is a pleasant town but has little to distinguish it from other Australian towns. Its new waterfront quarter is brimming with hotels and restaurants and boasts a new swimming lagoon that is kept stinger and crocodile free – a blessed relief from the sometimes unbearable heat and humidity. It is a town for settlers and immigrants. The few Aboriginal people we saw were those living hand-to-mouth on the street. This was a sight that was to repeat itself again as we visited Katherine and Alice Springs. Local attitude, as it appeared to us, falsely or not, still looks upon these people as something sub-human. Our attitude to white Australian prejudice towards the aboriginal people was informed by both the attitude and discourse we experienced while we were there. This, generally negative, attitude poisoned, to some extent, the view Mary and I took home of Australia.

The illegal expropriation of land by the early English settlers, was justified by regarding all of Australia as unoccupied (despite the very obvious, though in places transient, occupation by indigenous tribes), to the extent of inaccurately describing it as *terra nullius* (nobody's land). This precept of international law was used to justify appropriation of a whole continent. This spurious legal fiction was only successfully challenged as recently as 1992, when judgement in the *Mabo*[203] case held that native title to land still existed unless it had been extinguished by statute. The few legal successes that the indigenous people have had over the past 25 years have been diluted by subsequent legislation, largely as a result of the implications of such decisions for the rich and powerful. Paradoxically, the contention that Australia was *terra nullius* was given the lie by the white settlers themselves, as it was they who gave the indigenous people the title of Aborigines – whose definition implies those who inhabit or exist in a land from the earliest times, or from before the arrival of colonists.

Aboriginal people were, and in some cases still are, viewed as less evolved than whites and weak and degenerate in their habits. Many of the interventions to aid them, while well-meaning, were paternalistic, harsh, ignorant (particularly in terms of culture and traditions) and, in many cases inhuman.[204] Things now appear to be improving and many aboriginal people have carved successful careers and businesses for themselves. But,

---

203 Named after the Murray Islander (in the Torres Straits) Eddie Mabo who fought for decades for his land rights but, sadly, died before the ruling was given.

204 Incarceration, removal, relocation, break-up of families, requiring permits to move between reserves or to marry, indentured labour, taking away children of mixed race etc.

until Australians, who live in the cities, drop their prejudice and change their attitude progress will remain painfully slow. It was indeed disheartening to speak to some of our friends who live in Australian cities and hear their vociferous and negative opinions of the indigenous people.

Research commissioned by *Beyond Blue* in 2012 revealed that of those surveyed:

- 41% believe that Aborigines are given an unfair advantages by the government
- 37 % believe that Aborigines are sometimes a bit lazy (whatever 'sometimes' and 'lazy' mean)
- 29% believe that Aborigines should behave more like 'other Australians' (i.e. settled immigrant whites)
- 19% believe that terms (and jokes) usually considered racist are not that bad
- 21% would watch the actions of an Indigenous Australian in a retail environment

In a study by The Lowitja Institute, in Victoria,[205] 97 per cent of Aboriginal and Torres Strait Islander people surveyed experienced multiple incidents of racism. The survey showed that

- Almost every Aboriginal Victorian who participated in this survey had experienced racism in the previous 12 months.
- Most people had experienced racism multiple times, with more than 70% experiencing eight or more incidents a year.
- Racism occurred across a broad range of settings. It was most commonly experienced in shops (67%) and public spaces (59%).
- There were no differences in experiences of racism due to gender, age or rurality.

---

205 Ferdinand, A., Paradies, Y. & Kelaher, M. 2012, Mental Health Impacts of Racial Discrimination in Victorian Aboriginal Communities: The Localities Embracing and Accepting Diversity (LEAD) Experiences of Racism Survey, The Lowitja Institute, Melbourne.

- There were differences in experiences of racism due to education, with people educated at Year 12 or above reporting more experiences of racism compared to people with lower levels of education.

The more egregious manifestations of this type of abuse included....

- Being sworn at and being verbally abused - experienced by 84.1% of the study group

- Being deemed less intelligent - experienced by 81.9% of the study group

- Being spat at or having something thrown at them - experienced by 67.4% of the study group

- Being told they don't belong in Australia (despite being the first Australians) – experienced by 66% of the study group.

Casual racism appears endemic in Australia, especially where indigenous people are involved. Mary and I saw instances of it again and again as we travelled. No country, including my own, is free from intolerance (it is only necessary to look at how the Irish treat the Travelling community to show this) but, not excepting South Africa, Namibia and the USA, it appeared to us to be more overt and in your face, like a lot of things, in Oz.

The treatment by the Australian authorities of migrants, arriving by boat, by imprisoning them in offshore-detention facilities on two Pacific Island nations, Nauru and Manus Island (Papua New Guinea), has resonance in the 'White Australia' policy at the turn of the 20th century.[206] There is administrative cruelty in the futility inherent in the interminable processes of examining asylum claims. This process makes it clear that, irrespective of the merits of their case, the preordained outcome is that asylum seekers

---

206 Legislation specifically excluded 'any aboriginal native of Australia, Asia, Africa, or the islands of the Pacific, except New Zealand' from voting unless they were already on the roll before 1901. The *White Australia policy* did not represent any single policy but was the terminology used to describe a variety of historical policies that effectively barred people of non-European descent from immigrating to Australia. The policies were designed to exclude people from Asia (particularly China) and the Pacific Islands (particularly Melanesia). The policies were progressively dismantled between 1949 and 1973. https://en.wikipedia.org/wiki/White_Australia_policy accessed 07/08/2017

will never be permitted to settle on the mainland. People have been held in detention for years under a policy that is exclusive, mean-spirited, abusive, cruel and inhuman.

The Supreme Court of Papua New Guinea recently endorsed this view and ordered its Government to close the facility on Manus Island. The government has indicated it will comply. Despite this, the Australian Government is adamant that it will not change its policy. It knows this harsh and authoritarian stance has the support of the majority of voters – the very people who would also see more concessions to the Aborigines as diluting their own position and 'rights'.

One of my bucket list destinations was fulfilled when we got to visit Kakadu National Park. We had little time; so having driven along the Arnhem highway from Darwin we turned south at the small town of Jabiru and headed 50km further into the Park to reach an inland lagoon located at the end of Jim Jim Creek, a tributary of the South Alligator River, called Yellow Waters Billabong. We travelled with Aboriginal-owned Yellow Water Cruises. Before we went, I searched the web for a list of the birds we might see but to no avail. So let me, here, make a small start with the species I identified while in Kakadu –

| | English name | Latin name |
|---|---|---|
| 1 | Little Pied Cormorant | *Phalacrocorax melanoleucos* |
| 2 | Little Black Cormorant | *Phalacrocorax sulcirostris* |
| 3 | Pied Cormorant | *Phalacrocoeax varius* |
| 4 | Australian Darter | *Anhinga melanogaster* |
| 5 | Hoary-headed Grebe | *Poliocephalus poliocephalus* |
| 6 | Australasian Grebe | *Tachybaptus novaehollandiae* |
| 7 | Australian Pelican | *Pelecanus conspicillatus* |
| 8 | Jabiru (Black-necked Stork) | *Ephippiorhynchus asiaticus* |
| 9 | Brolga | *Grus rubicundus* |

| | English name | Latin name |
|---|---|---|
| 10 | Cattle Egret | *Ardea ibis* |
| 11 | Little Egret | *Ardea garzetta* |
| 12 | Intermediate Egret | *Ardea intermedia* |
| 13 | Great Egret | *Ardea alba* |
| 15 | Pied Heron | *Ardea picata* |
| 16 | Nankeen Night Heron | *Nycticorax caledonicus* |
| 17 | Black Bittern | *Ixobrychus flavicollis* |
| 18 | Australian White Ibis | *Threskiornis molucca* |
| 19 | Glossy Ibis | *Plegadis falcinellus* |
| 20 | Radjah Shelduck | *Tadorna radjah* |
| 21 | Magpie Goose | *Anseranas semipalmata* |
| 22 | Plumed Whistling-Duck | *Dendrocygna eytoni* |
| 23 | Wandering Whistling-Duck | *Dendrocygna arcuata* |
| 24 | Green Pygmy Goose | *Nettapus pulchellus* |
| 25 | Collared Sparrowhawk | *Accipter cirrhocephalus* |
| 26 | Whistling Kite | *Milvus sphenurus* |
| 27 | Osprey | *Pandion haliaetus* |
| 28 | White-breasted Sea Eagle | *Haliaeetus leucogaster* |
| 29 | Wedge-tailed Eagle | *Aquila audax* |
| 30 | Purple Swamphen | *Porphyrio porphyrio* |
| 31 | Comb-crested Jacana | *Jacana gallinacea* |
| 32 | Masked Lapwing | *Vanellus miles* |
| 33 | Black-winged Stilt | *Himantopus himantopus* |
| 34 | Caspian Tern | *Hydropogne caspia* |
| 35 | Whiskered Tern | *Chlidonias hybrida* |
| 36 | Bar-shouldered Dove | *Geopelia humeralis* |
| 37 | Sulphur-Crested Cockatoo | *Cacatua galerita* |
| 38 | Little Corella | *Cacatua galerita* |

| | English name | Latin name |
|---|---|---|
| 39 | Red-Tailed Black Cockatoo | *Calyptorhynchusmagnificus* |
| 40 | Rainbow Lorikeet | *Trichoglossus haematodus* |
| 41 | Hooded Parrot | *Psephotusdidissimilis* |
| 42 | Common Koel | *Eudynamis scolopacea* |
| 43 | Forest Kingfisher | *Todiramphus macleayii* |
| 44 | Little Kingfisher | *Ceyx pusilla* |
| 45 | Azure Kingfisher | *Ceyx azurea* |
| 46 | Rainbow Bee-eater | *Merops ornatus* |
| 47 | Dollarbird | *Eurystomus orientalis* |
| 48 | Rainbow Pitta | *Pitta iris* |
| 49 | Little Friarbird | *Philemon citreogularis* |
| 50 | Helmeted Friarbird | *Philemon buceroides* |
| 51 | Silver-crowned Firebird | *Philemon argenticeps* |
| 52 | Olive-backed Oriole | *Oriolus sagittatus* |
| 53 | Spangled Drongo | *Dicurus bracteatus* |
| 54 | Torresian Crow | *Corvus orru* |

This was not a bad haul for such a short stay, especially considering that we were travelling with a group of people following a fixed itinerary and not concentrating on birds.

Heading back towards Darwin we stopped off at the Adelaide River Crossing and took a jumping crocodile cruise. This is something very Australian and something about which I have very ambivalent feelings. It involves coaxing the saltwater crocodiles (*Crocodylus porosus*) that live in the river to jump up to 2m out of the water to snap at chunks of meat dangled from a bit of rope tied to a pole. The animals are repeatedly teased to get them to jump higher and higher until they manage to snatch a morsel. It is both disconcerting and exhilarating to sit in a boat and have a huge reptile surge out of the water right beside you, toothed mouth agape, and hear the loud clack of jaws as it snatches at the proffered bait. One of these days, it is going to see these happy snappers, gasping in awe in the boat, as a more accessible and larger meal than the pitiful morsel currently offered on the end of a stick by the crew.

We were in awe of the 80 year old, two tonne, and 5.5m (18ft) monster saltwater crocodile called 'Brutus' who jumped for food alongside our boat. My entire body would fit in his mouth alone. Brutus' right forelimb is missing – allegedly torn off by a shark in a fight. Well, Brutus had his revenge. In August 2014, pictures were published of Brutus attacking and then devouring a bull shark. However, the 'Match of the Monsters' was somewhat unequal as Brutus was about three times the size of his opponent. As well as Brutus, we saw several other crocodiles, one of whom was the flamboyantly named 'Dominator', who is believed to measure up to 6.1m (20ft), though nobody is willing to get in the water with a tape to measure him.

I have always held that you shouldn't feed wild animals. Indeed, most authorities frown on this sort of activity. It is particularly foolish when the animal is potentially dangerous to humans and you get it to associate humans with food. Ah! There's Australian macho for you.

Before we left Kakadu we had added a beautiful slender lizard called the northern water dragon and agile wallabies to our species list.

North of Jabiru at Ubirr, within the East Alligator region, is a group of rock outcrops. Here, several natural shelters hold a collection of Aboriginal rock paintings, some many thousands of years old. The art depicts creation ancestors as well as fish and other animals. From the top of Ubirr rock you have a panoramic view over the Nadab floodplain. In the distance we could see smoke from a couple of large bush fires – whether natural or controlled burning we could not tell. However, burning off has long been used as an effective land management technique by setting a number of small controllable fires in patches to stimulate new growth. Rangers in the National Park now apply the same technique, but the fires we saw were in November, outside the normal burning season of May and June.

We travelled from there via the stunning Burrunggui (previously called Nourlangie Rock), a sandstone formation of the Arnhem Land Escarpment. A number of shelters contain outstanding paintings representative of the Aboriginal Dreaming. Early art at the site is evidenced in handprints on the rock in red pigment. Some drawings depict introduced animals and European items and there are drawings of thylacines (Tasmanian tigers), which are known to have been extinct in the area for at least 3,500 years.

After over-nighting in the town of Katherine we started the day with a cruise through the Nitmiluk Gorge. The gorge is some 12 km long and was carved by the Katherine River through the ancient sandstone. The whole area is of great ceremonial significance to the *Jawoyn* people, the custodians of the National Park. As with some other areas that were sacred to the indigenous people, places in the gorge hold paintings and drawings of great significance.

We saw several of the freshwater crocodiles (*Crocodylus johnsoni*)[207] that frequent the river, but are harmless to humans. As a result, swimming is permitted in the gorge during the dry season when the water is low. In the wet season, when the water rises, saltwater crocodiles may be found and swimming is forbidden. These are removed when the water levels fall again – however, if one is missed … watch out.

Although the *Jawoyn* people own Nitmiluk Tours and are the custodians of the park, the café at the gorge provided us with another example of casual racism, when we saw a couple of indigenous people being demeaned and abused by a white employee.

We flew from Darwin to Alice Springs, which, surprisingly, I liked a lot. The town is low rise with leafy pedestrianised streets and a modern café/shopping culture.

In 1871, when surveying the route for the proposed overland telegraph line, the surveyor, William Whitfield Mills, followed a dry river bed which he

---

207 This species was named after the Australian policeman and naturalist Robert Arthur Johnstone (1843-1905). Gerard Krefft, who named it in 1873, made an error in writing Johnstone's name. In some references to this species it has been incorrectly named as *C. Johnston,* presumably to rectify the error in Krefft's spelling.

named the Todd River, after South Australia's Superintendent of Telegraphs, Sir Charles Hedley Todd.[208] This led him to a series of waterholes, the largest of which he named Alice Springs after Todd's wife.

'Alice,' as it is colloquially known, is almost at the geographic centre of Australia. Called *Mparntwe* (pronounced mbarn-twa) by its original inhabitants, the *Arrernte* people who have lived in the area for at least 40,000 years, the billabong is one of the sources of water Mills and his party used as they moved through the MacDonnell Ranges that run to the east and west of Alice Springs. The arid area surrounding Alice is known as the Red Centre, and is surrounded by desert: to the north is the Tanami Desert; to the east is the Simpson Desert; to the south are the Great Victoria and Perdika Deserts; and to the west the Great Sandy and Gibson Deserts.

Unfortunately, an increase in crime and a strong racial divide that has existed for years has plagued the town in recent years. Mark Schliebs reported in '*The Australian*' on February 23, 2011[209]...

*CRIME-PLAGUED Alice Springs is becoming a city divided along racial lines, with politicians, business owners and Aboriginal leaders agreeing that the influx of up to 1000 indigenous people is causing massive problems.*

*The Northern Territory Anti-Discrimination Commissioner, Eddie Cubillo, agreed there was a problem but said a "scaremongering" television advertising campaign funded by more than 100 business owners fed up with constant break-ins and alcohol-fuelled violence was fuelling racism in the small city.*

*Karl Hampton, the Minister for Central Australia, said he would contact his counterparts in South Australia and Western Australia to alert them to the fact that "large numbers of Aboriginal people from both states" were staying in Alice Springs.*

208 Also known as Charles Heavitree Todd

209 http://www.theaustralian.com.au/archive/in-depth/crime-wave-brings-racial-divide-to-alice/newsstory/108071993f6df4a81603c0760d78d357

When we were there, in 2012, the atmosphere between whites and indigenous people was strained, to say the least. We were treated with suspicion by the indigenous people and we observed several fights, drunken brawls and arrests.

A report by New Matilda in April 2015 suggested little improvement with time.[210] It stated ...

---

*'Locals are also making racist threats against Aboriginal people online, and posting about bashing, running over and even killing those involved in crime in the troubled Central Australian town.'*

---

It goes on to provide screen shots of some horrifying local reaction by whites against Aborigines, posted on the *Alice Springs Community Open Forum*, a closed Facebook page, who were either not afraid to include their name or were hiding behind pseudonyms, as follows:

1. Jacob Hutton posted: *'Beat the shit out of them.'*

2. Sean Parkinson posted: *'Be nice if you could load them in a road train of stock crates and send them back out bush. They wanna act like animals then get treated like one. Feel for my friend and family going they this horrible time (sic). Anyone think it's Africa.'*

3. Paul Vowles posted: *'If they walk out in front of me – I don't slow down. Yes I may hit a few But (sic) word will get around town soon enough.'*

4. Ricardo Barfuss posted: *'Typical dirty black fucks. Its* (sic) *obvious they are black good for nothing government funded animals that should be dumped out bush!'*

5. Lj Laurence Pomery posted: *'a good idea would be to declare an open season on them......naturally with a bag limit, possibly a bounty on matching pairs would be an incentive.'*

6. Jordi Little posted: *'Maybe we shoot the mulgar monkeys'*

---

210 https://newmatilda.com/2015/04/24/typical-dirty-black-fks-alice-springs-vigilantes-form-paramilitary-group/

7.  Michael Stiller posted: *Normal behaviour from these animals! It's disgusting! Time to string these animals up! Maybe a public stoning!*

I cannot think of another country where there wouldn't be a national outcry against such comments and calls for Facebook to remove the page. When I read this vitriolic diatribe, I couldn't believe that it emanated from a so-called civilised, modern democracy. With attitudes like this is it any wonder that Australia has problems. Multiculturalism, again, for many, seems to mean only one thing in Australia – you must be white and preferably European.

The Matilda report further stated…

*'Alice Springs residents are forming vigilante-style groups described as "paramilitary" forces and are threatening violent action against Aboriginal youths suspected of rock throwing, property damage and other criminal activity.'*

Why am I not surprised that this vigilante action was organised by a 'fellow' Irishman (albeit from Northern Ireland) and fairly recent immigrant, the bald headed, self-righteous, smug, Aran sweater wearing Garry Hall?[211] He must feel right at home having a new community to despise in his recently adopted homeland. He is the self-proclaimed spokesman for the AVF (Alice Springs Volunteer Force), described as a 'paramilitary force ready to defend.' No other members have been identified, but Hall – quite possibly its only member - has stated in interview that his 'group' will inflict 'bodily injury' as they see fit on lawbreakers. The ethos of this new group has chilling resonance with the UVF (Ulster Volunteer Force), which was responsible for much death and destruction in the land of Hall's birth. This is not coincidental. Hall admits that the UVF (widely regarded as a terrorist organisation) provided a template for this new organisation. I cringe in shame!

211  https://www.youtube.com/watch?v=ALmDuWTxU-0

Most white Australians I met were not racist, but, unfortunately, a significant minority were, and an atmosphere pervades that allows people of Hall's ilk slither to the surface. A huge part of the problem in Alice Springs is drink related. The most common solution tried? Ban the Aborigines from obtaining alcohol. The result? The secondary sale of alcohol has boomed, with the going rate for a bottle of rum in 2015 being $100 and a $10 bottle of wine selling on the street for $35. How do unemployed people get the money to fund their habit? Crime! QED.

In the 16 indigenous settlements on the edge of town, each representing a different tribal area of Central Australia, booze is banned, but is regularly smuggled in. The youth in these settlements have little to occupy them so frequently get drunk and get into trouble. This is the behaviour most often seen by whites and is what promotes the bulk of reaction. While indigenous people represent only 20% of the population of Alice, they are implicated in the bulk of antisocial behaviour. Short term solutions and punitive action is the common response. Banning alcohol doesn't work, especially when indigenous people can see it stored in profusion in the town's nine bottle shops for purchase by the whites.

Economic deprivation, squalor and sub-standard services in the settlements and camps add fuel to the problem. A solution that is not cross community and targets one sector of the population is doomed to failure. Examples abound of the failure of similar actions from around the globe, particularly in countries that were colonised. Perhaps a good start would be to ban alcohol for everyone – black and white. This would be a small price for whites to pay if it resulted in a decrease in antisocial crime and a better relationship with their fellow, but black, Australians.

Drinking booze is not a right, it is a choice. Perhaps the white population of Alice could make such a choice for the greater good. Maybe! But I doubt they would. Drinking culture is such an ingrained aspect of Australian life (as it is in many Western societies) that I could predict the outcry should such a simple remedy be proposed. Such selfless action is not impossible, but it is certainly difficult.

Another positive thing that could be done would be a strong nation-wide campaign to eliminate casual racism. This should not be a campaign built on penalties but on education. Asylum seekers should not be viewed as 'terrorists' simply because they want to escape economic deprivation or war in their homeland. Angry remarks such as *fucking Abbos, Chinks, Arabs, rag-heads, drunken Irish, whinging poms* and so on, may seem innocuous and merely an expression of frustration or stereotyping, but they have an un-derpinning regard of these groups as inferior. The irrational demand that people of colour, irrespective of when they arrived in Australia, should 'act Australian' (whatever that means) is meaningless – how do 'Australians' act that is different from other western countries? It is the unreasonable, the ignorant and generally shouted demand that people who are seen speaking together in their native language[212] should *'learn English or fuck off back home'*, even where their standard of English may be superior to that of the yob, that has the power to wound so deeply. The imputation that 'foreigners' are stealing 'our jobs' is also patently false as they are, in most cases, doing the type of job that Australians themselves refuse to take.

An ABC report in October 2017[213] shows that violence, particularly against Aboriginal children, continues in Alice Springs. The police indicat-ed that they were aware of vigilante groups operating in the town and that racist comment still regularly appears on Facebook. In the six years since we visited the country, it seems that little has changed.

But, I realise that I am in severe danger of being the pot that called the kettle black. In my own country we are intolerant of our Traveller com-munity. And some Travellers are intolerant of the 'new Irish' who arrived

---

212  In May 2018 two female American citizens at a Montana gas station were stopped by a US Border patrol agent who interrogated them and demanded proof of their identities. The reason he gave for doing so was that they were speaking together in Spanish, not English – to him a clue that they must be illegal aliens.

213  mobile.abc.net.au/news/2017-10-26-police-aware-of-vigilante-violence-on-alice-springs-streets/909058

from Africa when we had an economic boom during the so-called 'Celtic Tiger' days. Mary, when she was teaching in a Primary School, encountered Travellers complaining that Nigerians were sponging off the state and taking the bread from their mouth and that they should go back home. The same Travellers are frequently derided by educated Irish people as gypsies, tinkers and knackers. Maybe the initiatives I suggested might also have a place in Ireland – many of our social problems are caused by poverty and drink - and we, also, have an underlying rich vein of casual racism. We have made one small step forward in recent times when, in March of 2017, the Irish Government formally recognised Travellers as a distinct ethnic group in the state. In this respect, Australia was decades ahead of us.

Not far from the town of Alice Springs are the Telegraph Station and the School of the air. The Station is close to the billabong that gave the town its name. Nearby is the School of the Air, which provides distance education, through satellite technology, for children living on remote stations in the outback. In terms of area it certainly deserves its title of 'the largest classroom in the world,' covering some 1,300,000 square kilometres (about ten times the size of England), but in terms of numbers, it is really quite small having a total enrolment in 2017 of 143 pupils.

While we were there we had a chance to observe a class in progress. In recent times, looking back at my photographs of the school, I noticed one that showed a mural in the school building containing a large cartoon of Rolf Harris as a kangaroo – drawn and signed by the man, himself, when he visited in the 1980's. Given his imprisonment since for child sexual abuse, this has now been covered up.

Some 17km outside Alice, is the famous Simpsons Gap. This gorge was carved into the Western MacDonnell Ranges by Roe Creek, which flows through a small gap in the range. Here, we got our first sightings of the black-footed rock-wallaby (*Petrogale lateralis*) as well as nesting black-fronted dotterel (*Charadrius melanops*) and their endearing chicks. We also spotted a sacred kingfisher (*Todiramphus sancta*) on a branch near the creek. The morning sun beaming on the walls of the gorge illuminated their sublime red and orange surface. It is little wonder that it is sacred to the Central Aboriginal people.

Another place that is also sacred to the Aboriginal people is Standley Chasm. A short walk reveals stunning red cliff faces on either side of a narrow natural alleyway. The mid-day sunshine reflected off walls that glowed orange, like embers in a cooling fire. The track into the Chasm follows a small creek that supports an abundance of wildlife including ferns, cycads and gum trees.

We had refreshments in the small café that is owned and run by the Aboriginal descendents of the people who lived in this area for thousands of years. The *Iwupataka* Land Trust owns the private flora and fauna reserve that includes the Standley Chasm.

Our final stop in the afternoon was Glen Helen. Imposing quartzite cliffs mark the point where the West MacDonnell Ranges part at Glen Helen Gorge, to make way for the oldest river in the world, the Finke River.[214] Here, the permanent Finke River waterhole is an important refuge for migrating water-birds. The Finke River makes its way from Glen Helen into the Simpson Desert.

Some say that Glen Helen was named after Helen Grant, the niece of Alexander Grant, who took up the first lease of Glen Helen Station, the property on which the gorge is located, but there are diverging opinions. A favoured meeting place for the *Arrernte* Aboriginal people from the West and Central MacDonnell Ranges, they call the gorge '*yapalpe*' and know the Finke River as '*Larapinta*' which means 'serpent'. While tourists may cool off and swim in the waterhole, for the traditional owners of the land it is off limits. Their Dreamtime story indicates that it is the home of the ancient and powerful Rainbow Serpent.

---

214  Said to be between 350 and 400 million years old.

Driving 365km southwest of Alice Springs brings you to the large, domed rock sandstone formations of Kata Tjua/Mount Olga – known, geologically speaking, as bornhardts. Kata Tjua translates from the *Anangu* Aborigine as 'many heads.' The Olgas lie about 25km west of Uluru and are the second major landmark in this barren land. In the Dreamtime legends, the great snake king, *Wanambi,* is reputed to live on the summit of Kata Tjuta/Mount Olga and only comes down during the dry season. His breath is capable of transforming a breeze into a hurricane to punish those who do evil.

Foreigners and women are not privy to the detail of the mythology of Kata Tjua or Uluru. Both these sites are still used for religious ceremonies.

One of the main reasons for tourists coming to Alice Springs is to visit Uluru (formerly known as Ayer's Rock). We did the usual sunset and sunrise viewings to witness the rock change colour as the sun goes down and up. To be honest, I was underwhelmed. Visually, Uluru is a big rock stuck in the middle of featureless desert. The fact that it, along with Kata Tjua are the sole features for miles around and provide a source of scarce water is what makes them unique. This is what the *Anangu* people find meaningful and they remain for them a spiritual place.

Uluru is a massive sandstone inselberg[215] that shelters many springs, waterholes and rock caves. Its significance to the *Pitjantjatjara Anangu* people is evidenced in the many ancient paintings on its walls.

The Australian government returned ownership of Uluru to the local *Pitjantjatjara* Aborigines in 1985, with one of the conditions being that the *Anangu* would lease it back to the National Parks and Wildlife agency for 99 years and that it would be jointly managed. The *Anangu* requested that the walk to the top by tourists would be stopped and this was agreed by the government. The visitor's guide says '*the climb is not prohibited, but we prefer that, as a guest on Anangu land, you will choose to respect our law and culture by*

---

215 Literally 'island mountain'

*not climbing.'* When Prince Charles and Princess Diana visited in 1983 they climbed to the top, prior to the agreement with the *Aṉangu.*

Despite the agreement, records show that over one third of the 400,000 annual visitors still climb the rock. When we visited in 2012 several of the English people on our trip, showing a complete lack of sensitivity and empathy insisted on climbing, we stayed firmly earthbound. The fact that less than 20% of visitors make the climb was supposed to be a trigger to closing access to tourists entirely. Evidence shows that this level was reached in 2013.

The Uluru-Kata Tjuta management board announced in late 2017 that tourists will be banned from climbing Uluru, as and from October 2019 – the 34th anniversary of Uluru being handed back to the *Aṉangu* people.

The most interesting thing about Uluru is the walk along the base, where you can learn about the cultural and religious significance of the place to the *Aṉangu.* We followed two marked walks, the Mutitjulu walk to a waterhole and the Mala walk to the Kantju Gorge. The walks take you past waterholes and decorated caves. These caves serve as repositories of culturally important information to the indigenous people, and also as classrooms, where boys can be shown how to hunt and track. Paintings are rendered in natural pigments providing red, yellow, white and black colours. Some are naturalistic and others are very geometric. Concentric circles seem to indicate a waterhole and a sense of person is given by the many paintings of human hands. In some places it is forbidden to take photographs or to film sites. For example, *Mala Puta* is an *Aṉangu* women's site and is sacred under traditional law. For the *Aṉangu,* culturally important information must be viewed in its original location. It is deemed inappropriate that anyone who has not earned the right to this cultural knowledge should see it on film.

In the afternoon, after walking around the base of the Rock, we took a flight to Cairns. This was a town we both liked. Like much of northern

Australia, the climate here is hot and dry, but the desire to cool off by flinging yourself in the ocean is forestalled by the signs warning of the danger of saltwater crocodiles and the reports of hungry sharks. However, this did not deter one macho character who stood thigh deep in the water fishing with a throw net. Unsurprisingly, we saw no reasonable people in the ocean but many people enjoyed the swimming pools set beside the sea on the promenade. We had arrived in time to see the eclipse of the sun. Our arrival was coincidental with this great event, but many people had spent considerable sums to get here and the hotels were jammed. Huge crowds lined the waterfront to view the eclipse but this was partly spoiled by cloud cover. However, we did manage to get a reasonable view of it, when it appeared in a gap in the cloud cover.

I was able to spot many birds along the shoreline in Cairns and in the country to the north, including brown booby (*Sula leucogaster*); least frigatebird (*Fregata ariel*); eastern reef egret, dark phase (*Ardea sacra*); little egret (*Ardea garzetta*); intermediate egret (*Ardea intermedia*); royal spoonbill (*Platalea regia*); Australian white ibis (*Threskiornis molucca*); orange-footed scrubfowl (*Megapodius reinwardt*); masked lapwing (*Vanellus miles*); red-kneed dotterel (*Erythrogonys cinctus*); lesser sand-plover (*Charadrius mongolus*); red-capped dotterel (Charadrius ruficapillus); red-necked stint (*Calidris ruficollis*); sharp-tailed sandpiper (Calidris *acuminata*); great knot (*Calidris tenuirostris*); bar-tailed godwit (*Limosa lapponica*); whimbrel (*Numenius phaeopus*); eastern curlew (Numenius *madagascariensis*); common greenshank (*Tringa nebularia*); silver gull (*Larus novaehollandiae*); crested tern (*Sterna bergii*); little tern (*Sterna albifrons*); black-naped tern (*Sterna sumatrana*); diamond dove (*Geopelia cuneata*); peaceful dove (*Geopelia striata*); white-headed pigeon (*Columba leucomela*); Torresian imperial pigeon (*Ducula spilorrhoa*); rainbow lorikeet (*Trichoglossus haematodus*); double-eyed fig-parrot (*Psittaculirostris diophthalma*); white-rumped swiftlet (*Aerodromus spodiopygia*); welcome swallow (*Hirundo neoxena*); fairy martin (*Hirundo ariel*); white-winged triller (*Lalage tricolor*); mangrove robin (*Eopsaltria pulverulenta*); willy wagtail ( *Rhipidura leucophrys*);

zitting cisticola (*Cisticola juncidis*); varied honeyeater (*Lichenostomus versicolor*); brown honeyeater (*Lichmera indistinct*); zebra finch (*Poephila guttata*); spice finch (*Lonchura punctulata*); house sparrow (*Passer domesticus*); metallic starling (*Aplonis metallica*); common mynah (*Acridotheres tristis*); white breasted wood-swallow (Artamus leucorhynchus).

The common mynah was introduced to Tasmania and Australia in the 1860s and has now spread in an arc along the coast of eastern and northern Australia.

A highlight of any trip to Cairns is a visit to the Great Barrier Reef. I am not going to hype it or even try to describe it, except to say that while many television documentaries do it justice, it is impossible to describe the excitement, thrill and wonder you experience when you go under the water in this magical place. Try it, if you can.

Another highlight is a trip up to Daintree and on into the Cape York Peninsula. We booked a guided tour and enjoyed time in the stunning rain-forest bird watching, boating on one of the rivers, and observing crocodiles amongst the mangroves.

We were not so lucky with other animals and only saw some geckos. Fiddler crab (probably *Uca elegans*) and mudskippers (probably *Periophthalmus argentilineatus*) frolicking in the mud among the roots of the mangroves that fringed the shore. Mudskippers are amphibious fish that are fully terrestrial for some portion of the daily cycle.

The rest of our stay concentrated on the cities. First we visited Sydney. We loved the Harbour for its ambience, its restaurants and vibe. Bondi was interesting, particularly watching lifeguards in training and practicing with surfboards and boats. Indeed, we liked Sydney so much that we made it a stopover, several years later, as we returned home from New Zealand. We found it a great place to chill out for a few days. A side trip took us through the Blue Mountains to see the Three Sisters at Echo Point, Katoomba. This rock formation, according to Aboriginal legend, represents three sisters who were turned to stone. The story, to me, is more interesting than the reality. The Blue Mountains are a good day out, just not a great day out. A ride on what is reputed to be the world's steepest incline railway provides views over the Jimson Valley.

En route to Canberra we visited a typical sheep station for the obligatory demonstration of sheep-shearing – the activity beloved of muscular men dressed in jeans a white vest and a sweat stained Snowy River Akubra hat. The demonstration was followed by that mainstay of Australian cuisine, the barbecue.

Canberra was memorable only as a place to sleep between Sydney and Melbourne. We toured the town and visited the parliament building. The fact that it was selected as the site for the capital, as a compromise between Sydney and Melbourne, is proof that most compromises represent bad choices. The city is notable for the fact that it was entirely planned, with major roads following a wheel-and-spoke pattern rather than a grid; the outer areas of the city, built later, are not laid out geometrically. Overall, it has the appearance today of being conceived by someone with a ruler, protractor and compass but little soul and limited imagination. The competition was boycotted by the Royal Institute of British Architects. The chosen design was that of a pair of American architects. In the final analysis, however, this winning design was set aside and elements of it were amalgamated with the designs of the two runners up as well as a design from a Sydney architect. With this mishmash, they succeeded in designing a city of public servants for public servants, largely by public servants.

We left Canberra, with little regret, and headed for Melbourne. On the way we stopped off at Glenrowan which is famed as the place where the bushranger Ned Kelly made his last stand in 1880. Melbourne is a comfortable city, reminiscent of many cities around the world. We spent some time here with a couple of Mary's relatives, Irene and Frank, and had an enjoyable sojourn visiting the hinterland, sailing on Frank's boat in the bay and eating in some of the many restaurants. On our final night there, I took violently ill, as did Frank, and we had a duet in separate toilets evacuating the contents of our stomachs and bowels – or chundering, in the patois of the natives. I was to chunder regularly for the rest of my stay in Australia and this may, to some extent, explain my lack of awe when viewing subsequent sights.

From Melbourne we travelled along the Great Ocean Road to look at the famous Twelve Apostles and the Arch. When we got there we saw that there were only eight Apostles remaining, the other four having succumbed to the power of the Pacific Ocean. That they are still called the Twelve Apostles indicates an Australian attachment to the familiar in the face of simple mathematics. As rock formations go, they are interesting rather than astonishing. The viewing sites, roads and parking spots are also crowded, a testament to the lack of many other sights worth viewing.

After an overnight stay in the 'metropolis' of Warrnambool, we headed into the Barossa valley for a bit of wine tasting and lunch. I was still weak and chundering periodically, so Mary had to do all the tasting and eating and report to me. We visited two of the wineries that are well known to us in Ireland, Wolf Blass and Jacobs Creek. By the time we were finished Mary was in great good humour. I continued to nurse my delicate stomach – generally with a strained smile – as she explained the pros and cons of the vintages she had sampled. As a wine taster, she needs to learn to spit, not swallow.

A two night stay in Adelaide ended our tour. Mary informed me that Adelaide was nice, but my memories of it are dim. I struggled to get fit for our return trip, which saw us flying from Adelaide to Dublin with only stops in airports for connecting flights.

# CHAPTER 22

## *Isla de la Mala Gente – The Island of Bad People*

Growing up in the 1950s and 1960s, I was a prodigious reader – and I still am. My tastes as a youth were eclectic. While I enjoyed reading and swapping copies of the latest editions of the Beano, Dandy, Beezer, Topper, Eagle and Wizard as well as the more expensive glossy comics of Dell and Marvel (now, incomprehensibly, being made into successful blockbuster movies for adults), my reading wasn't confined solely to comics. We lived near a public library that my sister, Irene, and I would frequently visit to pick up the latest adventures of Frank and Joe, the *Hardy Boys*, which I then swapped for her copy of the latest exploits of the *Nancy Drew*. I devoured books on painting, science and natural history and supplemented my fiction reading with such classics as *Moby Dick, The Adventures of Tom Sawyer/Huckleberry Finn, The Swiss Family Robinson, Twenty Thousand Leagues under the Sea, Kidnapped, The Man in the Iron Mask, The Count of Monte Cristo, The Three Musketeers, Treasure Island* and countless others.

One of my favourite books, at this time, was *The Coral Island*.[216] This introduced me to a realm of shipwreck and cannibals. The image of fierce, glistening, bronzed natives in long canoes, hunting, killing and eating their enemies insinuated itself into my imagination when Jack Martin exclaimed …

---

216 The Coral Island: A tale of the Pacific Ocean – RM Ballantyne (1884); Thomas Nelson and Sons

*They are canoes, Ralph! Whether war-canoes or not I cannot tell, but this I know, that all the natives of the South Sea Islands are fierce cannibals, and they have little respect for strangers. We must hide if they land here, which I earnestly hope they will not do.'*

Books formed my vision, and my dread, of cannibals and I easily empathised with *Robinson Crusoe*[217] when I read...

*'for the dread and terror of falling into the hands of savages and cannibals lay so upon my spirits'*

This was only fiction but, to my young mind, made fact when I read Herman Melville's *Typee*[218], which recounts his voyage to the Pacific Island of *Nuku Hiva* (which I recently visited), where he lived for several weeks among the island's, allegedly, cannibal inhabitants before fleeing. His discovery of preserved heads and the probable remains of a cannibal feast left lasting impressions...

*'I ...caught a glimpse of three human heads, which others of the party were hurriedly enveloping in the coverings from which they had been taken. One of the three I distinctly saw. It was in a state of perfect preservation.... The sunken cheeks were rendered yet more ghastly by the rows of glistening teeth which protruded from between the lips, while the sockets of the eyes—filled with oval bits of mother-of-pearl shell, with a black spot in the centre—heightened the hideousness of its aspect. Two of the three were heads of the islanders; but the third, to my horror, was that of a white man....*

*Was I destined to perish like him—like him, perhaps, to be devoured, and my head to be preserved as a fearful memento of the event? My imagination ran riot in these horrid speculations, and I felt certain that the worst possible evils would befall me.'*

217 The Life and Adventures of Robinson Crusoe - Daniel Defoe(1719) W.Taylor

218 *Typee* - Herman Melville (1846) Dodd, Mead and Co, New York

Melville's fears were to be given substance when he.....

---

*'observed a curiously carved vessel of wood, of considerable size, with a cover placed over it...... I raised one end of the cover; at the same moment the chiefs, perceiving my design, loudly ejaculated, "Taboo! taboo!" But the slight glimpse sufficed; my eyes fell upon the disordered members of a human skeleton, the bones still fresh with moisture, and with particles of flesh clinging to them here and there!'*

---

Shortly after reading Typee, I purchased, in a second hand bookshop, a copy of *The Desert World* by Arthur Mangin.[219] Here, I first came across the word 'anthropophagy' and had to look up what it meant. The book provides a description of the cannibal behaviour of a number of tribes that is embellished by a gory illustration of the *Battas* of Sumatra slicing choice morsels of flesh from a naked victim bound to a stake and whom, custom dictated, must be eaten alive.

I thought this practice was restricted to the most remote areas of the world and was only engaged in by wild savages; and then I read about the Donner-Reed party in America in 1846-47. George Donner and James Reed set out with a wagon train, headed for California. Delayed by mishaps, loss of oxen and horses, rugged and difficult terrain and dissention, they were late reaching the Sierra Nevada and became snowbound near Truckee (now Donner) lake. Of the 87 pioneers who started only 48 made it out alive. Lack of food meant that many of them ate the dead to survive.

However, as far as I was concerned all this was history and took place in a distant past and that, with the possible exception of some of the yet to be explored inaccessible parts of the Amazonian jungle, head hunting and cannibalism no longer existed.

I was in my teens in the early 1960s, when my illusion that men stopped eating men in the previous century was instantly fractured. I sat in

---

219 *The Desert World* - Arthur Mangin (1872) T Nelson and Sons (translated from French)

a cinema in awe of what I was watching on the screen. In 1959, a six man Franco-Dutch team, led by Pierre-Dominique Gaisseau, headed on a perilous journey inland from the Arafura Sea to traverse Dutch New Guinea (now West Papua) from south to north. They were provided with a liaison officer and six armed policemen by the government, as the locals were known to be both head-hunters and cannibals.

They travelled by canoe and on foot some 700 kilometres through a large area of uncharted territory. It took them up rivers, through swamplands and dense rainforest, across high mountain ranges and unexplored valleys to the north coast in the vicinity of Hollandia (now Jayapura City). They spent seven months there; suffered deprivation; battled discomfort and disease; three of their *Muyu* porters died during the trek; eight members of their party were wounded; and twenty two got sick. While they were never in mortal danger from the inhabitants, they received a different welcome from the tribesmen who lived near the coast and those who lived in the interior. Those near the coasts invited them to live with them for a time and permitted them to observe rituals. In the interior, as they approached villages, they were warned off, the inhabitants refusing to have anything to do with them. This meant that they couldn't barter for food but had to rely on infrequent air drops from the port of Hollandia.[220]

Vojtech Novotny,[221] the Czech entomologist, provides a vivid example of the impenetrability of the New Guinea landscape in his description of the Jubilee Expedition of the British Ornithological Society. On the fourth of January 1910 the members of the expedition left the coast for a mountain ridge they could see on the horizon. After four hundred and eight days of bushwhacking they only covered forty miles and had to retreat having failed to reach their goal.

---

220 Their adventures were recorded as an Academy Award winning documentary – 'The Sky Above the Mud Below (also known as the Sky Above the Mud Beneath or *Le Ciel et la boue*).

221 Notebooks from New Guinea (2011) Oxford University Press

Gaisseau's journey, initially, took them deep into *Asmat* territory, a place where Michael Rockefeller, the twenty-three-year-old son of the New York Governor (who was later to serve as the 41st Vice President of America under President Gerald Ford), was to vanish only two years later. A recent book by Carl Hoffman[222] gives a detailed account that supports a theory that Michael was killed and eaten by *Asmat* tribesmen, from the village of Otsjanep, in revenge for the killing of five of the most important men in the village by the government controller, Max Lapré, several years earlier.

If Michael Rockefeller had been killed by the *Asmat*, it was a crime of opportunity. Gaisseau's Franco-Dutch expedition took place some time after Lapré killed the tribesmen and before Michael was lost. Although the expedition crossed through *Asmat* territory, there is no information to indicate that it ever came near the village of Otsjanep; and the presence of armed policemen, undoubtedly, acted as a deterrent to anyone with murderous intent, as the *Asmat* were well aware of the danger of guns, particularly machine guns.

Gaisseau spent some time with the lowland tribes and the images he shot of hundreds of naked men in feather headdresses, standing up and paddling long dugout canoes, chanting, stamping and banging their wooden shields, while hundreds more ran along the shore, remain with me today. He estimated that his small group was escorted up-river by two thousand natives.

Some of the men Gisseau met wore human skulls, hanging on a thong down their back, which provided an adornment during the day and a pillow at night. In one large village they witnessed a mock-birth ritual, involving two couples, one from the village and the other from an enemy village, with which it had been at war. Each couple became part of the opposite village

---

222 *Savage Harvest: A Tale of Cannibals, Colonialism and Michael Rockefeller's Tragic Quest for Primitive Art;* Carl-Hoffman (2015) William Morrow). The official cause of Michael's death was given as drowning. However, as remains were never found speculation as to the cause of his death abounded. Theories included that he'd been consumed by sharks or crocodiles; been kidnapped and kept prisoner; went native and lived his life out

and their re-birth into the opposite village was emblematic of a new, and, purportedly, permanent peace.

Men and women lived separately in most villages. In the men's hut, the sole furnishing usually comprised human skulls, either those of ancestors or enemies, and rings of human teeth hanging from the rafters. Each ring of teeth denoted a chopped off human head: the number of rings of teeth owned by an individual marked that man's importance in the tribe.

Gisseau and his party were formally adopted into one village. The adoption was sealed by the men breast-feeding from their new mothers.

This documentary, more than anything else, began my captivation by New Guinea and I resolved to go there; a resolve that only came to fruition in 2015.

New Guinea, in the South West Pacific region, is the world's largest tropical island and the second-largest island, in the world, after Greenland.[223] It has a land area of 785,753km². To the north it is bounded by the Pacific Ocean; the Bismarck and Solomon seas lie to the east; the Arafura Sea and the Coral Sea lie west and east along its southern coast; and the narrow Torres Strait separates the island from Australia.

Located in Melanesia, New Guinea is divided into two parts. The eastern half of the island, together with hundreds of offshore islands - the most prominent being New Britain, New Ireland, Bougainville and the Admiralty Islands - comprises Papua New Guinea (PNG). The western part and some 40 offshore islands comprise the Indonesian provinces of Papua and West Papua.

A massive unbroken mountainous spine, much covered with tropical rainforest, and with several peaks above 4,000 metres, runs the length of the island from the northwest to the southeast. Fringing the north coast, and running parallel to the central chain of mountain ranges, is a number of smaller mountain ranges.

---

223  2,400 km long from northwest to southeast; and approximately 650 km wide at its widest north to south.

In Papua New Guinea, the lowlands are dominated by swamps and floodplains. Major rivers include the Sepik, which wends its way some 1,126 km through lowland swamp plains in the north of the country, and the Fly, which flows southwards some 1,050km through the largest swamplands in the world. Both of these rivers provide major transport routes in a country still lacking a well developed transport infrastructure. Internal transport consists of a few roads (3,000km paved,[224]6349km unpaved), waterways (11,000km), and airways, with 21 airports with paved runways and 540 with unpaved runways.

Nestled within the central cordillera are elongated, fertile, highland valley basins. While the overall population density remains low, 40% of the population occupies the highlands, with a density of between 20 to 100 people per square kilometre. In the sparsely populated lowlands of the Western province there can be one person per square kilometre. The natural barriers created by the steep mountainous terrain meant that, until recent times, some groups, due to physical isolation or taboo, never mixed with neighbouring groups living in adjacent valleys only a few kilometres away. Both highlanders and lowlanders are still, predominantly, subsistence farmers. The traditional diet is mainly vegetarian. In the lowlands, yams, taro, sago and banana are staple foods, while sweet potato is the main highland food. Fish and shellfish are regularly eaten in the lowlands. Meat is sometimes eaten. Hunting supplements the diet with meat from birds, marsupials, turtles, and cassowaries. The main livestock species are pigs, poultry, cattle, goats, sheep and rabbits. Of these, by far the most important are pigs.

W. Ayalew et al[225] describe the relationship between rural communities and pigs in PNG thus...

---

224 Ireland, which is only 15% of the size of PNG has 96,036 km of paved road

225 W. Ayalew,G. Danbaro, M. Dom, S. Amben, F. Besari, C. Moran and K. Nidup (2011) 'Genetic and cultural significance of indigenous pigs in Papua New Guinea and their phenotypic characteristics' Animal Genetic Resources, 48, 37–46. © Food and Agriculture Organization of the United Nations, 2011doi:10.1017/S2078633611000026

*'In the largely traditional and subsistence rural communities of PNG, in particular in the fertile and densely populated highlands, pigs have strong socio-cultural significance. Pigs are culturally the most important animals used extensively in many forms of exchange, alms-giving, feasting, compensation and as symbols of social status and rank. Pigs are used for bride price payments, as gifts to establish or maintain social relations and as payments to resolve social disputes or strengthen relationships between individuals, families, clans and tribes. Pigs are also slaughtered during initiation rites, funerals for the dead and during elaborate ceremonies or gatherings where feasting is involved.*

*.....In many parts of PNG, the number of pigs owned and their body size and conditioning is used to judge the social rank of a person. Furthermore, the pig husbandry system followed reflects gender relationships whereby women in some communities look after the pig but do not own them, although pigs cannot be disposed off without their consent.'*

This was described to us more prosaically by a Huli woman when she said that the most important things to men in PNG were land, pigs and women - strictly in that order.

Pigs, as a symbol of wealth or influence, form the basis of feasts where chiefs or local 'big men' compete to outdo each other by distributing hundreds of pigs to guests. Eating, drumming, singing, dancing and speechmaking may go on for days at these events.

Human occupation of New Guinea dates back 40,000 to 50,000 years – depending on the source you read – with the migration of people from Southeast Asia to Australia and New Guinea. Evidence indicates that some 10,000 years ago, with the melting of ice age glaciers, the Arafura Sea rose to separate New Guinea from Australia. Evidence exists that, even then, sedentary agriculture, together with extensive swamp drainage and irrigation, was practiced in the highland basins. Food crops such as yams, taro and banana species were introduced from South-East Asia as well as pigs, chicken and other small ruminants.[226]

226 Kambuou, R.N. (1996) Papua New Guinea:Country Report to the FAO International Technical Conference on Plant Genetic Resources.

Indonesian and Asian seafarers knew of the island and its archipelago centuries before it was known to Europeans. Contact in the period before 1500 is described by Wright, Denham, Shine and Donohue (2012) …[227]

---

*'Trade in bird-of-paradise plumes, spices, betel nut, metal, glass beads and pottery has linked western New Guinea to Island South East Asia for at least 2000 years.*

*After AD 300, a decrease in demand for plumes led to a shift towards spices and aromatic woods, with Timor and the Banda Islands becoming important centres.*

*By the 12th century, commerce involving spices and bird-of-paradise plumes had escalated between wNG (west New Guinea) and ISEA (Island South East Asia), ultimately stimulated by increased demand from Eurasia.'*

---

References to New Guinea appear in the writings of the Arab Mas'udi,[228] in Chinese Sources and in Javanese poetry.[229] Wright, Denham, Shine and Donohue, citing other studies, note that by the 13th and 14th centuries Buddhist and Hindu missionaries were visiting west New Guinea in search of converts. They also record that by the 14th century, Islam had entered the Moluccas and the western edge of New Guinea.

Subsequent contact with the island was sporadic and, while many claimed it, few settled on it until the latter part of the nineteenth century.

- The Portuguese sailors Antonio d'Abreu and Francisco Serrano first saw the island in 1511 but made no attempt to land. Jorge de

---

227 An Archaeological Review of Western New Guinea (2012); Duncan Wright, Tim Denham, Denis Shine, Mark Donohue J World Prehist (2013) 26:25–73 DOI 10.1007/s10963-013-9063-8; Published online: 1 June 2013 Springer Science+Business Media New York 2013; http://austronesian.linguistics.anu.edu.au/historyd-ownloads/Wright_Denham_Shine_Donohue_2013_WestNewGuinea.pdf.

228 Abu al-Hasan Ali ibn al-Husayn al-Mas'udi (c. 896–956 AD)

229 Galis, K. W. (1953). Geschiedenis. In K. W. Klein (Ed.), Nieuw Guinea: De ontwikkeling op econo-mischsocial en cultureel gebied, in Nederlands en Australisch Nieuw Guinea. (p 7)The Hague: Stadtsdrukkerij; cited in Duncan Wright ,Tim Denham, Denis Shine and Mark Donohue (2013); An Archaeological Review of Western New Guinea, J World Prehist (2013) 26:25–73; Published online: Springer Science+Business Media New York 1 June 2013

Menezes landed at Biak[230] in 1526, where he was forced to winter. He called the region, including the western part of New Guinea, *Ilhas dos Papuas*. It is thought by some that he landed on Western New Guinea at Warsai on the Birdshead Peninsula. He is credited with being the European discoverer of New Guinea.

- In 1527, Hernán Cortés – the conquistador – who destroyed the Aztec civilisation in Mexico, prepared an expedition, commanded by his cousin Álvaro de Saavedra, aimed at finding a new land in the Pacific Ocean (or South Sea). In June 1528, Alvaro's expedition landed on Yapen an island south of Biak, where it stayed a month among the locals.

- In 1545, the Spaniard, Ynigo Ortiz De Retez sailed the north coast of New Guinea and claimed lands for the Spanish Crown. He named the mainland Neuva Guinea, due to the physical similarity he perceived between the natives and Africans from Guinea.

- On July 31 1678, Johannes Keyts was the first to plant the Dutch flag on New Guinea, at the west point of the Onin Peninsula (northwest of Fakfak).

- The Dutch claimed the western half of the island in 1828 as part of the Dutch East Indies.

- In the 1870's, Captain John Moresby of Great Britain surveyed the south-eastern coast, and by 1884 the south-eastern quadrant of New Guinea had been annexed by Great Britain. The German New Guinea Company took over administration of the northeast quadrant in the same year.

- The administration of British New Guinea was passed to Australia in 1904, and its name was changed to the Territory of Papua.

- Following World War I, German New Guinea was taken over by Australia as a mandated territory of the League of Nations in 1921.

---

230 The Schouten Islands, which include the main islands of Biak, Supiori and Numfor, as well as a number of smaller islands, lie 50 km off the north-western coast of the island of New Guinea. They were named after Dutch explorer Willem Schouten, who explored them in 1615.

- After Japan temporarily occupied large parts of the island during the early years of World War II, Australia combined its administration of the Territory of Papua and the New Guinea mandate into the Territory of Papua and New Guinea.

- Also after the war, the western half of the island, then known as Irian Barat, was returned to Dutch control. Indonesia became independent of Holland in 1949, and a plebiscite was held in 1969 to decide Irian Barat's future; as a result it was annexed to Indonesia.

- Papua New Guinea was granted independence within the British Commonwealth in 1975.

Bishop Couppe, in 1892[231] wrote about this region thus:

*'It is generally known that the islands of the South Pacific went for a long time under the name of "Land of the Bad People," and "Archipelago of Assassins." Among the many ancient maps hanging on the walls of the Vatican Library, I remarked one which exhibited the islands of those seas. The outlines of New Guinea are drawn very imperfectly. To the north-east of the great island, I found vaguely outlined under the name la terra di mala gente (Land of the bad people), the present Vicariate of New Pomerania.'* [232]

The early Spanish and Portuguese explorers who visited the region are purported to have given it this soubriquet (*Isla de la Mala Gente*) mainly as a reference to their opinion of the savage natives who lived there but they also referred to the island as Papua.

PNG has roughly one fifth of the world's languages. Its 6.8 million people speak nearly eight hundred distinct languages. However, with increasing urban drift many of these are rapidly disappearing. Preventing this

---

231 The Sacred Heart Review. VOL. 8.-NO. 12. Boston, Mass., August 13, 1892.

232 Now the Island of New Britain which is separated from Papua New Guinea by the Dampier and Vitiaz Straits

from constituting a national 'Tower of Babel' is the widespread use of *Tok Pisin*, or Pidgin English which acts as a *lingua franca* throughout the country.

The belief in sorcery and witchcraft continues to be widespread and pervades both public and private life. Most of the population of PNG believes in a supernatural (sorcery, witchcraft or taboo violation), rather than a natural, cause of illness or death. Rather they believe that an evil spirit, or *masalai*, is the cause. *Masalai are* sent by evil magicians or *sangumas* either for their own purposes or at the behest of a client. Whatever the misfortune that afflicts anyone, the suspicion that a sorcerer or witch has deliberately used supernatural powers to bring about this suffering is the first conclusion that will be drawn by relatives or friends of the victims. *Sanguma* hunts are not uncommon and retaliatory measures against the sorcerer range from destruction of their property or exile to torture and murder. Reports of retaliation include accounts of being buried alive, beheaded, pushed off cliffs, electrocuted, forced to drink petroleum, or being stoned , hacked or shot to death.

The problem is compounded where doctors and nurses, who may be unable to diagnose a specific illness or offer effective treatment options, suggest to patients and their families that '*sik bilong ples*' (literally 'illness from village'), hinting at a local, magical cause and that someone with a grudge had caused the sickness by sorcery or witchcraft. It is not surprising, therefore, that when people get sick they don't think in terms of the medical cause, but rather who they can blame. This has led to almost weekly reports of witchcraft killings and torture.

While many accusations of sorcery are frequently driven by strong beliefs, many other claims are fabricated for financial gain. Recent research by Oxfam found that in two in every three sorcery accusations resulting in dislocation, accusations were used as a means of possessing the wealth or resources, such as land, houses, or businesses of the person accused.

This belief in sorcery has not been diminished significantly either by (the somewhat uneven) availability of western medicine or by the exhortations of missionaries.

Missionary activity was, and still is, very active throughout PNG. This has resulted in 96% of Papua New Guinea's population, at least of those who answered the question in the census of 2000, identifying themselves Christian (mainly Protestants, along with a significant Roman Catholic minority). While only 3.3%, in the census, stated that they solely follow traditional beliefs such as ancestor worship, belief in evil spirits (*masalai*), sorcery (*puripuri*) and animism, it is clear that these religious beliefs and rituals are still deeply ingrained and widely practiced amongst many putative 'Christians'. Indeed traditional healers, who have the ability to identify and combat the underlying supernatural causes of illness, are more available and, therefore, more important to people in the villages.

In our trip through the highlands and along the tributaries of the Sepik River, it was not unusual to meet so-called witch doctors in some of the villages we visited, who readily demonstrated the ceremonies they used to ward off evil spirits and the techniques they employed to cure disease caused by evil spirits. We watched one healer 'cure' two teenage boys of malaria. While they lay face down, naked and moaning on the ground in his magical compound, he rubbed their backs with a magic stone, declared them cured and they sat up all smiles and healthy. Despite the discouragement of the Christian churches regarding such beliefs, we witnessed, in the village of Yamandim, where we had a homestay, a local healer carry out his magical duties, while nearby in a prominent place in the village stood a large, empty, stilted , palm leaf thatched church, inscribed 'St Lucas Cahtolic' (sic). Like the infrequent availability of western medicine, the sporadic attendance of a priest has resulted in many villagers adhering to the traditional in daily life and complying with the modern only when ordained ministers can fit them into their busy schedules. Sunday services are attended and led, in general, by an appointed deacon from the village. While the position carries recognition, it does not have the credibility of the local medicine man.

In the villages, men and women employ magic spells to ensure success in gardening, hunting and fishing; to prevent illness and cure ailments and to ensure success in lovemaking and procreation. Only a small number have knowledge of witchcraft or sorcery. This is generally regarded as a dangerous and malevolent skill and the adherent is shunned; but it may be regarded as a positive attribute where a clansman is adept at healing or war sorcery.

In the villages that are dependent on subsistence horticulture, there is a division of labour between the sexes. Men clear plots in the forest so that their wives can plant gardens and tend pigs. Men tend to plantations of sugarcane, bananas, coffee and cocoa. They are also responsible for building houses. Women do the cooking and tend gardens of taro, cassava, aibika, amaranth, and yams, to name a few. The dominant crop in the highlands is sweet potato, but in the lowlands a more diverse cropping system is used and generally consists of a banana – yam – cassava based system. In the wetlands and deltas of the main rivers (Sepik, Fly, Ramu and the Puerari) wild harvesting of sago, from the sago palm, predominates. Root crops, leafy vegetables and fish supplement the sago.

The extraction of sago from the sago palm is a very interesting procedure. In Kundiman Village, bordering the Karawari River in the Sepik Basin, we watched as members of the *Yokoim* tribe processed sago. Mature sago trees, between seven and sixteen years old are cut before they can produce seeds and when they are still rich in carbohydrate. After felling a tree, a man (and it appears to always be a man) used a stone axe and two long pointed poles to peel back the bark from the trunk. He then used the poles and his axe to chop the pith into smaller pieces, which a woman then placed in a closely woven basket over a canoe and poured water over the pulp and kneaded it to extract the starch. The dissolved starch filtered from the basket and settled in the bottom of the beached canoe. The water was left to evaporate in the sunshine and by the next day the starch would have settled out as a white paste in the bottom of the canoe. Any remaining water is then drained off. The starch is then peeled from the canoe, pounded into flour and left to dry.

The sago starch, which is eaten at every meal, may be cooked in two ways; either with boiling water to form a pinkish, gloopy paste, which is then served with boiled vegetables and fish; or dusted onto a pan to form a pancake, which is toasted over the fire. We were given the opportunity to taste both of these staples. Both were relatively tasteless, and I was not very keen on the texture of the gloopy porridge.

In the villages, both men and women look after small children, often with a father tending his infant while the mother weeds her gardens. 'Big men' need many wives and female helpers to raise food and pigs that they will give away at *moka* (gift giving) ceremonies to underpin their reputation. Although coming third in the ranking, behind land and pigs, of things that men value, hardworking women are a man's most valuable asset. However, men view women cautiously and try to limit contact to what is absolutely essential. Too frequent contact is thought to put men at risk from evil spirits or magic. Such is the caution that men and women have separate and designated bathing places in rivers – the men's bathing place being located, naturally, upstream of the women's to avoid contamination. God alone knows what consternation was caused when, one evening, some female members of our small group pitched themselves into the river near the canoe landing area, showing, at best, ignorance of protocol, or at worst, scant regard for local taboos. It is possible that after we left the entire village had to reorganise its bathing arrangements. Women are valued because of their procreative power but esteem is somewhat circumscribed by the belief that only men can create men. Men, through initiation ceremonies and complex ritual, go to great lengths to bring about biological and psychological transformation in adolescent boys. Part of this process involves the separation of the initiates from females and isolation in the spirit house, where ritual bloodletting takes place to expel the mother's postpartum blood and allow it to go back to the female line. These rituals are feared and are painful but are believed to be the necessary transformational elements that change a boy to a man.

The choice of a wife is serious business and is rarely left to the individual. After initiation into adult society, putative marriage partners are permitted to spend time in supervised courtship. To avoid inbreeding, clan exogamy is essential, even extending to marrying across enemy lines. However, in the battle between the sexes this puts men at greater risk from sabotage by the bride and from magic and evil spirits, so they need to strengthen themselves for contact with women. Repeated sexual contact between the husband and wife is thought to continuously dilute this danger.

Where possible, parents try to ensure that their daughters marry prosperous suitors, whose kin pay large bride-prices and who will be steadfast allies in commerce and war. Marriage is seen as a major transaction. The groom's family negotiates the bride-price - generally a dozen pigs, some cash and domestic goods; although, in mining and urban areas, vehicles, luxury consumer goods and money are the preferred payments that, in exceptional cases, may amount to as much as $100,000. Once the bride price has been paid, she will move to the hut he will build on his land. It is held by many in the towns that inflated bride prices are a disincentive to divorce as the husband may demand return of the bride-price from the wife's family and this, in many cases, could bankrupt them. As a result of such threats, many women are forced to tolerate very abusive relationships and PNG has the undesirable reputation of being one of the most dangerous places in the world to be a woman or girl, with an estimated 70% of women experiencing rape or assault in their lifetime.[233]

233 Human Rights Watch - World Report 2016: Papua New Guinea – events of 2015. https://www.hrw.org/world-report/2016/country-chapters/papua-new-guinea (accessed 9th November 2016)

Polygyny is the norm in PNG, where 'big men' attract a greater number of wives. With a sex ratio of 1.04 males to females, this is bad news for men. More men than women, and individual men having several wives (In *Gende* society, as many as 10 percent of adult males are polygynous at some time), leaves it as no surprise that men are more likely to be unmarried. Divorce, when it occurs, is frequently initiated by women. Remarriage is common, except where people are old and living with their children or grandchildren.

Women give birth, in relative isolation, in a birth hut or garden house where they can escape from malevolent spirits. Babies are nursed for several years and women carry their babies everywhere. Children are permitted to run free in the village, with girls, from the age of five or six, undertaking small chores – such as minding younger siblings, running errands and helping their mother in her garden or, in the Sepik basin, accompanying their mothers on fishing trips. Boys get a couple of years extra freedom before being required to collect firewood, fetch water, clear brush and hunt or fish. Children in PNG are believed, intrinsically, to be good. Bad behaviour is not the fault of the child but is caused by evil spirits. Children who behave badly are generally ignored or placed alone in a hut to allow their ill humour pass. If this does not work, then parents often engage the services of a medium to divine the spiritual source of the misbehaviour.

Many people have a perception of PNG being a very dangerous place. This is, in part, true. The UK foreign office travel advice site[234] had this to say when I accessed it on the 9th of November 2016…

*'Serious crime is particularly high in the capital, Port Moresby, and in the cities of Lae and Mt Hagen. Settlement or squatter areas of towns and cities are particularly dangerous. 'Bush knives' (machetes) and firearms are often used in assaults and thefts. Carjacking, assault (including sexual assaults), bag snatching and robberies are com-*

---

234 www.gov.uk/foreign-travel-advice/papua-new-guinea/safety-and-security

*mon. Banks and cash machines are attractive targets for criminals. Walking after dark is particularly dangerous in Port Moresby and other urban centres.*

*Known high-risk areas include the area around Parliament House in the Port Moresby suburb of Waigani, particularly outside of working hours, and along the highway between Lae and Nadzab Airport, particularly between Goroka and Kainantu. Criminals use roadblocks on roads outside towns to stop and loot vehicles and then attack the occupants. If you intend to travel in these areas, take great care and consider using a security escort.*

*If you have to travel at night, do so by car, with doors locked and windows up, and travel in convoy or with a security escort.*

*Most crime is random, but people have been abducted by organised gangs and forced to open office safes while others are held captive until the ransom has been paid.*

*Rape and sexual assault are problems across the country.*

*Don't carry large amounts of cash or openly display expensive jewellery and electronic equipment*

*Be vigilant at all times and leave travel plans with friends, relatives or reliable local contacts*

*Outbreaks of tribal fighting are common, especially in Port Moresby, the Highlands Provinces (particularly Southern and Western Highlands) and Enga Province. Ethnic disputes can quickly escalate and result in the widespread destruction of property, disruption of normal services and serious injury. Stay alert, monitor local media and consult local contacts, (accommodation or other service providers) before travelling to a new area. Tribal fighters and criminals are becoming increasingly well armed through the trade in drugs for guns.'*

This is all good advice, but it shouldn't deter you from visiting this magnificent country. As can be seen from the advice, most violent crimes occur in the urban areas or along roads leading to the mines. Much of this is caused by armed gangs of so called 'Raskols' who haunt the cities and highways. Useful advice when driving is *'drive fast, don't stop and always get someone else to open gates.'* All these elements were adhered to by our driver when we were in Tari, in the highlands, and this, coupled with armed security guards in the grounds of our accommodation, meant we never felt in danger. Given that most violent crimes occur in the towns and that most people live in the rural areas, which are the most fascinating parts of the country, spending as little time as possible in the uninteresting and relatively squalid towns and as much as possible in the countryside is both rewarding and sensible.

It is also useful to remember that most crimes that occur are crimes of opportunity. So taking the same normal safety precautions you would in any city (not flaunting your money or possessions, not walking alone or at night, if possible, and keeping away from known danger areas) will minimise the risk to health and wealth. Gangs don't, as a rule, attack tourists or *ex pats*. The investigations tend to be more thorough and penalties are much more severe. However, even though this is not the norm, it does happen. The message is, don't let fear prevent you from visiting PNG. We stayed in a number of the towns, including the infamous Port Moresby (dubbed by some the most dangerous city in the world) and in the highlands and the Sepik basin and never felt in danger at any time. Despite its much published problems (often magnified in the telling as opposed to the reality), PNG is probably one of the least spoilt and least developed countries on earth. That alone renders it a desirable destination for the open and adventure minded.

# CHAPTER 23

❦

# Big Hair, Bilum Bags, and Betel Nuts

The early afternoon Air Niugini flight took us from Jackson Field airport in Port Moresby, the capital of Papua New Guinea (PNG), to Kagamugu Airport, 15 minutes drive from Mount Hagen City, in the Western Highlands. Located some 1,677m (5,502ft) above sea level in the large and fertile Wahgi Valley, it is third largest city in PNG, with a population of 33,623.[235] An hour's drive from the airport brought us to our lodgings at Rondon Ridge, some 2164m (7100ft) above sea level and situated on the outer fringes of the Kubor Range. Rondon Ridge provides spectacular panoramic views over the Wahgi Valley below,

In 1933, Mick Leahy (1901 – 1979), the son of Irish immigrants Daniel Leahy and his wife Ellen (née Stone), together with his brother Daniel and government officer Jim Taylor, while conducting an aerial reconnaissance of the highlands, 'discovered' the heavily populated Wahgi Valley. Leahy was in PNG to prospect for gold and he, like most people at the time, thought that the centre of the country was uninhabited and was astonished to find so many 'primitive' people in the Valley.[236] A short time after this reconnaissance they walked in and became the first westerners to come into contact with the tribes.

---

235 http://worldpopulationreview.com/countries/papua-new-guinea-population/cities/ - accessed 09/08/2017

236 At that time it was estimated that it had a population of some 250,000

Leahy, on a previous expedition, having been caught unprepared, was wounded in a pre-dawn raid by a 'pineapple-stone' club wielding *Angu*[237] warrior and now travelled with a well supplied and armed patrol. Since the attack, he demarcated his camps with a fish-line perimeter and posted look-outs around the clock. If, as happened on a number of occasions, 'push came to shove,' Leahy and his retainers shot to kill. It is estimated that during these expeditions several hundred warriors were shot.

With bellicose warriors, Mick's view was clear; he said, '*I'd like to murder the murdering bastards.*' His skill in doing this was much admired by his native retainers who, when interviewed in the 1980s, stated admiringly that '*Masta Mick never missed.*' Mick Leahy never attacked women or children or peaceful tribesmen. He had fairly positive views about them to the extent of describing them as 'good kanakas'[238] (his brother Daniel described him as 'kind, but very hard'). Indeed, he partook freely of their lax attitude to sexual relationships, particularly when coupled with the ready availability of women, who were often offered as part of some transactual bargain or local hospitality.

An Academy Award nominated documentary, called *First Contact*, comprising photographs and footage taken by Mick Leahy, together with interviews with people who were around at the time of Leahy's expeditions, was made by Bob Connolly and Robin Anderson and released in 1983. Although poor quality black and white in many places, it is still a fascinating record.

Today, Mount Hagen hosts the famous annual Mount Hagen Cultural Show. Regional, provincial, and even national tribal dance groups gather to

237 Also known as Kukukuku (pronounced "cookah-cookah") or Toulambi by neighbouring tribes

238 "kanaka", once widely used in Australia to describe people from Melanesia. They were recruited as labourers from the 1860s on, from the Solomon Islands, New Hebrides (Vanuatu), New Caledonia and the Loyalty Islands. Some were kidnapped ("blackbirded") into long-term indentured service. Under the Pacific Island Labourers Act 1901 they were to be deported home. Those who were permitted to remain became known as The Australian South Sea Islander community and were recognised as a unique minority group in 1994, after a report by the Human Rights and Equal Opportunity Commission found they had become more disadvantaged than the indigenous Australians (https://en.wikipedia.org/wiki/Kanaka_(Pacific_Island_worker)

celebrate their cultural heritage in the form of a *singsing*. We were there to visit a number of tribal villages.

The *Melpa* were first encountered by the Leahy brothers during their expedition into the valley in 1933. In many ways, the lifestyle of the *Melpa* people remains little changed since first contacted by the Leahys. They are horticulturalists whose cultivation of sweet potato forms the basis of their diet and trade. Easy to cultivate, sweet potatoes will grow in all soils and can produce two to four crops per year. Having a surplus of sweet potatoes gives men the ability to purchase pigs. Pigs are a sign of wealth among the *Melpa*, and it is common to see women tending both their sweet potato gardens while looking after the family pigs. Indeed, in some uncommon cases, women have been known to suckle piglets to help them survive.[239,240]

True capitalists, the *Melpa* frequent the airport at Kagamugu, offering to sell modern bilum bags, stone axes and other artefacts. Some provide taxi or bus services to hotels and guest houses in Mount Hagen. They are strong believers in the 'Big man' concept and *moka* - a highly ritualized system of reciprocal gift giving. To become a 'Big man' in the tribe requires the single-minded accumulation of wealth and then, through *moka*, to give it away in a lavish ceremonial exchange. The purpose is clear - the bigger the *moka*, the bigger the 'Big man.' The size of the *moka* was previously judged by the number of pigs that were given away.[241] Nowadays, as well as pigs, cash, western goods and even vehicles are commonly given away.

Vojtech Novotny[242] describes *moka* thus…

---

239  Peter Dwyer and Monica Minnegal, "Person, Place, or Pig: Animal Attachments and Human Transactions in New Guinea," in *Animals in Person: Cultural Perspectives on Human-Animal Intimacies*, ed. J. Knight, Oxford and New York, 2005, pp. 37-60.

240  http://images.sciencesource.com/p/14116884/Chimbu-woman-breast-feeding-piglet-BT3013.html; http://blogofswine.blogspot.ie/2007/04/breastfeeding-pigs.html

241  See Chapter 22 for a description of the relationship between tribes and their pigs.

242  Vojtech Novotony (2011) Notebooks from New Guinea (2011) Oxford University Press (Translated from Czech by David Short)

*(It is) 'a system of moving capital around with zero gain is the gift-giving system known as moka. Here, one group, usually a clan, makes a public gift to another, usually an unpalatable neighbour, with whom it is in open competition for prestige, the gift consisting of considerable assets accumulated over many years. If the receiving side is not to be seen as guilty of a breach of etiquette, it is up to them , after some years of retaliatory saving, to respond in kind, and go one better at a similar ceremony.'*

In reality, this is a system of incremental exchange, not matching gifts. It locks people into an endless chain of escalating gift giving and often, as a result, debt. The status of a 'Big man' is really a reflection of how much people owe him rather than what he owns.[243] A side benefit, among what, otherwise, might be warring clans is that *moka* obligations underpin a fragile peace across hostile territories.

Ownership of land is central to existence in PNG. As Novotny noted...

*The idea of a homeless person, like that of a neglected orphan or little old lady was a novelty for traditional village communities, when the entire extended family would care for its kin. Nowhere have I seen the mentally or physically incapacitated so naturally integrated into society as in the villages of New Guinea.*

*The price of this felicity is that everyone is bound by a thousand bonds to dozens of more or less closely related kinsmen and dozens of neighbours near and far. There is no escape, since all reside until death on the selfsame hill where they have their plots of land.'*

But this is no rural idyll to be enjoyed by westerners. Novotny is graphic in his view about the effect that living within the confines of a

---

243 See THE KAWELKA: ONGKA'S BIG MOKA : https://www.youtube.com/watch?v=6D8o0mHSKMk Ongka is a charismatic big-man of the *Kawelka* tribe who live scattered in the Western highlands, north of Mount Hagen, in New Guinea. The film focuses on the motivations and efforts involved in organising a big ceremonial gift-exchange, or *moka,* planned to take place sometime in 1974. Ongka has spent nearly five years preparing for this ceremonial exchange, using all his big-man skills of oratory and persuasion in order to try to assemble what he hopes will be a huge gift of 600 pigs, some cows, some cassowaries, a motorcycle, a truck and £5,500 in cash.( www.therai.org.uk/film/the-series-of-disappearing-world/the-kawelka-ongkas-big-moka)

village would have on him … '*I personally would go berserk from the excess of attentive neighbours long before the absence of electricity got to me.*'

In PNG, clans are created through common descent from a shared male ancestor. Property is kept within the clan. Inheritance is patrilineal. Sons inherit from their fathers; the most important item that can be inherited is land. When a son gets married, he receives a parcel of land from his father. Spouses are chosen from outside the clans. Securing a wife is one of the most costly things facing a New Guinean. In some areas the purchase price can be in excess of US$8,000 – a truly gargantuan sum for those involved in a simple pastoral economy. However, the ties of kinship ensure that all members of his kin contribute according to their means and closeness to the groom. The bride's family distribute the bride price among their kin and in the fullness of time the cycle, in theory, and like the *moka*, is a zero sum game. However, in the short term, both the bride price and *moka* obligations result in winners and losers.

After marriage, the bride and groom set up home in the groom's father's village. A new woman's house is built for the wife.

As is common among different tribes in PNG, males and females are segregated in the villages due to the fear of pollution of males by females, especially through menstrual blood. Too frequent contact with women can leave men vulnerable to evil spirits or magic. Paradoxically, in many societies in PNG, the accumulation of wealth and power is frequently accompanied by the accumulation of wives. Male solidarity, with men and boys over eight years of age living separately from women, underpins the dominance of men over women.

The *Melpa* have two types of house. Men's houses are round with cone-shaped roofs; women's houses are rectangular and contain pig stalls. Men live with preteen and teenage boys, after they are separated from their mothers. Here, they undergo instruction and initiation into the ways of the clan. Women live with the younger boys, and their unmarried daughters.

Members of a clan live in the same area, with the different clan villages and gardens linked by paths.

Dress in Mount Hagen is a mixture of the traditional and the modern. In town most people wear Western-style clothes, but it is not unusual to see people in traditional dress, including a wig made from human hair that the men wear. Someone described this as… 'a juxtaposition of the stone age with the modern age.' Men usually wear shorts, T-shirts, and a knitted cap, and they carry a string (bilum) bag. Women generally wear simple floral print dresses and carry larger bilum bags than the men. Men and women may also wear shoes if they own them; this is more usual for men than women. Most people own only one change of clothing.

It is common during *moka,* ceremonial events and *singsings* to paint the face. We were keen to see it and our guide arranged that we attend a *Melpa singsing* in a village some distance away from the town.

The paint used for decoration is generally produced from local dyes mixed with pig fat.[244] In the case of the *singsing* we attended, we watched the women paint their faces with a white mask around the eyes that had two long streaks down the cheeks. This was then outlined in blue. They painted the tip of their noses with a circle of white outlined in blue and coloured red in the centre. Their lips were painted white (rather like the infamous black and white minstrels of the early 20th century) and this was incorporated as the crosspiece in a cruciform design that ran from the base of the nose to the chin. All areas painted white were outlined in blue. Any bare skin left on the face was painted scarlet. Around their necks they wore multiple heavy necklaces of shell and coral. The biggest was made from large cowry shells. A neck-plate, made from a kina shell, hung under the chin. The most valuable kina shells are cut from the gold-lipped pearl shell.

---

244 The American product Liquid Paper (white correction fluid known in Europe as 'Tipp-Ex') is frequently substituted for traditional white paint because of its better coverage and intensity. It was invented by Bette Nesmith Graham the mother of the singer/guitarist Mike Nesmith of the 1960s pop group *The Monkees*

Elaborate headdresses were decorated with feathers, especially bird of paradise plumes. These included lesser bird of paradise, King of Saxony bird of paradise and sometimes whole, dried, superb bird of paradise skins, together with wings poking from the side like comic Viking helmets, These, among the many other species I couldn't identify, made for a stunning, if somewhat sad display. I would much rather see these birds alive than mummified and, fortunately, later in our trip, I got to see several species.

Around their biceps they wore armbands stuffed with leaves. The ensemble was finished off with a buff coloured grass skirt fringed with a large bustle of green leaves. It was a stunning display that took a couple of hours to prepare. Some of the women were bare breasted; some wore simple brassieres of woven string, like bilum bags, to cover their breasts. The, drumming, singing and dancing was simple, fairly monotonous and hypnotising. No men danced for us, but several helped the women prepare their decoration.

After several dances we were treated to a pit barbecue known locally as a *mumu*. This comprised a fairly deep hole dug into earth, into which large stones were layered. A bonfire was lit over the stones and allowed burn for a long time until the stones were white hot. Some of the hot stones were set aside and a layer of banana leaves was placed over those that remained in the pit. Vegetables, such as yams, sweet potatoes and pandanus fruit, together with chickens, were wrapped in leaves and placed in the pit. More leaves were placed over the food and the reserved hot stones placed on top. These were, in turn, covered with leaves and soil and left for several hours so that the food could steam. Predictably, what we tasted was delicious. However, the cooking method is too long and impractical for my metropolitan lifestyle. The lack of sufficient banana leaves and the prevailing cold and damp Irish weather are sufficient disincentives to jettisoning my gas hob and electric oven in favour of a pit in my back garden.

Later we drove into the Waghi Valley to visit the *Asaro* Mudmen. Probably one of the most familiar 'cultural' symbols of PNG, Mudmen shows are now only put on for tourists or for the annual festivals at Garoka in the Eastern Highlands. We visited a clan in a rain-forest village in Pogla, about 50 km from Mt Hagen. We sat down on log benches around the perimeter of the village dance area and waited for the performance to begin. Several villagers, in native dress, sat to one side and displayed local goods they had for sale, including bangles, bead necklaces, bilum bags, and small models of Mudmen and their helmets.

After about fifteen minutes, a couple of wraith like figures drifted into view through the vegetation. A smudge fire, to the other side of the dance ground, billowed smoke that formed an opaque grey curtain through which they materialised. Each of the warriors was naked, apart from a dry-leafed thong covering his genitals, and had his body covered with thick grey clay. Some had tucked green leaves into the sides of their thong to add a spot of colour. One guy, sporting rather a sad looking helmet, had tucked ferns and a couple of twigs sprouting chains of red berries into his. Terrifying, he was not.

Upon the head of each warrior was a heavy, clay mask with exaggerated facial features; some of which were decorated with teeth. We watched as one bowman high-stepped slowly through the cloud of smoke, all the while aiming his arrow at us. Other Mudmen slowly appeared; some held bunches of leaves in each hand while others sported long sharpened tubes of bamboo on each of their fingers accentuating the menace of their helmets and ghostly body colour.

The show lasted a total of about ten minutes. This, in itself was a considerable feat of endurance as some of the mud helmets weighed in excess of 10kg. When the wearers removed them we could see that they were perspiring heavily.

The legend of the Mudmen has been embellished with each telling, so it is difficult to know what its true origin was. What we do know is that it came to prominence in 1957 when a group of *Asaro* participated in the Eastern Highlands Agricultural Show. They displayed this part of their heritage in the form of a *singsing* group for the tribal finery contest. The helmets (*girituwai*), which previously had the sole function of hiding the face, had by now became more sculptural and exhibited facial features with expressions. The entire body was covered in white clay. Some 200 *Asaro*, thus adorned marched into Goroka. They won the finery contest that year and the following two years.[245]

It is likely that the origin of the helmet began as a mask that the *Asaro* used, in times gone by, as a disguise, when raiding their neighbours from other clans. By doing this they intended to avoid recognition and the retaliation and revenge that would typically follow such raids. In time the masks became more elaborate. The original masks, apparently, were made by smearing mud over a bamboo frame covered with bilum material. Smearing the body with clay and mud was common practice among many tribes, particularly when in mourning. The new, entirely mud helmet appears to be a late 20th century development of the *girituwai*.

An alternative, more poetic, version of the helmet story suggests that centuries ago the *Asaro* of the Waghi Valley were attacked by enemies and forced to seek cover in a nearby muddy river. As they waited they got covered, head to toe, in sticky white mud. Sneaking away at dusk, they were spotted by their enemies who thought they were the returning spirits of the *Asaro* they had killed that day and they promptly ran away in fear. This then became a stratagem the *Asaro* continued to use to protect them from their enemies. While the first explanation has a ring of truth the second sings with romance. You pay your money and take your choice!

It was early morning and conditions were clear and bright when we boarded our P-759-XSTOL (Short Take Off and Landing), 9 seat, turbo prop aircraft to make the hop from Mount Hagen airport to our private bush landing strip on the banks of the Karawari River. Flying across primary rainforest in a

245 The Asaro Mudmen: Local Property, Public Culture? Ton Otto and Robert J Verloop https://scholar-space.manoa.hawaii.edu/bitstream/handle/10125/13111/v8n2-349-386.pdf?sequence=1

small plane is humbling. Below stretched a seemingly endless deep green tangle of vegetation; relieved here and there by the thin black or brown scars carved by streams and rivers. Here and there, in a valley or on a hilltop, we could see plumes of smoke from the village fires in those places where people had carved out gardens from the forest, but these were few and far between and so remote that it was difficult to comprehend how people could live there. The thought did occur to me that if we had to land, either voluntarily or otherwise, anywhere here, it would be game over for us. I should never have read the book '...*and then the engines stopped...*' [246] before we came.

We, patently, lacked the basic skills to survive in these conditions, unlike those who had made it their home for millennia. The map that our Australian pilot, Harold, had circulated to us, when we boarded, indicated 'Relief Data Incomplete' for the area beside our flight path - bringing little cheer to the gloomy thoughts I was having. I was reminded of the medieval maps of the world that showed great swathes as *'Terra Incognita'* and began to have the same apprehension and excitement that these explorers must have had. In our case, however, people knew where we were going and that we could expect a search should we go missing; in theirs it was a true voyage into the unknown with no hope of rescue should anything go wrong. After about an hour flying, we saw the brown ribbon of the Karawari River below us and Harold lined up for the landing on the small private grass airstrip belonging to the Karawari Lodge. Accessible only by small plane or by boat along the Karawari River, this is a remote and virtually unspoilt destination. The Karawari River is a tributary of the mighty Sepik River (1,126 kilometres long), which is the longest river on the island of New Guinea.

When we landed we were greeted by some native *Sepiks,*[247] who worked for the Lodge, and a small group of naked children, who had come to ex-

---

246 https://openresearch-repository.anu.edu.au/bitstream/1885/128830/1/And_Then_the_Engines_Stopped.pdf

247 Used here as a generic term to describe people from the many tribes and clans who occupy the catchment of the Sepik

perience the thrice weekly excitement of the arrival of the charter airplane. The airstrip is adjacent to the river so a short walk took us to the boats that were to take us upstream to the lodge. As we headed upriver we passes a couple of stilted villages built along the bank of the river and *Sepiks* in dugout canoes passed us as they made their way up and downstream on what was their main highway.

At a ramshackle riverside dock, we transferred to an ancient, rusted and rickety four-wheel drive vehicle that carried us and our luggage up the muddy path to the lodge, perched on a ridge some 300m above the river. From the deck of the lounge we were afforded stunning views across the Karawari River and the seemingly endless expanse of fecund and dense tropical lowland rain forest. This was to be our base for the next few days as we explored the villages and tribes in the adjacent area.

Located, as it is, on a windswept ridge, the lodge provides some relief from the mosquitoes that thrive in the Sepik basin. Given the prevalence of malaria in the area, mosquito nets and jungle strength DEET spray, as well as anti-malarial medication, is strictly *de rigueur*. The American cultural anthropologist Margaret Mead[248] in 1932, recorded in a letter home from the Lower Sepik region…

*'The mosquitoes have not been exaggerated; they are the most amazing, determined, starving crew imaginable.'*

While we were in the Middle Sepik region, the determination of the local mosquitoes to voraciously feed on our warm and pulsing blood was no less than that of their companions downstream.

Our visits to various villages was a significant learning experience, facilitated by our local guide - although it was sometimes difficult to tell

248  Margaret Mead (December 16, 1901 – November 15, 1978) in 1930 wrote the famous *Growing Up in New Guinea: a comparative study of primitive education (1ⁿ Perennial Classics ed. 2001)*; New York: Harper Collins. ISBN 978-0688178116

if he was telling us things he thought we wished to hear (especially about witchcraft and cannibalism) or was giving us real insight into local customs and culture. The answer probably lies somewhere between these extremes.

In the past, many people feared the inhabitants of PNG as vicious head hunters and cannibals. This view persisted right up to the middle of the 20th century. In a letter home from the Yuat River, in 1932, Margaret Mead, described the natives as being...

*'superficially agreeable... but they go in for cannibalism, head-hunting, infanticide, incest, avoidance and joking relationships and biting lice in half with their teeth.'* [249]

Despite infrequent reports to the contrary, it is unlikely that these practices persist anywhere in New Guinea today. Inter-tribal warfare and killing, as well as witch and sorcerer killing, certainly still takes place, but the occurrence of head-hunting and cannibalism appears to have, long since, been stamped out.

In the Middle Sepik region, people have beliefs related almost exclusively to their own clan or language group. This has left them vulnerable to the wide variety of sects of Christianity, whose missionaries associate Biblical stories directly with ancestral myths in order to increase their tally of 'converts'. Given that they do not remain in any of the villages permanently, but assign responsibility for services to a converted villager, it is not surprising that a type of syncretic religion is developing that borrows from both traditional beliefs and a PNG interpretation of Christianity.

Each village has its own spirit house, or Haus Tambaran, and some of them even boast Christian churches. The spirit houses are where men spend their time, store the sacred masks, ritual garb, statues, sacred flutes, war shields and, up to the fairly recent past, skull racks that held the dec-

---

249 Nancy Sullivan (no date) in 'A Brief Introduction to the History, Culture and Ecology of Papua New Guinea';Trans Niugini Tours , PTY LTD. P.O. Box 371, Mt Hagen, Papua New Guinea.

orated heads of slain enemies. The spirit houses contain many sago bark paintings that represent clan mythology. These are painted with both geometric and figurative designs.

The lounge in the Karawari Lodge has an impressive collection of sacred objects, including ornately carved posts and beams containing carved clan totems, statues and ancestral images of Sepik clans.

Most Middle Sepik people, including the *Karawari* are believed to have originated in the hills behind the Karawari River, where they lived a semi-nomadic existence. Here they spent much of their time avoiding headhunting raids from neighbours. The Karawari are still the most remote of these floodplain people. It is only since 'pacification' less than a hundred years ago that they settled near the river.

It is in the spirit houses that young boys are secluded and instructed by elders during the period of their initiation. Boys being initiated have their skin cut as a symbolic release of their mother's blood and as a means of eliminating any residual femininity. Girls also have their skin cut as part of a puberty rite, although any formal initiation process is rare. We came upon one young mother whose extensively scarred back was intended to represent the skin of the crocodile, in deference to a belief in ancestral ties to the crocodile.

One of the most important activities that can be seen in the villages is sago palm (*Metroxylon sagu*) culture. All the river people seem to depend on it for food and trade. PNG has vast natural stands and a high genetic variation of sago palm trees. Starch is accumulated in the pith and, as a result of its size and lengthy vegetative phase, vast quantities of sago starch are stored in the stems.

To cultivate sago, a planting site near a creek or in a damp place is chosen and cleared of vegetation. Next, a suitable sucker, chopped from an old sago clump, is planted in a shallow hole and left to grow. Occasional thinning, weeding and the cutting back of encroaching vegetation, from time to time, over the next twelve to fifteen years is all the attention needed. The sago palm is then ready to be cut down and harvested.

As mentioned in the previous chapter, after lunch on the day we arrived, we travelled by motorised dugout canoe a short distance up river and over to the opposite bank to Kundiman village, to learn about the harvesting and preparation of sago. While a display was laid on for us, it was part of normal everyday life in the village and was not false or embellished for tourists. The members of the *Yokoim* tribe we met were friendly and natural in both their dress and behaviour. Village life, with the exception of the antics of curious children, proceeded around us as if we weren't there. Villagers were friendly but were not distracted from the imperatives of daily life by our presence. However, they did recognise an economic opportunity when they saw one and, after a suitably discrete interval, some of the women placed straw mats on the ground and laid upon them wooden carvings and simple jewellery crafted from shells, seeds and nuts.

The women were dressed solely in simple grass skirts made up of bunches of differently coloured grasses (green, yellow, brown, maroon and black) and had painted their faces and smeared their bodies with white clay. Some women had stuffed large bunched of green leaves into the back of their skirts to make a comfortable cushion when they sat down. A small number of women wore caps decorated with shells and boar tusks as well as elaborate necklaces of seeds and nuts. These women also had much more elaborate designs painted on their faces.

The men wore lap-laps,[250] and cloaks of loose, long, green leaves and a woven cap decorated with cowry shells and boar tusks. Like the women, the men had painted their faces - in this case black - and had smeared their bodies with white mud. The children, generally, were naked but some fashioned miniskirts of twigs and their attached leaves and draped them around their waists with pieces of chord.

---

250 A lap-lap is a loincloth woven from the same material as a bilum bag. It consists of three parts: a front flap, a back flap, and a belt or thread to tie them around the waist. The sides are generally open. How much is covered by the front and back flap varies.

Early the next day we boarded our canoe, which was hollowed out from single sandalwood tree, and headed upstream to have a 'home stay' in one of the villages. The distance involved should have taken only two to three hours, but as we were also scheduled to stop at another village, the home of some of the staff of the Lodge, it was to take most of the morning. At the first village it seemed everyone turned out. People here were more finely dressed and decorated than had been the case the previous day. We were greeted by the headman and a group of the villagers started a *singsing* by dancing and singing to the beat of kundu drums, slit drums (or garamuts) and flutes. Here, some of the women painted their entire face red and decorated it with lines and patterns painted in black, yellow and white. Many wore necklaces heavy with shells and seeds, and hats (some of which were woven from human hair) or headbands that were decorated with plumes, kina and cowry shells. Armlets, tied around the biceps and made of either bunches of grass, leaves or bunches of flowers, decorated both the men and women. As in the previous village, I noticed a number of women whose backs were completely scarified, but I failed to detect any similar scarification on the men.

Our second stop, Wamut village, was the site of our homestay. This was also the home of our boatman, Sixtus, a member of the *Yamandin* clan.

The diminutive headman, more than a head shorter than me (and I am only 1.625m - the extra 0.025 is important to my self esteem), and who was dressed in a lap-lap and leaf skirt, and a necklace of three large kina shells and a circle of bone, greeted us at the top of the bank. Sixtus translated his greeting in which he stated that the village was delighted to welcome white people to stay with them and we discovered that some of the villagers, and in particular many of the children, had never seen a white person before. As a result, every activity we indulged in while we were there was the subject of great and open curiosity. It was impossible to traverse the village in any direction without being accompanied by hordes of giggling children.

The villagers had decorated the steep slope up the bank with fronds of leaves strewn along the path and branches stuck in the ground. Some of the villagers were dressed in tattered t-shirts and shorts others were in traditional grass skirts and lap-laps and had their bodies and faces painted and decorated with leaves, grasses, bird plumes and flowers. We were greeted with wide smiles that exposed red teeth stained from chewing betel nut. Once again we stood and watched as a selection of the villagers performed a *singsing* for us.

The village, as is typical, was divided into men and women's houses. We were housed in two separate houses divided by gender. As I was the only married member of the group, and a white man, I was permitted to share the women's house with my wife and our travelling female companions. The houses were constructed on stilts and consisted of walls made of vertical poles, a palm thatched roof and a split bamboo floor. Entry was gained by clambering up a ladder made by chopping notches in a tree trunk and laying it at a 45 degree angle against a raised patio.

The company we were travelling with had laid on mattresses, pillows and sheets as well as the all important mosquito nets. These had travelled up from the lodge in a separate boat. This boat also brought all our food supplies, as the company was unwilling to subject us to the test of local hygiene. Thoughtfully, or in the hope of repeat business, the villagers had dug and screened a pit toilet for us, some way to the edge of the village and at the edge of the bush. Evacuation should have been a relaxed affair, as there are no large predators in PNG, but the thought of being joined by one of the many poisonous snakes in the country had the laxative effect of quickly scaring the shit out of you.

While we dined separately at the edge of the river under a palm roofed pergola, the villagers watched with interest. Communication was difficult but not impossible. We had unimpeded access to all parts of the village. It is highly likely that we broke many taboos in our peregrinations, but we were white people and expected to know no better. Most of us used the buckets and basins provided by the lodge to carry out our ablutions, but two of the women felt in need of something more and went for a swim in the river. They were required to bathe in the women's area, which is downstream from the men's to ensure that they would not pollute the men. I presume they checked before entering the water. Disregarding this taboo would have been a step too far.

We visited several other villages as we travelled down-river on our way back to the Lodge. At each we were greeted with a *singsing*. Everyone was friendly and, although craft goods were left on display for us, there was absolutely no pressure to buy. We also had the pleasure of watching a group of women in canoes fish, using nets, and cook their catch on small fires they lit in the canoe. The women stood as they paddled, while children sat in the bottom of the canoe. Overhead, a white-bellied sea-eagle (*Haliaeetus leucogaster*) and a couple of brahimny kites (*Halistur Indus*) scanned the water for any morsel that might be missed or left behind.

A second flight in our P-759-XSTOL over the rainforest brought us from Karawari to the southern highland town of Tari. Here, we transferred to a vehicle, armoured with steel mesh over the windscreen and windows, for the journey up the mine road to Ambua Lodge (2133m; 7000ft above sea level), which is tucked in between the Doma Peaks. We were informed that the steel mesh was to protect the windows from flying rocks fired up as mine trucks careered down the road. If this was so, we felt that it was doing an incredibly bad job as the windscreen was already starred with cracks. The validity of the explanation was further eroded when we arrived at the roadside gate to the lodge, and it was opened by security guards armed with AK47s. Inside the lodge grounds similarly armed guards patrolled. This level of security was required, we were informed, because of tribalism, hooliganism and violence in Hela Province in general, but in Tari in particular.

A 2010 report by Oxfam tried to put this in context. It stated...

*Recent economic growth in PNG has not translated into an increase in living standards for ordinary Papua New Guineans. Unequal wealth distribution, a lack of economic opportunities and poor service delivery to the rural majority has been accompanied by an increase in criminal activities and corrupt practices, although causal relationships between these factors are hard to establish. A resource rich region, the SHP has one of the highest provincial revenues in the country, but per capita Provincial revenue is lower than the national average. SHP is one of the worst performing provinces in the country in terms of socio-economic indicators. Conflict and lawlessness have contributed substantially to this lack of progress, accompanied by corruption in political affairs at the provincial and district levels.[251]*

Jo Chandler writing in The Sydney Morning Herald on 3ʳᵈ September 2011 reported...

*Tari is no place to be without friends. The wild west outpost - a clearing in the endless jungle, little more than a long airstrip surrounded by a cluster of thatch huts and ramshackle buildings without phone lines or power - is a place where wigmen warriors in grass skirts and running shoes brandish bows, arrows and, when things get lively, shotguns.*

*They are lively the day 'The Saturday Age' arrives. A local man has just been beheaded with a machete in a tribal fight in a nearby village, a school burnt to the ground, women and children have fled and two foreign workers on ExxonMobil's new Komo air strip site have been attacked by locals with bush knives. The project workforce is locked down for security.*

*It might sound like the badlands, but Tari and the nearby mountains are the epicentre of PNG, crucible of economic hope and political strife. Down the road is buried*

---

251  https://www.oxfam.org.nz/sites/default/files/reports/Tari-report-final_2011.pdf

*treasure, the $US16 billion ($A14.9 billion) PNG liquefied natural gas project.'*

In November 2014, the year before we arrived, we were informed that the minibus transferring guests from the airfield to Ambua Lodge had been attacked by 'raskals' attempting to steal the staff wages. Thankfully, they failed and no one was hurt.

February 2016, a year after we had been there we noted the following headline[252]

'Dozens of police officers in the Papua New Guinea Highlands centre of Tari have been arrested and charged with various offences.'

*The Post Courier reports the arrests came as the PNG police hierarchy cracked down on ill-discipline.*

*The Tari police station commander Daniel Yangen said 26 police personnel had been arrested and charged with criminal offence such as theft, assault, alcohol-related and firearms offences.*

*He said there would be more police arrested and charged in coming weeks.*

*Furthermore, another 22 police men and women will be put off the payroll for disciplinary breaches.'*

Today the Australian Government[253] gives the following advice about visiting '…reconsider your need to travel'…

*'(there have been) recent violent tribal clashes. Clashes between clans have occurred in and around Tari in the 2016-17 holiday period. Security forces have been deployed to restore law and order.'*

---

252 http://www.radionz.co.nz/international/pacific-news/295477/dozens-of-police-arrested-in-png's-tari
253 http://smarttraveller.gov.au/Countries/pacific/Pages/papua_new_guinea.aspx (accessed 19th August 2017)

A report in 2017 stated[254] …

*'More than 300 police and military personnel have been deployed to Papua New Guinea's Hela province as an operation to end a spate of lawlessness gets underway.*

*The province, home to the lucrative LNG gas project, has been gripped by widespread tribal fighting and a build-up of firearms, which local police have been at a loss to prevent.'*

On 19th August 2017 an article in NBC/PNG Today read…

'Army call-out in PNG's Hela Province starts today'[255]

*'A Defence Force call out into Papua New Guinea's Hela province to end the continuous tribal fighting and general lawlessness starts operation today .*
*The Parliament Member for Tari-Pori and Finance Minister, James Marape, will launch the operation on Christmas Eve.*
*The Defence Force is being assisted by members of the police.*
*The Mobile Squad in Port Moresby is sending three units to assist in the operation.*
*There has been a surge of deadly tribal clashes in Hela this year, which has spread into the provincial capital, Tari, forcing it into locked down (sic) at times.*
*The operation is the beginning of a wider effort to establish a permanent police and court structure for the province to try and instil law and order.'*

Remarkably, in the year we visited PNG, 2015, there were few reports of violence, other than the endemic domestic violence, from Tari. Nonetheless, we remained vigilant throughout our time there.

The Tari valley is the home of the famous *Huli* Wigmen. They are proud and strong people, with an intricate culture. They believe that they

254 http://www.radionz.co.nz/international/pacific-news/322018/hundreds-of-police-deployed-to-end-lawlessness-in-png's-hela

255 http://news.pngfacts.com/2016/12/army-call-out-in-pngs-hela-province.html#ixzz4qCcZOFjG

are descended from a single ancestor called *Huli* and who, it is said, introduced gardening into their territory. The men and women tend separate gardens because of an abiding fear by the men of pollution from females, particularly from female menstrual blood. They live in separate houses and cook and eat their meals separately. Sexual contact is believed to be especially dangerous, even life threatening, and is only permitted under strict traditional rules.

The predominant crops grown are sweet potatoes, taro, beans, corn, pumpkin, cabbage and a variety of other greens. Pineapples, papaya trees and banana are also cultivated in suitable areas. Sweet potatoes are the main staple of the *Huli* people. Men are reported to eat between seven to ten large tubers a day and to carry some extra in their bilum bags for snacks.

As well as crops, the *Huli* keep pigs and chickens. The importance of pigs for food is reflected in the *Huli* love of pork, but it is subservient to their role as currency, in bride price and in ritual sacrifice.

The *Huli* are fierce warriors who frequently indulge in inter-clan as well as inter-tribal warfare. *Huli* territory is criss-crossed with great trenches, each up to several metres deep. These define family and clan boundaries; help keep the pigs under control; and guard against incursion by enemies. Warfare seems endless. When we were visiting one of the villages, a woman told us of an incursion by a rival clan the previous year in which two men were killed in a tit-for-tat battle. This was stated in such a matter-of-fact way that it underscored the philosophy that vengeance is the appropriate response to injury, preferably by inflicting greater injury on the enemy. Previously, bows and arrows were the weapon of choice, with battles being fought between opposing sides lined up just outside effective range, charging, dodging and screaming while firing arrows at each other. This type of ritualised warfare meant few casualties. The recent proliferation of shotguns has changed this dynamic.

Both men and women are very conscious of their appearance and invest considerable energy in self-beautification. Both men and women wear some facial paint almost every day. At a minimum, this involves daubing spots of yellow paint and red paint at the corners of the eyes, over the eyelids or under the eyes, and on the tip of the nose. During dances, like the Mali dance we were to attended, or other ritual events, they apply greater amounts of paint to their faces and their bodies.

The face is generally painted yellow on the top half and red below; sometimes separating these colours with a band of white.

Men individualise their look with thin lines of white dotted with red painted on top of the basic yellow and red undercoat. The men dress in a woven apron that hangs above the knee, over which they wear a shorter apron. Another short apron, decorated with dangling pig tails, may be worn during dances. All of this is held in place by a thick, red, woven belt. A huge bunch of red and green cordyline leaves, bound together with rope and attached to the belt, covers the buttocks. Men commonly wear a kina shell breast plate, earrings, neck bands, cowry shell necklace, a hornbill beak and pig tusk necklace worn on the back of the neck, and a shaft through their nasal septum. They make their bodies shine by the liberal application of tree oil and a stiff belt of woven cane and bark is tied tightly around the torso to emphasise their physique. The whole ensemble is topped by a large cap-like wig made from their own hair and decorated with feathers, many taken from parrots, cockatoos and Birds of Paradise. Up close it was possible to identify several species of bird of paradise used in decoration. Wigs contained the breast plates of superb birds of paradise, beautiful eye plumes from the Duke of Saxony bird of paradise, long tail plumes of the black sicklebill bird of paradise, Stephanie's astrapia tail plumes and golden plumes from the raggiana bird of paradise as well as sulphur crested cockatoo crest feathers and cassowary plumes.

Given the difficulty I had experienced in sighting the few species of bird of paradise I managed while in PNG, my feelings were mixed - sad at the end of these exceptionally beautiful creatures but astonished by the use to which they were put.

The Mali dance is simple and repetitive and consists of a simple jumping step which the dancers silently perform to the beat of small kundu drums carried by the dancing men. To my mind it is the sight of the dancers, rather than the dance that has appeal; to them it is the ritual significance of the dance, to which they pay homage by dressing up, that is important.

*Huli* wigs are crafted by young men out of their own hair. Why this tradition developed is obscured by the mists of time. Males in their late teenage years and early 20's leave their community to attend 'Bachelor' school, where a wig-master teaches them about manhood and how to craft these unique wigs. The process takes between 18 months to three years.

We got to visit a 'wig school' where four initiates were several months to two years into the process. As would be expected, it starts with the bachelors growing out their hair. When sufficiently grown, the shaping of the wigs begins. A circular band of bamboo is used to train the hair into a saucer-like shape. Eventually, as the hair continues to grow, this band is replaced by an oblong one to produce a shape similar to a toreador's hat. During this period the men bathe their hair daily at a purifying spring. After 18 months the hair is clipped off close to the scalp and reshaped to create the typical ceremonial wig. During this entire time the men must sleep using a headrest that prevents the nascent wig being squashed.

Some men wear a wig daily, although it is more commonly reserved for special occasions like the Mali dance. In the absence of a wig, Huli men usually adorned their hair with feathers, everlasting daisies, leaves, or tree kangaroo fur.

The traditional dress for women consists of a long grass skirt that hangs below the knees. Today, most women wear a European smock purchased from a store in Tari. Young *Huli* women are forbidden to expose their breasts - older women, however, may go about topless. In contrast to what we experience in western culture, Huli women tend to wear less body decorations than men. Typical adornment is restricted to kina shell breast plates, neck beads and flowers in the hair.

Ubiquitous in PNG, among both men and women, is the bilum bag. This is a type of woven string bag traditionally fashioned from plant fibre - such as reeds or grasses - fur from tree kangaroos, or, increasingly in urban areas, store bought string or wool based yarns. The designs woven into the bilum may be reflective of a particular tribe or clan, the region in which they were made, a major festival or event, or, increasingly, patterns that are entirely individual to a weaver.

We watched women weave bilums when we visited the *Huli* Villages in the Tari Valley. We were informed that a single large bilum can take up to one month to complete. In recent times bilum weaving has become an important source of income for PNG women. It is not unusual to see them being sold in village markets, near tourist hotels or beside airstrips and airports. In a classic example of cultural piracy, a company in the west has appropriated the title of this unique PNG icon and has registered the name as a trademark for its own bags.

Bilum bags serve a multiplicity of roles depending on their size - from purses to handbags, shopping bags, baby carriers or man-bags. The woven string can stretch to an amazing size due to its resistant and elastic structure, making them ideal for carrying awkward and heavy loads. The bilums that women use tend to have short handles that permits them sling the handle across their foreheads and drape the bag down their back. Women frequently carry prodigious loads - both within the villages and travelling to and from market. It is not unusual to see women who are pigeon-toed and who have deformed foreheads sustained from the back breaking effort of lifting and balancing and porting. Women also use their bilum bags as cradles, or carry cots, for children. It is not uncommon in a village to see a large bilum bag containing a peacefully sleeping infant dangling from a branch near a vegetable garden, while the child's mother weeds her sweet potato patch.

Men generally prefer bilums that have a long strap like handle permitting them to be worn over the shoulder, thus keeping the hands free. For men, the bag is used to carry necessities of daily life such as sweet potatoes for snacking, smokes, *kina*[256] and *buai'* (betel nut).

Almost, but not quite, as ubiquitous in PNG as the bilum bag is the habit of chewing betel nut or *buai'* (boo-ayeh) in Tok Pisin - the *lingua franca* of PNG. Evidence abounds in the form of the bright red gobs and splashes of spit that festoon pavements, lamp-posts and walls, together with the husks and the chewed remains of the 'nut', referred to as *buai pekpek* locally.

The betel nut is the seed of the areca palm (*Areca catechu*), which grows in much of the tropical Pacific, Asia, and parts of east Africa and has flourished for centuries in the coastal areas of Papua New Guinea. The areca seed is not a true nut, but a berry. In PNG it is generally sold in its green, fresh, form with the 'nut' inside soft enough to be bitten through or cut with a knife.

For chewing, a lump of 'nut' is bitten off or the whole 'nut' may be popped into the mouth. Some chew only one betel nut at a time, while others chew several together. Average daily consumption is reported to be between 8 to 10 nuts.

To be effective, it is chewed with a mustard stick (*daka*) dipped in lime powder (*cumbang*). The mustard is grown from seed while the lime powder is refined by drying, burning and sieving stag horn corals from the coastal area. The nut is chewed until juice is released. The mustard stick, moistened with saliva, is dipped in the lime powder and chewed with the betel nut. It is the reaction between the betel nut juices the mustard and the lime that creates the bright red colour. The habit results in strong staining of the mouth, teeth, tongue and lips. Users are immediately obvious when they smile or spit.

---

256 the currency of PNG

Various compounds, but especially arecoline (the primary psychoactive ingredient that is similar to nicotine) act as mild stimulants, and are said to promote a warming sensation in the body and to heighten alertness and depress appetite.

The World Health Organization (WHO) has estimated that, globally, 600 million people chew some form of betel nut. Consumption lies in fourth place after nicotine, alcohol, and caffeine.

Like tobacco use, however, the effects of betel nut chewing are less than benign. It is a carcinogen that has been implicated, amongst other conditions, in cancers of the mouth and oesophagus. The World Health Organization cites PNG as having the highest incidence of mouth cancer in the world - 32.3 cases per 100,000 men and 26 cases per 100,000 women.

PNG currently has one of the highest infection rates with tuberculosis in the world. Control of the increasingly multiresistant strains is significantly compromised by the requirement to spit out the excessive saliva produced by chewing *buai*.

It has also been shown that if chewed during pregnancy it significantly increases adverse outcomes, such as higher incidences of preterm birth and low birth weight and height, for the baby.

Since 2013, Port Moresby, the capital of Papua New Guinea, had enforced a ban on *buai*. Numerous billboards and posters in Port Moresby encouraged people to respect the town and not to chew and spit betel nut '*Lukautim town. Noken kaikai em spitim buai*'. Fines for transgression ranged from 500 *Kina* (about €130) to 9000 *Kina* (€2400). At the time of its introduction it was estimated that the cost of cleaning the town would exceed 6 million Kina annually (about €1.6 million).

In May 2015, a police raid in the stilt village of Hanuabada, just north of Port Moresby, saw the police confiscate over 1,000 bags of betelnuts, with a value of some €150,000. Earlier in the year, two betel nut vendors were killed in Hanuabada after police reservists, enforcing the ban, fired on a crowd.

In August 2016, police set up road blocks to check for people who might be chewing betel nuts, after the public largely ignored the ban. As an added incentive to quit, it has been reported that some *buai* sellers were beaten by the authorities. Despite this, trade continued. As Peter Rasta, a seller in Port Moresby told a correspondent for 'The Telegraph'[257] '*It is simple - betel nut cannot be stopped by imposing such fines as it is the daily income for unemployed youths and families that are struggling to survive in the city.*'

Given the prevalence of the habit across the nation, the authorities have found that it is not simply a matter of checking the population for chewing and spitting; they also have to develop processes to ensure that the police and military carrying out implementation of the ban are not, themselves, chewing on the job.

Like all bans, the effectiveness of this one was compromised by the extent to which the sale and consumption of *buai* is embedded in the population. It only served to encourage smuggling, drive the sale underground and greatly increase the price of the product, with the consequent and growing criminality this fostered. One major success of the ban, however, was a noticeable change to the streets of Port Moresby. Many areas were entirely spit free.

The futility of the efforts to ban the selling and chewing of betel nut was highlighted in May of 2017 when the ban in was lifted.[258] Clearance was given to vendors to return to selling betel nut from their street-side stalls, and the police were warned not to impede the business of vendors.

Like everything that happens in Papua New Guinea, nothing is simple, and little is certain. This is what makes the country unique; this is a major part of its attraction. I can't wait to go back.

---

257 http://www.telegraph.co.uk/news/2016/08/02/betel-nut-checkpoints-set-up-as-papua-new-guineans-defy-ban/

258 http://www.radionz.co.nz/international/pacific-news/330172/betel-nut-ban-lifted-in-png-capital

# CHAPTER 24

# The Shamwari and Sanbona Safaris

*We desire to bequeath two things to our children; the first one is roots, the other one is wings (Sudanese proverb)*

Almost from the time she could speak, my granddaughter, Holly, has called me 'Grandad Beard' – to distinguish me from her other granddad 'Grandad Mick'.

This has now become the family tradition, with my wife, my elder daughter and her husband and my grandson, Liam, all using the same appellation. The fact that, in appearance, I look like a hybrid between 'Papa Smurf' and a leprechaun renders the nickname somewhat appropriate. I do not object to it; in fact I'm rather proud of it.

The relationship between grandparents and grandchildren is something special. This nickname endorses that special bond. Becoming a grandparent is a wonderful thing. The angst and uncertainty you felt bringing up your own children disappears, allowing you relax into this new role with assurance and diminished responsibility. You have the time and the patience to indulge the antics of this newer generation. This leaves your grandchildren, at least in the beginning, believing that their grandparents know everything and will tolerate almost anything. However, they are wily enough to appreciate that, although the boundaries might be wide, they are still there and should not be transgressed. Unfortunately, they don't extend the same courtesy to their parents, as pushing boundaries seems to be a compulsory child/parent activity. Their interaction with their parents is a matter for them as a family and is territory upon which grandparents have no right to intrude. Our role is to support, to inform, to care for and to enjoy – not to discipline, argue or spoil; although grandparent's indulgence is frequently seen as spoiling – but only by parents.

Children have boundless curiosity. They constantly seek explanation of what is going on around them. They have an innate interest in all living things. Unfortunately, the road to adulthood has meant, for many, that this curiosity has been stifled and they have developed a dislike for many creatures based on irrational value judgements. A consequence of this understandable, but distorted, view is that many place their own material development high above the need to preserve wilderness and its inhabitants from human encroachment.

There are things I have had the privilege to see that I fear will be gone by the time my children reach my age and will be long gone by the time my grandchildren are parents themselves. This has led me to seek out opportunities when I could show them some of the wonders of the world and instil in them a passion for nature; and foster a deep desire to preserve the best of this planet for the benefit of future generations. It was also stimulated by a desire to see the wonder on their faces when they first encountered rare animals in the wild. Thus were the Shamwari and Sanbona Safaris born.

South Africa was chosen because the areas we planned to visit were malaria free; January provided relief from the grey, cold and wet weather of post-Christmas Ireland; private wildlife reserves provided an unaccustomed level of comfort for our safaris – a change from the two man tented bush camps we had become familiar with in the past; and, especially in 2015, the fact that we could take Liam – then just over 4 years old - on game drives

343

was a big plus. We had intended this trip to be a one-off event. However, it proved so successful that we repeated it twice more – each trip becoming more special as the children grew up and their appreciation for nature, landscape and people grew.

In January 2017, Dylan, our wildlife Game Ranger, asked Holly what she would like to see most. Having been in Shamwari previously and having failed to see them, she answered promptly 'leopards!' 'We will try' answered Dylan, 'but they are very difficult to see.' 'And what about you Liam?' asked Dylan. 'Snakes' he replied. 'Well we will have to see what we can do about that' replied Dylan.

This was the second time of the three times that we had left Ireland, just after Christmas, and travelled to South Africa. When we first went to Shamwari at the end of December 2014, Holly was eight and a half years old (the half was important then) and Liam was just over four years old. Several factors influenced me in suggesting that we should go *en famille* on safari. High among these was my desire to ensure that my grandchildren would be able to see large mammals in the wild before they disappeared entirely.[259]

So with this in mind, Holly and Liam together with Grandad Beard, Granny Mary, mum and dad – Helen and Michael – and Auntie Niamh headed off on a great family adventure.

Shamwari was not our only stop. In our three safaris (January 2015, January 2017 and January 2018), we watched Cape fur seals (*Arctocephalus pusillus*) chill out on the wooden jetties in the Victoria and Alfred waterfront of Cape Town; the kids strutted and waddled along the boardwalks of Boulders Beach at Simon's Town in giggling imitation of the African black-footed (or jackass) penguins (*Spheniscus demersus*) that have lived here since 1985. Also observed on the rocks and in the water was the now

---

259 Mary and I had been on safari with Helen, Niamh (our daughters) and Michael (our son in law) previously in Botswana and Zambia. This was before Helen and Michael had children.

endangered all black Cape cormorant (*Phalacrocorax coronatus*), with its piercing turquoise eye and orange-yellow gular skin below its beak. Gathered in a large flock at the edge of the tide we observed a group of mainly juvenile swift terns (*Thalasseus bergii*) which have grown accustomed to human activity in South Africa. As well as diving for food, such as sardines and other fish, this bird follows fishing boats for jettisoned by-catch. It has also taken to nesting on the roofs of buildings and artificial islands in salt pans and sewage works. Studies of the bird in Australia show that on Lizard Island, near the Great Barrier Reef, swift terns (or great crested terns as they are also known) may supplement their diet with vertebrate prey such as agamid lizards and green turtle hatchlings.[260]

The first time we travelled south to the Cape of Good Hope, Holly and Liam saw wild ostriches (*Struthio camelus*) near the seashore and promptly got out the cameras they got for Christmas and started filling up their memory cards. In the car park and near the Cape of Good Hope sign, they spotted small troops of dark grey-brown chacma (or Cape) baboons (*Papio ursinus*) as they arrogantly strutted around looking for any exposed food that visitors may have left unguarded. They learnt that this is the longest species of monkey, with a male body length of 50–115cm and tail length of 45–84cm; it is also, at up to 45kg, one of the heaviest. Feeding mainly on fruits, but also insects, seeds, grass, and smaller vertebrate animals, the chacma baboon at the Cape of Good Hope is notable for eating shellfish and other marine invertebrates it gathers from the shoreline.[261] Conflict with the baboons, who have become accustomed to humans, sometimes occurs when visitors set up barbecues and picnics. Attempts to share in the food has led to the baboon dashing in to snatch a morsel and visitors to the park attempting to chase or beat them off.

---

260 *Blaber, S. J. M.; Milton, D. A.; Smith, G. C.; Farmer, M. J. (November 1995). "Trawl discards in the diets of tropical seabirds of the northern Great Barrier Reef, Australia" (PDF). Marine Ecology Progress Series;127: 1–13. doi:10.3354/meps127001*

261 Christine Davidge (1978) Ecology of Baboons (Papio Ursinus) at Cape Point, Zoologica Africana, 13:2, 329-350, DOI: 10.1080/00445096.1978.11447633

Holly and Liam also got to see their first antelopes in the wild in the Cape of Good Hope Nature Reserve. They were lucky enough to see the elegant chocolate-brown coloured bontebok (*Damaliscus pygargus pygargus*). Its rich dark coat contrasts with a white underside, a white stripe from the forehead to the tip of the nose, and a distinctive white patch around its tail. It also sports knee-length white socks. Previously regarded as pests by landowners, they were hunted and killed to the point of extinction. At one time, there were only 17 animals left in the wild. Since then numbers have recovered. The IUCN Red List of Threatened Species now lists them as 'Least Concern' as '*the species is reasonably abundant in both formal conservation areas and on private land, the population is stable/increasing, and there do not appear to be any major threats to its long-term survival.*'[262]

We took the Flying Dutchman funicular (named after the local legend of the Flying Dutchman ghost ship) from the car park up to the museum and looked out at the cliffs and the old lighthouse. Here we spotted a four-striped grass mouse(*Rhabdomys pumilio*) and a hovering rock kestrel (*Falco rupicolus*). Luckily for the mouse, or its days would have been numbered, it escaped detection by the bird.

On the way down we eschewed the funicular and walked back to the car park. Grazing on the cliff-side meadows we saw several eland (*Taurotragus oryx*). In size, this is the second largest antelope being slightly smaller than its north-western or central African cousins the giant eland (*Taurotragus derbianus*). These big, bulky, antelope are the slowest of all the antelopes but they can jump a considerable height (up to 3m) from a standing start. When on the move, eland herds are accompanied by a loud clicking sound that carries a considerable distance. It is speculated that the weight of the animal causes the two halves of its hooves to splay apart, and the clicking is the result of the hoof snapping back together when the animal raises its leg. In areas where predators occur, adult eland have little fear and frequently

---

262 IUCN is The *International Union for Conservation of Nature. ref at*http://www.iucnredlist.org/details/30208/0

confront and see off lions. As there are no large predators, such as lion and hyaena, in the Cape of Good Hope Nature Reserve, the eland here live a relatively comfortable life.

Near the restaurant we spotted another four-striped grass mouse and a southern boubou (*Laniarius ferrugineus*) – a black and white, cinnamon breasted bushshrike, notable for its distinctive bell-like calls. Belying its reputedly shy and skulking nature, the birds we saw eagerly flitted from table-top to table-top and between table legs looking for morsels that had fallen from the plates of diners.

Another animal Holly and Liam particularly liked was the dassie (*Procavia capensis*) or rock hyrax. We first encountered it at the top of Table Mountain as it scuttled along the rocky edge beneath boulders, where courting rock pigeons (*Columba guinea*) billed and cooed – the males trying to impress the females by pushing out their chests and puffing up their neck feathers. In the nearby trees speckled mousebirds (*Colius striatus*) fed on the abundant fruit. Holly and Liam were fascinated to learn that the closest living relatives of the dassie – a small (up to 50cm), squat but heavily built mammal - were the elephants and sirenians (dugongs and manatees).[263] People in South Africa have been gathering dassie poo for years, as it contains a large amount of hyraceum—a sticky mass of dung and urine. This has been used in folk medicine to treat epilepsy and convulsions. Today the natural musk from hyraceum is being used in the manufacture of perfumes. Isn't it interesting to ponder that the scent some women dab behind their ears to make themselves more attractive is derived from the dung of a miniature relative of the elephant.

Sunning themselves on the rocks on Table Mountain we also observed the black girdled lizard (*Cordylus niger*) and several blue-headed male agama lizards (*Agama atra*) in full breeding dress.

---

263 The name sirenian is derived from the sirens of Greek mythology. This comes from a legend about their discovery, involving lonely sailors who mistook them for mermaids. When you see one, it looks rather like a huge seal with a broad, paddle-like tail

Interesting birds we saw as we travelled from the cape towards Shamwari included the beautiful tiny southern double-collared sunbird (*Cinnyris chalybeus*) – one of Africa's versions of a hummingbird - the African hoopoe (*Upupa africana*), Egyptian goose (*Alopochen aegyptica*), African sacred ibis (*Threskiornis aetiopicus*), hadeda ibis (*Bostrychia hagedash*), Hartlaub's gull (*Chroicocephalus hartlubii*), Cape canary (*Serinus canicollis*), Cape sparrow (*Passer melanurus*), Cape bulbul (*Pycnonotus capensis*), and the olive thrush (*Turdus olivaceus*).

High on the list of 'must-see' attractions, each time we visited Cape Town, was the excellent Two Oceans Aquarium. The kids were particularly taken by the ragged-tooth sharks (*Charcharias tarus*), a cousin of the great white shark (*Carcharodon carcharias*), long one of Holly's favourite animals. The ragged-tooth shark, like its relative – but much more infrequently - has been known to attack humans.

A new attraction for 2018 – the sunfish (*Mola mola*) – had both Holly and Liam enthralled. The magnificent new I&J ocean exhibit has a 10m long tunnel that allows you stand still while fish swim beside you and above you. Entered through a dimly lit hall with pillar tanks containing a myriad of shimmering jellyfish of a variety of sizes, the tunnel permits close up views of rays – such as the eagle ray (*Myliobatis aquila*), giant guitarfish (*Rhynchobatus djiddensis*), giant yellowtail (*Seriola lalandi*) and green sea turtle (*Chelonia mydas*), to name but a few.

In recent days (January 8, 2018), a disturbing report has emerged about the effect of global warming on the green sea turtle. Rising temperatures appear to be turning all turtle eggs in certain beaches into females. Sea turtles lay their eggs on shore, buried in sandy beaches. At this time the sex of the animals in the eggs is undefined. It appears that the sex of most turtles – and that of alligators and crocodiles - is determined, not by X and Y chromosomes as in mammals, but by the temperature of the sand in which their eggs incubate. This is known as temperature-dependent sex determination

(TSD). A very narrow and specific temperature range produces a clutch where 50% of the babies are born male and 50% female. A shift by just a few degrees on the cooler side can produce 100% males. A few degrees on the hotter side can turn a whole clutch female. On some northern Great Barrier Reef beaches in Australia over 99% of the hatchlings are female, while the female sex bias is 65% to 59% in the cooler southern Great Barrier Reef beaches.[264] Such a skewed sex ratio bodes ill for the survival of this species and others that reproduce in the same way.

As we drove through the main gate into Shamwari for the first time in 2015, we were immediately greeted with the sight of a herd of Burchell's zebra (*Equus burchellii*). This is a southern subspecies of the plains zebra and is the only subspecies of zebra which may be legally farmed for human consumption.

Zebras are members of the horse family and are only found in Africa. The basic colour of the zebra is black with white stripes. A distinguishing feature of Burchell's zebra is the fact that the stripes continue underneath the belly, unlike other zebras that have completely white bellies; and it also has shadow stripes, which appear as brownish stripes on the white between the black stripes. Like our fingerprints, the pattern of stripes is unique to each individual animal. The function of the stripes is unclear - several theories have been proposed, the most convincing include:

- The stripes may help to confuse predators, such as lions, by motion dazzle - a moving group of zebras may appear as one large mass of flickering stripes, making it more difficult for the lion to pick out a single target

- Some say that the stripes are effective in attracting fewer flies, including blood-sucking tsetse flies and horseflies

---

264 Environmental Warming and Feminization of One of the Largest Sea Turtle Populations in the World
Michael P. Jensen, Camryn D. Allen, Tomoharu Eguchi, Ian P. Bell, Erin L. LaCasella, William A. Hilton, Christine A.M. Hof, Peter H. Dutton
http://www.cell.com/current-biology/fulltext/S0960-9822(17)31539-7

- Stripes may be used to cool the zebra. Air may move more quickly over black light-absorbing stripes while moving more slowly over white stripes - a sort of natural air conditioning.

Zebras have excellent eyesight, hearing and acute senses of smell and taste. They must be constantly wary of lions and hyenas. A herd provides many eyes and ears alert to danger. If an animal is attacked, its family will come to its defence, circling the wounded zebra and attempting to drive off predators.

Not much further on, we found a herd of waterbuck (*Kobus ellipsiprymnus*) relaxing on the grass. These were common waterbuck and are easily distinguished from their central and western African cousins (defassa waterbuck) by the white band that circles their rump. Many liken it to the animal sitting on a newly painted toilet seat. Spiral horns,[265] present only on males, curve backward, then forward and can reach a length of up to 1m. A local African story explains how the waterbuck got its white circle.[266] One dark, moonless, night a waterbuck mother and her calves were grazing very close to a hut that a tribesman had been whitewashing. He had left the pots outside. One of the calves knocked over the bucket of paint and the tribesman rushed out of the door to determine what was going on. When he saw the overturned paint pot he picked it up and angrily flung it at the mother waterbuck, which was running away. It hit her on the rump and left a white circle on her russet coloured hide. Rather than being upset, the mother waterbuck was delighted as the bright white circle acted as a guide to her calves as they followed her through the dark night. Other waterbuck saw how useful this white ring was and adopted it themselves and no waterbuck is seen today without one. The mystery, however, is where do they get the paint?

---

265  Antelope have permanent horns; deer have antlers that the shed and re-grow each year.

266  courtesy of Shamwari

As we drove towards Riverdene Lodge we saw black wildebeest (*Connochaetes gnou*), springbok (*Antidorcas marsupialis*) and helmeted guineafowl (*Numida meleagris*) – all before we had even checked in.

After lunch, in the cool of the afternoon, we headed off on a game drive with our Game Ranger, Ntobeko Ngcala, who was to stay with us for the rest of our time in the Reserve. Ntobeko was great with Holly and Liam and they kept asking him questions every time we went on a drive. He had those characteristics, shared by Dylan van Aardt, our Game Ranger in 2017, of patience, knowledge and the ability to talk to children and adults on equal terms. Both of these Game Rangers added immeasurably to our enjoyment of Shamwari and Holly and Liam learnt an enormous amount from each of them.

Our first encounter was with a lion (*Panthera leo*) and two lionesses. They had fed earlier and so they just wandered around slowly before lying on the ground for a post-prandial snooze. Further out on the plain, where they could see all around them, were a pair of cheetahs (*Acinonyx jubatus*), who were likewise engaged in doing nothing. Had the lions not been so well fed, it is unlikely that they would have tolerated the cheetah being so close. In the grass ahead of us, a brilliantly coloured orange-throated longclaw (*Macronyx capensis*), a member of the wagtail and pipit family, hunted for insects.

Holly and Liam were thrilled at these sightings. I think both of them preferred the cheetahs as they, at least, sat up and allowed them take good photographs – the lions remained supine and unbothered by our presence. Although we were within yards of some of the most dangerous animals in Africa, both children showed only interest and asked many whispered questions of me, their parents and Ntobeko. The whispering was not out of fear but in obedience to the instruction not to talk out loud or stand up suddenly in the vehicle – it was a mature example of good game drive etiquette for such young children.

Nearby we saw a pale chanting goshawk (*Melierax canorus*) on the ground. It was obvious that this elegant mid-sized bird of prey had caught something to eat, either a lizard or a small mammal, but we were too distant to properly identify what it was clutching in its talons in the grass. For a first day's safari, we all agreed that this was wonderful and headed back to the lodge for a superb dinner.

Back out on a game drive before dawn the following day, we saw some red hartebeest (*Alcelaphus buselaphus caama*) and their calves. This is the most colourful of the ten hartebeest subspecies. Its general russet body colour and pale/whitish rump are highlighted by black markings on the face and upper part of its limbs. It has a longer face that other hartebeest subspecies, and its head is armed with complex curving horns that are joined at the base. Although adults are only occasionally taken by lions or leopards the young are vulnerable to both of these big cats, as well as to cheetahs and hyaena. To escape, when being pursued, hartebeest run in a zigzag pattern to confuse their predators.

Much to our delight, and that of Holly and Liam, we were to see more lions that day. Unlike many adults, children don't seem to get tired of seeing the same things over and over again. This time we saw two lionesses, one of which was blind in one eye. This was immediately evident as she stared intently at us; one of her eyes had the appearance of a solid blue lifeless marble; the other was a vibrant yellow with a small dark pupil vivid with life and threat. Every so often one of the lionesses would open her mouth or yawn widely and reveal her four long, pointed, canine teeth in her black bordered mouth. Although we were parked within a few metres of them, most of the time they just rested on the grass or groomed themselves by licking their limbs with their coarse pink tongues. That they had eaten fairly recently was evident from the blood on the side of the face of the half blind female and from streaks of blood on her legs, picked up while she squatted to feed. We sat and watched them for about twenty minutes while Holly and Liam took several photographs with their new colour coded cameras (pink for Holly, blue for Liam).

A little distance further on, we observed a fairly large leopard tortoise (*Stigmochelys pardalis*). This one was, obviously, a female as she was digging in the ground with her hind feet, an activity these tortoises only indulge in when they are making make nests in which to lay eggs. For shelter, they squat in abandoned fox, jackal, or aardvark holes but do not excavate homes themselves. These are very long lived animals and, in captivity, have been known to live for up to 80 years.

Nearby a female greater kudu (*Tragelaphus strepsiceros*) browsed on some bushes. The males of this species are, to my mind, the most handsome and elegant of the antelopes – an accolade others, mainly hunters, give to the endangered sable (*Hippotragus niger*), some of which have been introduced into Shamwari for conservation purposes. Personally, I don't think there is any competition. Its long spiralling horns and slim proportions, together with its patterned face and coat, make the Kudu the hands down winner.

Kudu, or koodoo, is the name given to this animal by the Khoi-Khoi[267] people of South Africa. While it was not unusual for us to spot groups of female kudu, all the males we encountered were solitary. The males are not usually aggressive, but will fight by locking horns and pull and push each other during the mating season. The large spirals of their horns sometimes means that they become locked together in a fight and, in such cases, the males involved will die from hunger and thirst if they cannot disengage.

A favourite antelope, with all of us, is the graceful impala. Like the kudu, it is a slim and elegant animal that sports a soft rufous-brown coat on its back that gradually becomes paler down its flanks and fades to white on the belly. The males carry a distinctive and glorious pair of wide-set lyre shaped horns that curve backwards, sideways and then upwards. Down the

---

267 Called 'Hottentots' by 17th century Dutch – a description that today is thought both offensive and derogatory

middle of the tail and running as two lines along the edge of the rump are distinctive black markings forming a large letter 'M' shape. For this reason some safari Game Rangers describe them as the 'McDonald's of Africa.' Indeed the pattern on the impala's rump has a lot in common with the McDonald's logo and the animals themselves are regarded by many of the larger predators as tasty take-away snacks.

In subsequent game drives we enjoyed the antics of families of warthog (*Phacochoerus africanus*). Regarded by some as ugly, but by us as interesting and highly comical, this medium sized pig has very little hair and what they have is confined to a long black or brown mane on the neck and shoulders. They have a large head, distinguished by a large flat face sporting two sets of large 'warts' – one set on the side of the head below the eyes and the other on the sides of the face between the eyes and the mouth.

Two pairs of tusks protrude from the mouth and curve outwards and upwards in a semi-circle. The shorter lower pair is razor-sharp as a result of rubbing against the upper pair every time the warthog opens or closes its mouth. The tusks are used for digging, for combat with other hogs, and in defence against predators such as lion, leopard, cheetah, hyaena and wild dogs. Its general colour is grey, but after wallowing in mud holes, as we watched them doing near our lodge when we revisited in 2017, it can take on the colour of the mud as it bakes dry on its skin. Its tail is long and ends with a tuft of hair. When fleeing danger, the warthog holds his tail aloft, like a warning banner. Warthogs are powerful diggers, using both their snouts and feet as shovels. Whilst feeding, they often bend their front feet backwards and move around on the calloused pads that protect their wrists.

Dotted here and there, and particularly near bushes, we could see the fading sunlight shine pink through the long thin ears of the many grizzled-grey scrub hares (*Lepus saxatilis*) that grazed on the grass. These are solitary animals, only coming together to breed. The young are born fully haired, have open eyes, and are capable of taking care of themselves within a short time after being born.

In the late evening sunset we spotted a pair of yellow mongooses (*Cynictis penicillata*) playing in the grass at the edge of a copse. Nearby, a blesbok (*Damaliscus pygargus phillipsi*) stopped and looked back at our vehicle to determine if danger was near.

Blesbok are variant subspecies of the bontebok we had seen at the Cape of Good Hope.

Late in the afternoon, at about 17.30, as we drove down a track between some trees, we heard crashing and breaking noises. Ntobeko cut the engine and we waited in silence to see what was making the commotion. Just beside us the bushes parted and revealed the head and ear of an elephant (*Loxodonta africana*). We sat and watched as he browsed on leaves and chomped through young branches. Suddenly, with a heave, he emerged from the bush and stood right beside us. You couldn't hear a sound from us other than the initial gasp for breath we made – almost in unison. We were astonished to be so close to this huge animal. He did not feel threatened by us and we, in turn, although in awe of him, were not afraid.

We sat there conscious of his smell, his breathing, the slapping of his ears and the rumbles of his belly. Slowly, he walked past us and became lost in the bush again.

Delighted at what we had seen, we headed to a high ridge for sundowners. We were all buzzing with the excitement of the game drive. As we sipped our drinks and feasted on snacks we were able to look down on the plains below. As we did so, we saw a herd of elephant pick their way through a small forest and out at its edge several giraffe (*Giraffa camelopardalis giraffe*) browsed the treetops. Nearby, perched at the top of a thorny acacia branch, a Fork-tailed Drongo (*Dicrurus adsimilis*) emitted a grating call.

Subsequent drives brought more sightings of all these animals and Holly and Liam watched with interest as red-billed oxpeckers (*Buphagus erythrorhynchus*) fed on the ectoparasites that were in turn feeding a variety of different animals such as giraffe, kudu, impala, eland, and rhino. The birds like to feed on the blood-engorged female ticks that parasitize these animals. However, their actual preferred food is blood, so while they may take the ticks, they also like to feed on blood directly, pecking at any wounds or scabs the animal may have to keep them open and the blood flowing.

A new encounter with lions had both Holly and Liam fascinated. A pride of four lions, fed on a recently killed warthog. Sated from the feast, one of them idly played football with the pig's stomach, while the remaining three tore at what remained of their prey. It was possible to hear the grinding of their teeth on bone and, as they ate, their muzzles became gory with blood. Holly and Liam looked on in fascination. They didn't express any sympathy for the prey or revulsion at the savagery they were witnessing. They took it in their stride – this was what happened in nature and you couldn't change it - nor did they wish it changed.

We were also fortunate to see rhinoceros on both of our visits to Shamwari. The name rhinoceros means 'nose horn'. There are two types in Africa - the rare white rhinoceros (*Ceratotherium simum*), and the very rare black rhinoceros (*Diceros bicornis*). We observed white rhinoceros adults and young, on two occasions in 2015 and several occasions in 2017 and also in Sanbona in 2018; we only had a fleeting sighting of a black rhinoceros crossing the Bushman's river in 2015, but in 2017 we spent about 30 minutes with a family of mother, father and their calf.

Rhinoceros are very easily poached - they visit water holes daily and can be easily killed while they drink. They are generally killed for their horns. They have two horns on their snout - a large horn in front and a shorter one behind. Rhinoceros horns are used in traditional medicines in parts of Asia, such as China and Vietnam and for dagger handles in Yemen and Oman.

Shortly after our first trip, when we had come home and I was driving Holly and Liam somewhere and we were talking about our first Shamwari visit, Liam said '*Grandad! I hate poachers*'. Even at his tender age he realised the damage they were doing to these animals. I tried to explain to him that he shouldn't hate the person, just what he was doing. I think he understood.

Neither the white rhino nor the black rhino have teeth at the front of their mouths, relying instead on their lips to pluck food. The white rhino has a heavy head and a square shaped face that usually points towards the ground; this is so that the rhino is able to use its wide lips to eat short grass. Black rhinos have a triangular shaped face. The upper lip is prehensile and is able to hold and pull leaves, as well as branches, which can then be bitten off and eaten. An interesting difference!

It is interesting to observe rhinoceros mothers and calves flee from danger. The white rhinoceros calf runs in front of the mother, so the mother is able to protect it from a chasing predator, or draw attention away from the calf to herself. With black rhinos, the calf will run behind the mother. Black rhinos live in very bushy vegetation, therefore the mother runs ahead of the calf to break through the bushes and trees so they can make a speedy getaway.

Near where we saw three white rhinoceros together in 2015, we came across a dung midden, a couple of metres across, containing a steaming pile of recently dropped dung in the middle. Rhinoceros middens are used as communication centres. They provide information on the health and status of the local population. A male can use it to discover if a female is ready to mate or subordinate males can use it to find out whether there is a dominant male nearby. Only a dominant male, as was the case with this midden, defecates in the centre of the dung-heap. He is also the only one who will kick his dung. This is done to spread his scent over that of other users of the midden. This midden was covered with hundreds of brown-veined white butterflies (*Belenois aurota*). This is known as mud-puddling and the butterflies do it to gather liquid nutrients, such as salts and amino acids.

As we watched the white rhinoceros groups, we noted that they were often accompanied by fork-tailed drongos and Cape glossy starlings (*Lamprotornis nitens*). This, most likely, was because the ambling rhinoceros disturbed insects upon which the birds could feed. On one occasion we saw a glossy starling grab a leathery brown insect grub about as thick as my thumb and as long as its own head. Once it got inside the leathery exterior it had a supper that would last it for quite some time.

As we searched in vain for leopards, visiting the spots where they had been seen in the past, we came across a secretive chocolate brown bushbuck (*Tragelaphus scriptus*) skulking at the edge of the track. Across his back he had half a dozen white stripes and white spots on his flanks. Some time earlier, in another part of the Reserve, we had seen a female hiding in the bushes.

Our trip in 2017 added some new species to our list as well as giving us a chance to see some familiar ones. In some ways it was better, as we were more relaxed and had little in the way of unrealistic expectations. Holly and Liam now understood that nature sometimes lets you see its glory, other times it hides it from you. We went on game drives intent on observing as much as we could, not expecting to see anything in particular, but not regretting things that did not appear.

This time, on arriving at Riverdene Lodge, we were greeted in the garden by a male pintailed whydah (*Vidua macroura*). This is a small black and white bird, with a scarlet bill and a pennant like tail nearly three times its body length. This conspicuous bird sings from a high perch and his undulating and hovering flight is intended to show off his magnificence to any observing female.

In the restaurant and open hallways between the rooms, we noted that the greater striped swallows (*Hirundo cucullata*) that had nested there during our previous visit continued to make use of the place as their own exclusive avian hotel. In the gardens, malachite sunbirds (*Nectarinia famosa*) fed on the abundant blossoms, while small common waxbills (*Estrilda astrild*) fed on the grass. These waxbills are the main hosts of pintailed whydahs, who, like cuckoos, are brood parasites, laying their eggs in the nests of other birds. The large trees in the gardens were festooned with the nests of Cape weaver birds (*Ploceus capensis*).

Down at the Bushman's river we saw the long necked African darter (*Anhinga melanogaster*), known to some as the 'snake bird' and looking like a thin long necked cormorant. A particularly exciting observation was the African finfoot (*Podica senegalensis*) that made its way across the river, just below the observation deck. And flying overhead was one of my favourite birds, an African fish eagle (*Haliaeetus vocifer*).

While we saw many of the same animals as we did on our previous safari, I had asked Dylan to make sure Holly and Liam also saw the smaller creatures that most people ignored. Although termite mounds abound and are unmissable, few people actually see the termites. We saw a few mounds that had been damaged by aardvarks (*Orycteropus afer*), although, unfortunately, we never got to see these nocturnal creatures themselves. The termites, however, could be seen around the damaged area.

Termites are tiny ant-like insects. There are three groups of termites in a mound. The workers, who are solely responsible for getting the food and for the upkeep of the mound; the soldiers, who protect the mound from enemies using their large jaws and toxins as deadly weapons; and the king and queen, who are responsible for producing the next generation of termites. The queen produces up to 30,000 eggs a day and may live for 30 years.

Each mound, which is riddled with tunnels to ensure air flow, is as strong as concrete and populated with millions of termites.

Once again, on this safari, we looked for leopard, and once again we failed to find them. Although there are leopards in the Reserve, they are nocturnal in habit and very secretive. Our chances did not look good. Dylan told us it was five months since he had last seen one.

However, we did get to see some in the flesh in the *'Born Free'* cat rescue centre that is located in the Reserve. The centre houses rescued captive animals in as near to natural conditions as possible, but because these animals were brought up in close contact with humans they can never be returned to the wild, as they lack the skills to survive.

Leopards are not rare, just elusive. The rest of the family, except for Holly and Liam had seen them in the wild elsewhere in Africa. This was the closest the grandkids were going to get this trip. Ah well! There was always the next year, when we would safari in Sanbona Reserve.

As we travelled around this time we saw gemsbok (*Oryx gazella*) in a part of the Reserve we hadn't visited the previous time, when we were busy chasing leopard. We also saw Cape buffalo (*Syncerus caffer*) up close. Previously, in Shamwari, we had only seen them in the distance. On our previous visit in 2015 we did not scout along the Bushman's river. This time we went specifically to look at hippopotamus (*Hippopotamus amphibious*). Unfortunately, they were in the water beneath very steep banks and there were predators around. This meant that only the adults got to see them and Holy and Liam had to remain with Michael in the vehicle. Dylan, who was armed, acted as a guard for those of us who ventured to the edge of the high bank. Holly and Liam got their chance in 2018 when they were able to observe Hippo in the reservoir at Sanbona.

We saw our one-eyed lioness again, this year, and followed her as she walked along the track heading to where she had left her almost fully grown cubs. It was nice to renew acquaintance. As she walked, she paused to lap up water from a puddle formed by rain water gathered in a wheel rut on the track. All around, giraffe were alert, watching her every move. After a while she lay in the grass and began to groom. Several times she rolled over on her back with her legs in the air, finally ending up in a sitting position, paying attention to everything that was going on. We drove on a bit and a moving shape in the grass caught our attention. We stopped near a cross track and slowly a russet coloured caracal (*Felis caracal*) emerged from the long grass stalking prey we couldn't see. This was a wonderful close up sighting.

The caracal is normally nocturnal but sometimes hunts at twilight or during the day. This is the biggest of the small cats in Africa and it is sometimes described as Africa's version of a lynx. Much smaller than a cheetah it is regarded as an awesome predator, regularly killing the animals it targets.

'One-eye' eventually got up and joined another female who was attending four cubs. Three were quite small and one was half grown. Eventually they all got up, crossed the road and headed into the bush.

Just down the road we stopped and picked up a dung beetle. This relatively large coleopteran uses dung for food and as a nursery for its eggs. The front legs are used to make a large ball of dung which is rolled away and buried with the beetle's eggs inside. Interestingly, when the dung ball is being moved the beetle does a 'hand stand' and pushes backwards. The dung ball can be as much as 250 times heavier than the beetle rolling and burying it.

We saw several new reptiles this trip – the angulate tortoise (*Chersina angulata*), The Cape skink (*Trachylepis capensis*), the very large water monitor (Varanus niloticus) and the boomslang (*Dispholidus typus*).

As Liam particularly wanted to see some snakes, Dylan caught a boomslang near the lodge and brought it out with us on our game drive so that we could study it close up and he could release it in a spot remote from the lodge. It is a shy, generally non-aggressive, but dangerous snake. When disturbed it puffs up its throat and strikes repeatedly but because it is rear fanged, although with relatively large fangs, it can only bite properly if it strikes small appendages like fingers and toes, or ears and nose - if it strikes at the face. Its venom clots the blood, causing huge blockage in the major blood vessels. In man the dosages are generally too low to cause fatal clotting but cause uncontrolled bleeding and haemorrhaging over a period of several days. This can be fatal unless treated with the specific antivenom.

Boomslang venom is slow acting. Symptoms of a bite may not be obvious for several hours. Sometimes, this lures human victims into a false sense of security, believing that the bite was dry (i.e. without envenomation), thus underestimating its seriousness.

Boomslangs feed on chameleons and other arboreal lizards, frogs, birds and birds' eggs, and the occasional small mammals, all of which are swallowed whole.

Other mammals we saw that are worth noting were vervet monkeys (*Chlorocebus pygerythrus*) - their antics in fording the Bushman's River by leaping from the high branches of a tree on one bank to lower branches of a tree on the opposite bank were truly entertaining. The chacma baboons we saw were generally lazing around and paid us no attention whatsoever. Cape clawless otters (*Aonyx capensis*) were present in the river one day as we lunched on the riverbank. We also saw black-backed jackal (*Canis mesomelas*), small grey mongoose (*Galerella pulverulenta*), water mongoose (*Atilax paludinosus*), bushpig (*Potamochoerus larvatus*), and among the antelopes we added were the common duiker (*Sylvicapra grimmia*) and steenbok (*Raphicerus campestris*).

We added many new birds to our list with highlights, in no particular order, including the jackal buzzard (*Buteo rufofuscus*), booted eagle (*Aquila pennatus*), the spotted thick-knee (*Burhinus capensis*), the southern red bishop (*Euplectes orix*), Denham's bustard (*Neotis denhami*), long-billed crombeck (*Sylvietta rufescens*), the bokmakierie (Telophorus zeylonus), giant kingfisher (*Megaceryle maximus*), fiery-necked nightjar (*Caprimulgus pectoralis*), spotted eagle owl (*Bubo africanus*), the long-tailed widow bird (*Euplectes progne*) and the stately secretary bird (*Saggitarius serpentarius*). I could go on, but the list is endless.

The third of our safaris, undertaken in January of 2018, was to Sanbona in the Western Cape. This is completely different habitat to Shamwari. It is arid semi-desert and, as a result, does not support large herds of antelope. Fewer antelope means fewer large predators, so you have to work much harder to see animals in Sanbona than in Shamwari. If the only objective is to see big animals, then Sanbona is not as fruitful as Shamwari. This, however, was not our objective. Shamwari is rich in vegetation suitable for a variety of animal species. Large numbers of ungulates sustain a healthy population of predators such as lion, cheetah and leopard. Grassy plains sustain a number of white rhino and subtropical thicket provides browsing for elephant and black rhino; hippos are found in the Bushman's River.

Sanbona is different; its mountain fringed plains; its seemingly vast landscape and vistas; its stillness; and its isolation create a completely different feeling. You have to be tough to survive here whether you are a plant, an animal or a human.

Sanbona represents an on-going conservation project that aims to restore ecological balance in the area. Plant life includes acacia thickets, renosterveld, succulent Karoo and central mountain fynbos. Various species of succulents thrive and sport unique names such as baby's bottoms, ostrich toes and pig's ears. Herds of zebra and antelope – such as springbok, gemsbok (oryx) and eland – are present, together with hartebeest, kudu and buffalo, but numbers are much smaller than Shamwari, as the carrying capacity of the land is lower.

This reserve, like Shamwari, was fashioned out of former farms - now being rehabilitated to their previous wild condition - and is situated in the Little Karoo a 290-km-long valley, ranging in width from 40km to 60km, and formed by two parallel Cape Fold Mountain ranges, the Swartberg to the north, and the continuous Langeberg-Outeniqua range to the south.

We had explained carefully to Holly and Liam the difference between the two areas before we travelled, so their expectations were realistic. In Sanbona they would have the chance to see the intimate relationship between the organisms and environment that characterise arid habitats.

Sanbona is named for the '*San*' hunter-gatherer people who, before the European settlement of the land, occupied the area, and '*bona*' means 'vision'. It is well named as it requires vision and the combined senses of hearing, smell and touch to properly appreciate the complexity and variety within this seeming wilderness.

The *San* people were the hunter-gatherers, who originated on the north coast of Africa but were driven south into more arid lands by stronger tribes. They have been called by many names: 'Bushmen', '*San* or '*Son-qua*', '*Soaqua*', '*Sarwa*' or '*Basarwa*', and '*Twa*' all basically meaning, 'those without domestic livestock'. They were excellent trackers and lived in caves or shelters, made of branches, close to waterholes for drinking water and so that animals could be easily hunted.

A related group, the *Khoi-Khoi* (men of men) practiced extensive pastoral agriculture (a nomadic lifestyle based on herding of cattle) in Southern Africa for about 30,000 years before the European settlers arrived in 1652. The settlers knew them as Hottentots. They lived in simple dome-shaped huts made from branches that could easily be taken apart and transported to a new location. Their huts were erected in a circle, surrounded by a fence of thorny acacia branches to protect themselves and their animals from predators and other intruders. In the minds of the settlers these two tribes were frequently conflated into one grouping that they called the *Khoisan*. The *San* and *Khoi-Khoi* lived in this area up to 100 years ago.

Much strife developed when the San and the *Khoi-Khoi* interacted with the settlers, both black and white, who invaded their traditional territory. The nomadic *San* regarded the settlers' cattle as game that they could hunt. As a result conflict arose and many of the *San* people were killed and the rest were driven north into Namibia and Botswana - and particularly into the Kalahari desert. The name the Dutch colonists gave them was *Bosjes-mans* which was transliterated into English as Bushmen. The attitude of the settlers to the *San* was irrational and one of odium. This is exemplified by the view of the colonial historian George McCall Theal who, at the beginning of the 20<sup>th</sup> century, stated that they…

> *'were of no benefit to any other section of the human family, they were incapable of improvement, and it was impossible for civilised men to live on the same soil with them, it was for the world's good that they should make room for a higher race.'*

While viewed as objects of derision, the *San* and the *Khoi-Khoi* were also treated as objects of curiosity. This was particularly true of the *Khoi-Khoi* (renamed by the settlers as Hottentots in imitation of the click sound consonants that are unique to the Khoisan language). The colonists noted that these people had substantial levels of tissue on the buttocks and thighs, tapering to the knees that produced a curvaceous figure. Known as Steatopygia, the term derives from the Greek *stéar* meaning 'tallow' and *pugè* meaning 'rump'.

Steatopygia is a genetic characteristic found mainly in women of sub-Saharan African origin, most notably (but not solely) among the *Khoisan* people of southern Africa. Charles Darwin wrote about *Khoisan* steatopygia in *The Descent of Man* in 1882, thus…

> *'It is well known that with many Hottentot women the posterior part of the body projects in a wonderful manner; they are steatopygous; and Sir Andrew Smith is certain that this peculiarity is greatly admired by the men.'* [268]

The *Khoi-Khoi* saw the colonists as unwanted intruders on their grazing pastures. The colonisation of the Cape forced them to change their lifestyle, as they witnessed their population being progressively and severely reduced by wars, epidemics (e.g. smallpox) and economic deprivation. As a result, they eventually became detribalised and cease to exist as a nation.

---

268  http://darwin-online.org.uk/content/frameset?itemID=F955&viewtype=text&pageseq=1 p.578

Negative views of the *San* persist. Since 1996 the *San* have been subjected to evictions and resettlement programmes. The United States Department of State[269] described ongoing discrimination against *San*, or *Basarwa*, people in Botswana in 2013 as the 'principal human rights concern'.

Today there are about 86,000 *San* living on the brink of cultural extinction, mostly located in sub-Saharan Africa. They live in the outer reaches of the Kalahari Desert in Botswana (47,500), Namibia (25,000), South Africa (10,000), Angola (< 5,000), and Zimbabwe (1,200) and speak a variety of *Khoisan* languages.

Sanbona is known for its ancient rock art. The seven recorded sites throughout Sanbona date back more than 3,500 years and are depictions of what the *San* and the *Khoi-Khoi* shamans saw in drug induced trances.

It is generally possible to identify the origin of the painting from both its colour and its theme. The *San* paintings tend to be more representative of animals, people, and spirit beings. Due to the amount of ochre in the paint, they are usually a dark red colour. *Khoi-Khoi* paintings are more symbolic in style and a lighter orange colour. The paint was also made with ochre, but included a mixture of calcrete, animal blood, animal fat, plant sap, and ostrich eggs, ground to a paste.

A link between the *San* and *Khoi-Khoi* heritage of both Sanbona and Shamwari can be found in the 2000-year-old *Khoisan* mummy that was discovered in 1999 in a cave in the Baviaanskloof Mountains, not far from Shamwari. The mummy was found to be male, aged between 30-40 years old, and was 135-145cm tall. He was nicknamed 'Moses' by the local newspapers and is the only mummy ever to be found in South Africa.

'Moses' was buried lying in the foetal position in a large woven basket, placed in a hole and covered with a decorated rock, within a small cave. Around his head were beads made of stone and sea-shell. He was embalmed with the scales of the *Boophone* bulb, which was believed to have the

269 *Bureau of Democracy, Human Rights and Labor;Botswana 2013 Human Rights Report (PDF)*. United States Department of State

power to transport the dead through a doorway to the afterlife. The body was also covered by *Boophone disticha* leaves for preservation.

*Boophone disticha* is indigenous in Sanbona and was pointed out to us by our Game Ranger, Brenda Gunter. The Latin name *Boophone disticha* is derived from the Greek *bous* (ox) and *phontes* (killer of) referring to the poisonous properties of the bulb and possibly the experience of the early colonists whose cattle inadvertently consumed it. To the *San* and *Khoi-Khoi* it had many medicinal uses, particularly in the treatment of pain and wounds. The outer covering of the bulb is applied to boils and abscesses and fresh leaves are used to stop the bleeding of lesions.

The plants are known to be poisonous to cattle and sheep and the bulb is very poisonous to humans. The principal compounds are eugenol - an aromatic, volatile oil smelling of cloves and having analgesic properties - and the toxic alkaloids buphandrin, crinamidine and buphanine, the latter having an effect akin to that of scopolamine,[270] and if taken in quantity may lead to agitation, stupor, strong hallucinations – an effect sought by *Khoisan* shamans - and (if over-ingested) coma or death. *Khoisan* people once used its poison for their arrows. Not only is the bulb poisonous but the attractive and sweetly scented, pink to scarlet,single, dense umbel has earned the name of 'sore-eye flower' as a result of the fact that a person exposed to the open flowers in a confined space may suffer from sore eyes or headache. After flowering (July to October), the large seed heads break off the stalk and tumble across the veldt dispersing seed. This gives the plant its other common name - 'tumbleweed'.

*Boophone disticha* is even more conspicuous in leaf than in flower. The specific name *disticha* indicates that the 50cm long and up to 6cm wide and undulating erect leaves, numbering between 8 and 16, are arranged in a neat fan shape. This is often the most noticeable indication of the plant as you look across the veldt.

---

270 See Chapter 1

Having already seen most of Africa's big animals, we were all keen to see animals that we hadn't seen before.

Justin Fox, the travel writer and photographer from Cape Town, drew up a list of what he believed to be South Africa's most elusive animals. He called this list South Africa's impossible five - Cape mountain leopard, aardvark, pangolin, riverine rabbit and naturally occurring white lion. Of these, Sanbona held the slight possibility that we would be able to see three – the aardvark (Sanbona had a picture of a recent sighting on its website), the white lion, several of which had been introduced into the reserve and the riverine rabbit – as Sanbona is one of two protected areas with a population of riverine rabbits. Riverine rabbits are classified as the 13$^{th}$ most endangered mammal on earth. The Cape mountain leopard also occurs here, but is even scarcer than the other three.

In the event, we only got to see one of the impossible five – the white lion. Scarcity, a nocturnal lifestyle and the fact that Sanbona and the western Cape was experiencing its worst drought in 100 years, conspired to prevent us from seeing the others.

On our game drives we reacquainted ourselves with springbok, eland, kudu, gemsbok, giraffe, plains zebra, white rhino, hippo, elephant, lion, cheetah and chacma baboon. New sightings for Holly and Liam included the black-backed jackal (often called the Cape jackal here), Karoo bush rat and klipspringer.

The black-backed jackal (*Canis mesomelas mesomelas*), which we had previously only glimpsed in Shamwari, is a fox-like canid with a reddish-brown coat that sports a black saddle extending from the shoulders to the base of the tail. The black-backed jackal is both monogamous and territorial.[271] Territories are marked out through depositing faeces and urine on the range boundaries. It is a highly vocal species, and it's yelping, woofing, whining and growling helps minimise territorial disputes and provides an eerie sonic backdrop to the dark South African night.

---

271  Individual territories can be up to 10.6 square kilometres

Black-backed jackals are omnivores, feeding on beetles, grasshoppers, crickets, termites, millipedes, spiders, and scorpions, as well as rodents, hares, and young antelopes. When the opportunity arises they will feed on carrion, lizards and snakes, birds, birds' eggs, fish and mussels. Occasionally, they will eat fruits and berries. This eclectic diet means that they can survive in a wide variety of environments and in a range of environmental conditions. Predators of the black-backed jackal include leopards, caracals, African wild dogs, and martial eagles.

In Khoi -Khoi folklore, black-backed jackals are often described outsmarting the lion. One traditional story explains that it came by its dark saddle when it got burnt after offering to carry the sun on its back.

Black-backed jackals can be a serious problem for goat and sheep farmers. Attempts to eradicate them through hunting and with dogs, poison, traps and gas have had varying levels of success but, ultimately, have all ended in failure.

The black-backed jackal is prone to the diseases which are common in canines such as rabies, canine distemper and canine parvovirus. As a result, they can act as a reservoir for rabies and can be responsible for outbreaks in domestic dog populations. This and its proclivity to predate livestock, where possible, means that, in many places, it is still persecuted. However, its widespread range and adaptability have resulted in its conservation status being listed by the IUCN as of least concern.

The second new species that Holly and Liam saw was the klipspringer (*Oreotragus oreotragus*).[272] The rest of us had seen this species before in East Africa and in Namibia.

We spotted a group of three high on a cliff bordering the track, beside a dried up river bed. Standing prominently on the rocks has the dual function of advertising their possession of territory and spotting potential predators – such as leopards.

---

272 It reaches 43–60 centimetres (17–24 in) at the shoulder and weighs from 8 to 18 kilograms

'Klipspringer' literally means 'rock jumper'. Klipspringers are mostly found in pairs or family groups of three. A male and female will mate for life. Females are slightly larger and heavier than the males. Short, spiky horns are present only on males.

Always wary, klipspringer take turns feeding. If a potential predator is spotted, they will emit a piercing whistle and continue to do so until the predator realises that the element of surprise is lost and departs to seek out less vigilant prey.

The boundaries of territories are marked with secretions from preorbital gland and also by large dung middens. Both males and females scent mark twigs and rocks using their preorbital gland. This leaves a sticky, sickly-sweet smelling, black smear about 5cm long. Over time, repeated marking of the same places leads to the build up of a black blob. The male usually over-marks his mate's marks. Klipspringers refresh the odour from scent marks by licking them.

These graceful little antelope are incredibly agile, leaping with ease from boulder to boulder and using the smallest of cracks and ledges to climb cliffs. They stand on the tips of their oval hooves, which have soft pads in the middle and hard rims to provide grip. Klipspringer's hair is actually hollow. It was formerly prized for stuffing saddles. Today, there are no major threats to the survival of the klipspringer, as its habitat is inaccessible and unfavourable for hunting. Natural predators include the baboon, black-backed jackal, caracal, serval, leopard, martial eagle, and Verreaux's eagle.

Klipspringers browse on young plants, fruits and flowers. Grasses form only a minor part of their diet. They depend mainly on succulent plants, and not on water bodies, to meet their water requirement. This adaptation will surely stand them in good stead during the prevailing drought in Sanbona.

The Karoo bush rat or bush vlei rat (*Myotomys unisulcatus*) has a natural habitat in temperate shrubland. However, it uses behavioural adaptations to cope with a dry arid climate, such as that prevailing in Sanbona. They are rather endearing, chubby animals with chocolate hair, black eyes and hairy round ears.

Unlike most rodents, the Karoo bush rat creates lodges made of interwoven sticks, sited on the surface, rather than in a burrow. We saw them frequently in the garden at Gondwana lodge in Sanbona. They survive by eating foliage and succulent stems from up to 60 different plant species, which they bite off in lengths and drag back to one of their lodges for consumption. Between their lodges and their food plants are foraging pathways. On average, they do not travel more than 5m from the lodges. Multiple lodges are constructed in a territory, thus ensuring that the animal is never far from shelter. Their diet varies seasonally. In the winter they feed mainly on succulents; in spring they eat succulents, non-succulents, and annual vegetation; in the summer and autumn months they consume succulent and annual plants equally.

While a lodge may accommodate up to eight individuals, the relationship between them all is uncertain – but they probably represent one family group. Although the Karoo bush rat lives in this arid region, it is poorly adapted physiologically to these harsh conditions. Protection by their stick lodges and feeding on highly hydrated plant material is clearly critical for its survival, even more so during the drought of the past two years.

Our one success with finding one of the impossible five was our sighting of the white lion. This was no real success as Sanbona had introduced white lions into the reserve and these now coexist with several tawny lions in a single pride. As they are a key species in the Reserve, they are never particularly difficult to find.

White lions are not albinos but are the result of a recessive white gene among some of the prides in the Greater Timbavati/Kruger park region of South Africa. The notion that white lions cannot survive in the wild due to a lack of camouflage has been studied and seems to lack any scientific basis. A ten year study by Jason A. Turner, Caroline A. Vasicek and Michael J. Somers[273] clearly showed that they could hunt as successfully as tawny lions.

White lions, also known as blond lions, are leucistic and are uncommon in the wild. Killing by big game hunters in the past for trophy animals – and a white lion was a highly desired and rare trophy – ensured that mutations would have been eliminated from the population before they could be passed on.

In 2003, a white lion named *'Jabulani'* and white lioness called *'Queen'* were purchased and released into Sanbona Wildlife Reserve. In May 2004, this pair produced 3 cubs (2 males, 1 female). In June 2004, a white lioness and her 3 five month old cubs joined them at Sanbona. These lions have made their own kills in addition to receiving carcasses of zebra and kudu.

Sanbona provided me with a unique opportunity to test out my new Echo Meter Touch bat detector. This tiny, featherweight, but snazzy, bit of kit that attaches effortlessly to the charging port of an iPhone is linked to an App that is being beta tested for identifying bats in South Africa. I noted that no bat species were recorded for the Reserve so one evening I plugged in the detector and tried it out in the grounds of Gondwana Lodge. To my surprise, and that of the resident Game Rangers, within a one hour period I had recorded six species around the lodge. These were the Cape serotine bat (*Neoromicia capensis*), the Cape hairy bat (*Myotis tricolor*), the little free-tailed bat (*Chaerophon pumilus*), Hildebrandt's horseshoe bat (*Rhinolophus hildebrandtii*), the Egyptian free-tailed bat (*Tadarida aegyptiaca*), and the African yellow bat (*Scotophilus dinganii*). There is something innately satisfying in recording new species for an area. Although this is a tiny contribution to biogeography it was an enormous contribution to my personal satisfaction. I was able to tell a number of extremely knowledgeable Game Rangers something about their own patch that they didn't know. For me, this changed things from being solely in receipt of information to being able to share new knowledge.

---

273 http://www.open-science-repository.com/biology-45011830.html

Sanbona is one of the very few places the riverine rabbit continues to have a chance of survival. It lives almost exclusively in seasonal river basins and habitat loss, more than anything, has rendered its continuing survival haphazard. The population in Sanbona and the conservation efforts of the owners of the reserve represent its best chance. Seemingly, it is easier to see them at night during the new moon. We never saw one during the day and were additionally handicapped at night as we had arrived after one of the rare supermoons when the moon is at perigee (the closest distance to the Earth in its elliptic orbit). In the Little Karoo, which is renowned for star-gazing and has little light pollution, such a moon illuminates the arid land keeping shy nocturnal creatures hugging cover. The fact that night drives were not available further ensured our lack of success.

One of the joys of Sanbona is the clear dark night, unpolluted by background light. This makes it a delightful place to stargaze. Brenda, our guide, used a laser pointer to show Holly, Liam and the rest of us the constellations. Even here, in the Southern Hemisphere, the influence of Greek mythology is strong and the celestial sky is interpreted through Northern Hemisphere heroes, stories and images.

Orion, The Hunter, accompanied by his two dogs (Canis Major and Canis Minor) can be seen trampling on the hare (Lepus) and being menaced by a charging bull (Taurus). Ophiuchus, the god of medicine, has his hands full with the serpent. The centaurs, half man and half horse, are represented by Centaurus, who can be seen fighting a wolf (Lupus). Sagittarius (the Archer), can be seen shooting Scorpios (the scorpion) with an arrow. Orion is killed by a sting from Scorpio, so Zeus the sky and thunder god and king of all the gods ordered that the killer and the victim be kept apart, so they can be seen at opposite ends of the sky – one rising while the other sets. This is a story I am familiar with from my childhood.

However, African mythology sees things differently. According to the *Khoi-Khoi*, the three stars of Orion's belt appear as three zebras – a male in the centre flanked by two females.

Prominent in the southern sky, The Southern Cross is a brilliant constellation consisting of several bright stars more or less in the shape of a cross. The brightest is Alpha Crucis. Beta Crusis is a blue star, and Gamma Crusis, at the head of the cross, is an orange coloured star. The star denoting the right-most corner on the cross (Delta Crusis) is the faintest of the four. Within this constellation, the *Basotho* Bushmen saw a giraffe with an outstretched neck. Other Bushmen saw a pride of lions, while the *Zulu* saw the Southern Cross as the Tree of Life.

The Milky Way, our galaxy, so difficult to see in our light polluted country, shimmers like a lace curtain in Sanbona. According to *Khoisan* legend, the Milky Way was created when a girl threw wood ashes from a campfire into the sky to help a lost hunter find his way back to camp. She later created some of the brighter stars by throwing roots into the sky. According to the legend, the white stars are ready to eat, but the red stars are old roots that are no longer edible.

Over the course of my life, I have watched with growing dismay, and sometimes disgust, the mess we are making of the planet. I have long been concerned by the destruction of habitat and the consequent reduction in biodiversity this entails. I have long believed, also, that those of us in the west, who enjoy the comfortable armchair spectacle of wildlife documentaries, and those who have the means and inclination to exploit the opportunity to see species in their natural habitat, have a responsibility to share in the cost of conserving these magnificent places and their unique inhabitants. Our enjoyment and the richness of experience we get from these efforts should not come free. To do so only devalues both the difficulty of access and the rarity of what we are looking at. The local people, who are constrained economically by our desire that these wild places be kept sacrosanct, should share in any profit made. As actors and singers are paid fees and residuals for filmed performances and subsequent screenings (such as television reruns), so should local communities receive a continuing benefit from the exploitation of their resources that are central to the production of documentaries and the enjoyment of visitors from far away lands. Visits to National Parks should be low impact in terms of limitations on access and the number of visitors permitted – to protect the environment; but they should also be of sufficiently high cost to ensure that the revenue generated can be used to offset the disadvantages to the community of maintaining such places in pristine condition.

It cannot be left to economically disadvantaged local populations to bear the entire burden of preserving habitats and species for our enjoyment and entertainment. We must share the burden. This is beneficial for the local people and also good for the planet. Decisions to conserve large areas of unique habitat should not result in impoverishment of the people who traditionally occupied the area but should be agreed in a manner that would provide locals with a tangible asset from which they can continue to derive material benefit. Too often, in the past, decisions to gazette large areas of so called 'wilderness' as National Parks or Natural Reserves have resulted in the usurpation of traditional rights, exclusion from traditional lands and punitive action to keep designated conservation areas free of people and human activity. This has created resentment and fostered poaching and criminality. Instead of excluding local people from conservation areas they should be directly employed in the effort of education, development and protection; encouraged to develop supporting enterprises or obtain employment that will underpin the success of conservation effort; and supported with resources derived from those of us in the west who wish to see these efforts succeed.

The same economic argument can be used in relation to deforestation and global climate change. If we do not want a country to cut down its rainforest because it is detrimental to our climate, then we should be willing to pay them not to do so. We require them to forego an asset that would be economically beneficial to their economy and the welfare of their people, so it is only right that we pay for it.

Leaving aside the penchant of elite groups for self-enrichment and corruption when it comes to money and power, it seems possible that, through international agreement, a dedicated agency (possibly under the auspices of the UN) could administer a global conservation effort through a levy on all nations. This could start with global climate change, with the money that is raised being used to lease rainforests from the poorer countries where they flourish. Leasing, rather than buying ensures continuing income for communities and minimises the chance of individuals enriching themselves by selling off community property. Ownership of the asset would remain with the people. Such revenue could be used by local and regional authorities to subsidise populations, where they have to surrender right of use to habitat or resources that the world believes should be conserved. Allied to this would be the need for new international law and international enforcement that would help national authorities deal with those whose rapaciousness and greed motivates them to cut down protected forests; to pollute waterways and groundwater in the illegal pursuit of mineral or oil wealth; illegally dispose of waste or emit toxic pollutants into the air. A pipe dream, you may well think. Maybe so! But the changing dynamics on our planet may rapidly turn this from a dream into a reality, as the tide of self interest flows from wealth accumulation to simple survival.

I want my children and grandchildren to continue to experience the wonder and awe appropriate to seeing the plants, creatures and other peoples with whom we share this magnificent planet. While you can get information and entertainment from books or visual media, you can only get true appreciation through personal experience. You get it by making the effort to travel, to be uncomfortable, to be unfamiliar, and to be open to new experience, new cultures, new tastes, new smells, new sounds and new sights. Even though a lifetime is not long enough to experience everything this little planet has to offer, it is well spent by making every effort, within our means, to experience all that we can fit in.

Over several decades Africa has gotten into my blood. It has also infected Mary, Helen, Michael and Niamh. It is like a disease. The Shamwari and Sanbona Safaris have spread the contagion to Holly and Liam – may they never recover.